历届美国总统就职演说

(第 4 版)

主　编　郑家顺　蒋　玮
副主编　张海蓉　李世勇　白秀琴
编　委　张长明　祝一宁　李玉影
　　　　赵彦阳　王劼华　张小凤

东南大学出版社
SOUTHEAST UNIVERSITY PRESS
·南京·

图书在版编目(CIP)数据

历届美国总统就职演说:英汉对照/郑家顺主编.
—4版. —南京:东南大学出版社,2021.6
ISBN 978-7-5641-9540-3

Ⅰ.①历… Ⅱ.①郑… Ⅲ.①英语-汉语-对照读物
②总统-就职演说-汇编-美国 Ⅳ.①H319.4:D

中国版本图书馆 CIP 数据核字(2021)第 100778 号

历届美国总统就职演说

出版发行	东南大学出版社
出 版 人	江建中
社　　址	南京市四牌楼 2 号
网　　址	http://www.seupress.com
电　　邮	press@seupress.com
经　　销	全国各地新华书店
印　　刷	南京京新印刷有限公司
开　　本	700 mm×1000 mm　1/16
印　　张	15.25
版　　次	2021 年 6 月第 4 版
印　　次	2021 年 6 月第 1 次印刷
字　　数	400 千字
书　　号	ISBN 978-7-5641-9540-3
印　　数	1～3000 册
定　　价	37.50 元

＊凡有印装质量问题,请与我社读者服务部联系,电话:025-83791830。

历届美国总统就职演说
前 言

一本好书如同一座随行的漂亮花园(A good book is like a beautiful garden carried in the pocket.)。

古人云:"读书破万卷,下笔如有神。"可见读书的重要性。"熟读唐诗三百首,不会作诗也会吟",因此读好书尤为重要。

《历届美国总统就职演说》乃英语阅读中的精品。每一篇总统就职演说词都经过了撰稿人字斟句酌,因此语言铿锵、词句华美、逻辑严密;不仅展现了总统的个人风采,而且表达了总统的雄才大略和美好期望;内容涵盖美国生活的多个层面,可以说是美国社会、政治、文化的发展史,更是英语语言千年生活的结晶。

花点时间细细品味,不但可以突破传统英语学习窘境,洞察美国国家生活动态,了解国际政治、经济,快速提高英语口语,轻松提高英语(四六级、专业四八级、国外考试)写作水平,更可以感悟社会、感悟人生,从中体会"读总统就职演说——轻松学英语"的乐趣。

为方便阅读,"演说词"采用英汉对照排版,并加上标题与简介,这样就给您省去了"查资料、问老师"等麻烦。

★欢迎本书读者光临"郑家顺英语博客(http://blog.sina.com.cn/zhengjiashun)"或"英语考试网(www.zgyyksw.com)"!

这里既有作者在英语学习、教学中的一些心得体会,也有"英语专业四八级、大学英语四六级、全国大学生英语竞赛、考研英语、MBA英语、同等学力申请硕士学位英语、自主招生、公务员面试"等考前做题技巧以及最新试卷及答案,希望能对你的英语学习有所帮助;同时也希望能借此收到更多的反馈与意见,让我们一起进步,谢谢您的参与!

郑家顺

E-mail:1522074077g@qq.com

历届美国总统就职演说

目 录

乔治·华盛顿　美国人民的实验	1
约翰·亚当斯　宪法和政治体制	7
托马斯·杰斐逊　政府的基本原则	17
詹姆斯·麦迪逊　坚守正义　维护和平	24
安德鲁·杰克逊　总统职责	29
亚伯拉罕·林肯　联邦和政府	34
亚伯拉罕·林肯　战争和上帝旨意	50
尤利西斯·S.格兰特　为最大多数人谋最大利益	54
格罗佛·克利夫兰　和睦互让的精神	59
西奥多·罗斯福　自由的自治政府	66
伍德罗·威尔逊　正本清源的工作	70
卡尔文·柯立芝　国际上寻求更好了解,国内厉行节约和减税	77
赫伯特·胡佛　向更高的标准前进	89
富兰克林·罗斯福　建立健全国家经济	100
富兰克林·罗斯福　持久进步之路	108
哈里·杜鲁门　主动权在我们手中	116
德怀特·艾森豪威尔　以正义建立和平	125

约翰·肯尼迪　我们的许诺…………………………………………………… 133

林顿·约翰逊　美国公约：公正、自由、团结…………………………… 140

理查德·尼克松　伟大孕育于质朴无华…………………………………… 147

吉米·卡特　不变的原则…………………………………………………… 157

罗纳德·里根　我们是美国人……………………………………………… 163

乔治·H. W. 布什　团结、多样、包容…………………………………… 174

比尔·克林顿　复兴美国的新时代………………………………………… 184

乔治·W. 布什　超越自我的信念………………………………………… 192

巴拉克·奥巴马　为艰巨的使命付出一切………………………………… 201

巴拉克·奥巴马　继续先驱开创的事业…………………………………… 211

唐纳德·特朗普　美国利益至上…………………………………………… 221

乔·拜登　团结是前进的道路……………………………………………… 228

George Washington
乔治·华盛顿(1732-1799)
1st President of the United States (1789-1797)

乔治·华盛顿:美利坚合众国奠基人,首任总统(1789年)。美国历史上唯一以全部选举人票两次当选的总统。任满后拒绝三连任,传为历史佳话。本篇表达了他在结束隐退、出山任职时的惶恐心情,和他要在君主大国控制的世界上进行共和制"实验"的决心。

就职典礼原定3月4日在临时首都纽约举行,但由于交通不便,华盛顿4月中旬才接到当选通知,所以不得不延至4月30日举行。

George Washington
乔治·华盛顿(1732-1799)
1st President of the United States (1789-1797)
Political Party: Federalist

The Experiment Entrusted to the Hands of the American People
美国人民的实验

Fellow-Citizens of the Senate and of the House of Representatives:

  Among the vicissitudes incident to life no event could have filled me with greater anxieties than that of which the notification was transmitted by your order, and received on the 14th day of the present month. On the one hand, I was summoned by my Country, whose voice I can never hear but with veneration and love, from a retreat which I had chosen with the fondest predilection, and, in my flattering

参议院和众议院的公民们:

  在人生沉浮中,没有一件事能比本月十四日收到你们送达的通知更使我焦虑不安。一方面,国家召唤我出任总统一职,对于她的召唤,我只能肃然从命。而隐退是我以挚爱心情、满腔希望和坚定决心所选择的暮年归宿,由于爱好

hopes, with an immutable decision, as the asylum of my declining years—a retreat which was rendered every day more necessary as well as more dear to me by the addition of habit to inclination, and of frequent interruptions in my health to the gradual waste committed on it by time. On the other hand, the magnitude and difficulty of the trust to which the voice of my country called me, being sufficient to awaken in the wisest and most experienced of her citizens a distrustful scrutiny into his qualifications, could not but overwhelm with despondence one who (inheriting inferior endowments from nature and unpracticed in the duties of civil administration) ought to be peculiarly conscious of his own deficiencies. In this conflict of emotions all I dare aver is that it has been my faithful study to collect my duty from a just appreciation of every circumstance by which it might be affected. All I dare hope is that if, in executing this task, I have been too much swayed by a grateful remembrance of former instances, or by an affectionate sensibility to this transcendent proof of the confidence of my fellow-citizens, and have thence too little consulted my incapacity as well as disinclination for the weighty and untried cares before me, my error will be palliated by the motives which mislead me, and its consequences be judged by my country with some share of the partiality in which they originated.

Such being the impressions under which I have, in obedience to the public summons, repaired to the present station, it would be peculiarly improper to omit in this first official act my fervent supplications to that Almighty Being who rules over the universe, who presides in the councils of nations, and whose providential aids can supply every human defect, that His benediction may consecrate to the liberties and happiness of the people of the United States a Government instituted by themselves for these essential purposes, and may enable every instrument employed in its administration to execute with success the functions allotted

和习惯，且时光流逝，健康渐衰，时感体力不济，越来越感到隐退的必要和珍贵。另一方面，国家召唤我担负的责任如此巨大而艰巨，足以使国内最有才智和经验的人度德量力，而我天资愚钝，又没有民政管理的经验，应该倍觉自己能力的不足，因此必然感到难以担此重任。怀着这种矛盾的心情，我唯一敢断言的是，通过正确估计可能产生影响的各种情况来恪尽职责，乃是我忠贞不渝的努力目标。我唯一敢祈望的是，如果我在执行这项任务时因沉溺于往事，或因由衷感激公民们对我高度的信赖，因而过分受到了影响，以致在处理从未经历过的大事时，忽视了自己的无能和消极，我的错误将会出于使我误入歧途的各种动机而减轻，而大家在评判错误的后果时，也会适当包涵产生这些动机的偏见。

既然这就是我在遵奉公众召唤就任现职时的感想，那么，在此宣誓就职之际，如不热情地祈求全能的上帝将是一件非常不当的事，因为上帝统治着宇宙，主宰着各国政府，它的神助能弥补人类的任何不足。愿上帝赐福，保佑一个为了美国人民的自由和幸福而组建的政府，保佑它为这些基本目的而作出奉献，保佑政治的各项行政措施在我负

George Washington
乔治·华盛顿(1732-1799)
1st President of the United States (1789-1797)

to his charge. In tendering this homage to the Great Author of every public and private good, I assure myself that it expresses your sentiments not less than my own, nor those of my fellow-citizens at large less than either. No people can be bound to acknowledge and adore the Invisible Hand which conducts the affairs of men more than those of the United States. Every step by which they have advanced to the character of an independent nation seems to have been distinguished by some token of providential agency; and in the important revolution just accomplished in the system of their united government the tranquil deliberations and voluntary consent of so many distinct communities from which the event has resulted cannot be compared with the means by which most governments have been established without some return of pious gratitude, along with an humble anticipation of the future blessings which the past seem to presage. These reflections, arising out of the present crisis, have forced themselves too strongly on my mind to be suppressed. You will join with me, I trust, in thinking that there are none under the influence of which the proceedings of a new and free government can more auspiciously commence.

By the article establishing the executive department it is made the duty of the President "to recommend to your consideration such measures as he shall judge necessary and expedient." The circumstances under which I now meet you will acquit me from entering into that subject further than to refer to the great constitutional charter under which you are assembled, and which, in defining your powers, designates the objects to which your attention is to be given. It will be more consistent with those circumstances, and far more congenial with the feelings which actuate me, to substitute, in place of a recommendation

责之下都能成功地发挥作用。我相信,在向公众利益和私人利益的伟大缔造者献上这份崇敬时,这些话也同样表达了各位和广大公民的心声。没有人能比美国人更坚定不移地承认和崇拜掌管人类事务的上帝。他们在迈向独立国家的进程中,似乎每走一步都有某种天佑的迹象;他们在刚刚完成的联邦政府体制的重大改革中,如果不是因虔诚的感恩而得到某种回报,如果不是谦卑地期待着过去有所预示的赐福的到来,那么,通过众多截然不同的集团的平静思考和自愿赞同来完成改革,这种方式是难以同大多数政府在组建过程中所采用的方式相比的。在目前转折关头,我产生这些想法确实是深有所感而不能自已。我相信大家会和我怀有同感,即如果不仰仗上帝的力量,一个新生的自由政府就无法做到一开始就事事如意。

根据设立行政部门的条款,总统有责任"将他认为必要而适宜的措施提请国会审议"。但在目前与各位见面的这个场合,恕我不进一步讨论这个问题,而只是提一下伟大的宪法,它使各位今天欢聚一堂,它规定了各位的权限,指出了各位应该注意的目标。在这样的场合,更恰当、也更能反映我内心激情的做法不是提出具体措施,而是称颂将

of particular measures, the tribute that is due to the talents, the rectitude, and the patriotism which adorn the characters selected to devise and adopt them. In these honorable qualifications I behold the surest pledges that as on one side no local prejudices or attachments, no separate views nor party animosities, will misdirect the comprehensive and equal eye which ought to watch over this great assemblage of communities and interests, so, on another, that the foundation of our national policy will be laid in the pure and immutable principles of private morality, and the preeminence of free government be exemplified by all the attributes which can win the affections of its citizens and command the respect of the world. I dwell on this prospect with every satisfaction which an ardent love for my country can inspire, since there is no truth more thoroughly established than that there exists in the economy and course of nature an indissoluble union between virtue and happiness; between duty and advantage; between the genuine maxims of an honest and magnanimous policy and the solid rewards of public prosperity and felicity; since we ought to be no less persuaded that the propitious smiles of Heaven can never be expected on a nation that disregards the eternal rules of order and right which Heaven itself has ordained; and since the preservation of the sacred fire of liberty and the destiny of the republican model of government are justly considered, perhaps, as deeply, as finally, staked on the experiment entrusted to the hands of the American people.

Besides the ordinary objects submitted to your care, it will remain with your judgment to decide how far an exercise of the occasional power delegated by the fifth article of the Constitution is rendered expedient at the present juncture by the nature of objections which have been urged against the system, or by the degree of inquietude which has given birth to them. Instead of undertaking

要规划和采纳这些措施的当选者的才能、正直和爱国心。我从这些高贵品格中看到了最可靠的保证：其一，任何地方偏见或地方感情，任何意见分歧或党派敌视，都不能使我们偏离全局观念和公平观点，即必须维护这个由不同地区和不同利益所组建的大联合政权；因此，其二，我国的政策将会以纯正不移的个人道德原则为基础，而自由政府将会以赢得民心和全世界尊敬的一切特点而显示其优越性。我对国家的一片热爱之心激励着我满怀喜悦地展望这幅远景，因为根据自然界的法则和发展趋势，在美德与幸福之间，责任与利益之间，恪守诚实宽厚的政策与获得社会繁荣幸福的硕果之间，有着密不可分的关系；因为我们应该同样相信，上帝亲自规定了永恒的秩序和权利法则，他绝不可能对无视这些法则的国家慈颜含笑；因为人们理所当然地、满怀深情地、也许是最后一次地把维护神圣的自由之火和共和制政府的命运，系于美国人所遵命进行的实验上。

除了提请各位注意的一般事务外，在当前时刻，根据激烈反对共和制的各种意见的性质，或根据引起这些意见的不同程度，在必要时行使宪法第五条授予的权利究竟有多大益处，将依靠你们来加以

George Washington

乔治·华盛顿(1732-1799)

1st President of the United States (1789-1797)

particular recommendations on this subject, in which I could be guided by no lights derived from official opportunities, I shall again give way to my entire confidence in your discernment and pursuit of the public good; for I assure myself that whilst you carefully avoid every alteration which might endanger the benefits of an united and effective government, or which ought to await the future lessons of experience, a reverence for the characteristic rights of freemen and a regard for the public harmony will sufficiently influence your deliberations on the question how far the former can be impregnably fortified or the latter be safely and advantageously promoted.

To the foregoing observations I have one to add, which will be most properly addressed to the House of Representatives. It concerns myself, and will therefore be as brief as possible. When I was first honored with a call into the service of my country, then on the eve of an arduous struggle for its liberties, the light in which I contemplated my duty required that I should renounce every pecuniary compensation. From this resolution I have in no instance departed; and being still under the impressions which produced it, I must decline as inapplicable to myself any share in the personal emoluments which may be indispensably included in a permanent provision for the executive department, and must accordingly pray that the pecuniary estimates for the station in which I am placed may during my continuance in it be limited to such actual expenditures as the public good may be thought to require.

Having thus imparted to you my sentiments as they have been awakened by the occasion which brings us together, I shall take my present leave; but not without

判断和决定。在这个问题上，我无法从过去担任过的职务中得到借鉴，因此我不提具体建议，而是再一次完全信任各位对公众利益的辨别和追求；因为我相信，各位只要谨慎，避免作出任何可能危及团结而有效的政府利益的修订，或避免作出应该等待未来经验教训的修订，那么，各位对自由人特有权利的尊重和对社会安定的关注，就足以影响大家慎重考虑应在何种程度上坚定不移地加强前者，并有利无弊地促进后者。

除上述意见外，我还要补充一点，而且觉得向众议院提出最恰当。这条意见与我有关，因此应当尽量讲得简短一些。我第一次荣幸地响应号召为国家效劳时，正值我国为自由而艰苦奋斗之际，我对我的职责的看法要求我必须放弃任何俸禄。我从未违背过这一决定。如今，促使我作出这一同样决定的想法仍然支配着我，因此，我必须拒绝对我来说不适宜的任何个人津贴，因为这些津贴可能被列入并成为政府部门常设基金不可分割的一部分。同样，我必须恳求各位，在估算我就任这个职位所需要的费用时，可以根据我的任期以公共利益所需的实际费用为限。

我已经把有感于这一聚会场合的想法告诉了各位，现在我就要向大家告辞；但在此

resorting once more to the benign Parent of the Human Race in humble supplication that, since He has been pleased to favor the American people with opportunities for deliberating in perfect tranquility, and dispositions for deciding with unparalleled unanimity on a form of government for the security of their union and the advancement of their happiness, so His divine blessing may be equally conspicuous in the enlarged views, the temperate consultations, and the wise measures on which the success of this Government must depend.

以前,我还要再一次以谦卑的心情祈求仁慈的上帝给予帮助。因为承蒙上帝的恩赐,美国人民有了深思熟虑的机会,有了为确保联邦的安全和促进幸福,用前所未有的一致意见来决定政府体制的意向;因而,同样明显的是,上帝将保佑我们逐步扩大眼界,稳定地进行协商,并采取明智的措施,而这些都是本届政府取得成功所必不可缺少的依靠。

John Adams
约翰·亚当斯(1735-1826)
2nd President of the United States (1797-1801)

约翰·亚当斯:美国第 2 任总统（1797—1801），美国形成两党后第一次由政党提名参加竞选的总统,也是最长寿的美国总统之一（享年 90 岁）。本篇发表于临时首都纽约。

John Adams
约翰·亚当斯(1735-1826)
2nd President of the United States (1797-1801)
Political Party: Federalist

The Constitution and System of Government
宪法和政治体制

When it was first perceived, in early times, that no middle course for America remained between unlimited submission to a foreign legislature and a total independence of its claims, men of reflection were less apprehensive of danger from the formidable power of fleets and armies they must determine to resist than from those contests and dissensions which would certainly arise concerning the forms of government to be instituted over the whole and over the parts of this extensive country. Relying, however, on the purity of their intentions, the justice of their cause, and

早先,当有识之士第一次认识到,美利坚不可能在无限制屈从于外国立法机构与主张完全独立之间采取中庸之道时,他们并不害怕必须下定决心抵抗令人生畏的强大舰队和军队,而是担忧在我国广大领土上实行何种政体来管理全国及其各个州的这一问题必然会引起争论和分歧。但是,这个国家的代表们,当

the integrity and intelligence of the people, under an overruling Providence which had so signally protected this country from the first, the representatives of this nation, then consisting of little more than half its present number, not only broke to pieces the chains which were forging and the rod of iron that was lifted up, but frankly cut asunder the ties which had bound them, and launched into an ocean of uncertainty.

The zeal and ardor of the people during the Revolutionary War, supplying the place of government, commanded a degree of order sufficient at least for the temporary preservation of society. The Confederation which was early felt to be necessary was prepared from the models of the Batavian and Helvetic confederacies, the only examples which remain with any detail and precision in history, and certainly the only ones which the people at large had ever considered. But reflecting on the striking difference in so many particulars between this country and those where a courier may go from the seat of government to the frontier in a single day, it was then certainly foreseen by some who assisted in Congress at the formation of it that it could not be durable.

Negligence of its regulations, inattention to its recommendations, if not disobedience to its authority, not only in individuals but in States, soon appeared with their melancholy consequences—universal languor, jealousies and rivalries of States, decline of navigation and commerce,

时人数还不到现在的一半,凭着自己出发点的纯洁和自己事业的正义感。依靠人民的团结和智慧,在一开始就格外护佑这个国家的上帝的指引下,不仅砸碎了正在炼制的镣铐和向他们举起的钢鞭,而且毅然切断了捆绑他们的绳索,开始向动荡不定的海洋进发。

在革命战争期间(即1775－1783年美国独立战争),人民的热诚和奋发奠定了政府的地位,保持了至少足以暂时维持社会的某种秩序。人民最初感到有必要建立邦联时,是根据巴达维亚和海尔维希的邦联模式进行筹备的。(巴达维亚是雅加达旧称,指17世纪的荷属东印度群岛;海尔维希指13世纪末在永久同盟旧称上形成的瑞士联邦,今为瑞士西北部一地区)。它们是历史上仅有的、详细而确凿地实行邦联制的例子,而且无疑也是到那时为止全人类曾经考虑采用邦联制的唯一例子。但是,考虑到美国与它们在许多具体问题上的显著区别,例如在这些国家,邮差在一天之内便可从政府所在地抵达边陲,因此,邦联国会的某些筹备者必然预见到这种政体不可能持久。

很快,不仅有一些人,而且有一些州,开始无视政府的规定和不听政府的建议。这些现象即便不是反抗政府的权威,也造成了令人忧郁的后

John Adams

约翰·亚当斯(1735-1826)
2nd President of the United States (1797-1801)

discouragement of necessary manufactures, universal fall in the value of lands and their produce, contempt of public and private faith, loss of consideration and credit with foreign nations, and at length in discontents, animosities, combinations, partial conventions, and insurrection, threatening some great national calamity.

In this dangerous crisis the people of America were not abandoned by their usual good sense, presence of mind, resolution, or integrity. Measures were pursued to concert a plan to form a more perfect union, establish justice, insure domestic tranquility, provide for the common defense, promote the general welfare, and secure the blessings of liberty. The public disquisitions, discussions, and deliberations issued in the present happy Constitution of Government.

Employed in the service of my country abroad during the whole course of these transactions, I first saw the Constitution of the United States in a foreign country. Irritated by no literary altercation, animated by no public debate, heated by no party animosity, I read it with great satisfaction, as the result of good heads prompted by good hearts, as an experiment better adapted to the genius, character, situation, and relations of this nation and country than any which had ever been proposed or suggested. In its general principles and great outlines it was conformable to such a system of government as I had ever most esteemed, and in some States, my own native State in

果——意志普遍消沉、州与州互相猜忌和倾轧、海运和商业衰落不堪、必需品的制造萎靡不振、土地和农产品价值普遍下降、个人与公共信念遭到鄙视、对外交往事务欠审慎以致对外信誉丧失,这一切终于出现了种种不满、仇恨、结帮、偏激的集会和骚乱,预示着一场全国性浩劫的到来。(各地人民不断爆发起义,规模最大的是1786-1787年由贫农出身,参加过独立战争的军人谢斯领导的马萨诸塞州农民起义。这些起义促使美国建立起强有力的联邦政府。)

在此危急时刻,美国人并没有失去惯有的良知、镇静、决心和正直。他们想方设法共谋大计,以便组成更完善的联邦,确立公理正义,保障国内安定,提供共同防御,促进公共福利和保障自由幸福。通过公众的一系列研究、讨论和斟酌,才产生了目前这部令人满意的宪法。

在这一转折的整个过程中,由于我在国外执行公务,所以在异邦第一次见到了合众国宪法。我以极大的喜悦阅读了这部宪法,我既不为围绕宪法措辞的争吵而激怒,也不为公开辩论而激动,更不为党派仇恨而激愤。我认为,这部宪法是襟怀坦荡的有识之士的作品,它是胜过迄今任何其他的提议或建议的一种试验,它更能适合这个美国和美国人民的才能、性格、环境和

particular, had contributed to establish. Claiming a right of suffrage, in common with my fellow-citizens, in the adoption or rejection of a constitution which was to rule me and my posterity, as well as them and theirs, I did not hesitate to express my approbation of it on all occasions, in public and in private. It was not then, nor has been since, any objection to it in my mind that the Executive and Senate were not more permanent. Nor have I ever entertained a thought of promoting any alteration in it but such as the people themselves, in the course of their experience, should see and feel to be necessary or expedient, and by their representatives in Congress and the State legislatures, according to the Constitution itself, adopt and ordain.

Returning to the bosom of my country after a painful separation from it for ten years, I had the honor to be elected to a station under the new order of things, and I have repeatedly laid myself under the most serious obligations to support the Constitution. The operation of it has equaled the most sanguine expectations of its friends, and from an habitual attention to it, satisfaction in its administration, and delight in its effects upon the peace, order, prosperity, and happiness of the nation I have acquired an habitual attachment to it and veneration for it.

各种关系。就这部宪法的总则和总纲而言，它与我迄今最推崇的政府体制相一致，而且某些州，尤其是我的出生地所在州，为确立这种体制作出了贡献。我与公民们一样有权投票决定是否采纳这部宪法，因为它将要管束我和我的后代，管束同胞们及其他们的后代。我毫不犹豫地赞同这部宪法，不管在公众场合，还是私下里。无论在当时还是此后，我都不认为行政部门和参议院不能维持长久的想法。我也从未想过要促成修改宪法，除非人民经过多年实践经验看到和感到有必要或暂时有必要进行修改，并通过他们的国会和州议会代表根据宪法本身的精神予以采纳或作出规定。

在与祖国痛苦地分别了10年后，我又回到了她的怀抱，并有幸在一片新气象中当选就职。(亚当斯于1778年起长期在法国、荷兰和英国从事外交活动，1788年回国并当选副总统，他就任此职的日期〔1789年4月21日〕比华盛顿就任总统早9天。)我不断地投身到支持宪法的最庄严的义务之中。宪法的实施没有辜负拥护者们的最乐观的期望。由于我习以为常地关注宪法，对宪法的实施感到满意，而且宪法对国家的和平、秩序、繁荣和幸福等方面产生的作用使我感到喜悦，因此，我一如既往地对宪法热爱和崇敬。

John Adams
约翰·亚当斯(1735-1826)
2nd President of the United States (1797-1801)

What other form of government, indeed, can so well deserve our esteem and love?

There may be little solidity in an ancient idea that congregations of men into cities and nations are the most pleasing objects in the sight of superior intelligences, but this is very certain, that to a benevolent human mind there can be no spectacle presented by any nation more pleasing, more noble, majestic, or august, than an assembly like that which has so often been seen in this and the other Chamber of Congress, of a Government in which the Executive authority, as well as that of all the branches of the Legislature, are exercised by citizens selected at regular periods by their neighbors to make and execute laws for the general good. Can anything essential, anything more than mere ornament and decoration, be added to this by robes and diamonds? Can authority be more amiable and respectable when it descends from accidents or institutions established in remote antiquity than when it springs fresh from the hearts and judgments of an honest and enlightened people? For it is the people only that are represented. It is their power and majesty that is reflected, and only for their good, in every legitimate government, under whatever form it may appear. The existence of such a government as ours for any length of time is a full proof of a general dissemination of knowledge and virtue throughout the whole body of the people. And what object or consideration more pleasing than this can be presented to the human mind? If national pride is ever justifiable or excusable it is when it springs, not from power or riches, grandeur or glory, but from conviction of national innocence, information, and benevolence.

确实,还有其他什么形式的政体能值得我们如此尊敬和热爱呢?

古代有一种似乎不甚严密的观念,即从圣哲的眼光来看,人类聚集而形成城市和国家,乃是最令人感到愉快的目标;但无可置疑的是,在仁慈者的心目中,任何国家所显示的情景都比不上我们这个政府的会议更令人感到喜悦、高尚、庄严和受人尊敬,这样的会议在国会两院屡见不鲜,而政府的行政权和国会各个机构的立法权,是经过定期选举的公民来行使的,是为公众利益而制订和执行法律的。难道皇袍和钻石能为此增添实质性的东西吗?难道它们不只是些装饰品吗?难道通过偶然继承或远古制度而继承的权力,会比诚实而有见识的人民凭借觉悟和判断而产生的权力更可亲可敬吗?这样的政府唯一代表的是人民。它的每个合法机构,无论表现为何种形式,反映的都是人民的权利和尊严,并且只为人民谋利益。像我们这样的政府,不论存在多久,都是知识和美德在全人类传播的充分证明。难道还有比这更令人喜悦的目标或设想能奉献给人类观念吗?如果说民族的自豪感是正当的情有可原的,那么这种自豪感必须不是来自权势或财富,不是来自豪华和荣耀,而是唯独来自坚信民族的纯真、见识和仁爱。

In the midst of these pleasing ideas we should be unfaithful to ourselves if we should ever lose sight of the danger to our liberties if anything partial or extraneous should infect the purity of our free, fair, virtuous, and independent elections. If an election is to be determined by a majority of a single vote, and that can be procured by a party through artifice or corruption, the Government may be the choice of a party for its own ends, not of the nation for the national good. If that solitary suffrage can be obtained by foreign nations by flattery or menaces, by fraud or violence, by terror, intrigue, or venality, the Government may not be the choice of the American people, but of foreign nations. It may be foreign nations who govern us, and not we, the people, who govern ourselves; and candid men will acknowledge that in such cases choice would have little advantage to boast of over lot or chance.

Such is the amiable and interesting system of government (and such are some of the abuses to which it may be exposed) which the people of America have exhibited to the admiration and anxiety of the wise and virtuous of all nations for eight years under the administration of a citizen who, by a long course of great actions, regulated by prudence, justice, temperance, and fortitude, conducting a people inspired with the same virtues and animated with the same ardent patriotism and love of liberty to independence and peace, to increasing wealth and unexampled prosperity, has merited the gratitude

当我们沉浸在这些令人愉快的想法时,如果任何片面和枝节问题影响了我们纯洁的、自由的、公平的、公正的和独立的选举,使我们竟视而不见自由所面临的危险,我们就会自欺欺人。如果选举中出现了一票之差将决定谁赢得多数票的局面,而一个政党可以通过耍诡计和搞腐败来达到目的,那么这个政府就有可能成为政党为自身目的而作出的选择,而不是国家为人民利益而作出的选择。如果其他国家有可能通过奉承、威胁、欺骗、暴力、恐怖、阴谋或收买等手段获得这张独特的选票,那么这个政府就可能不是美国人民作出的选择,而是其他国家作出的选择。那样,就可能是外国统治我们,而不是我们人民来自己管理自己。在这种情况下,公正的人士就会认识到,选择胜于命运或机遇的优越性就所剩无几和不值得夸耀了。

这就是使人感到亲切的有趣的政治体制(及其可能暴露的某些弊端)。八年来,美国人民在一位公民的执政下展示了这种政治体制,引起了各国贤达的赞赏和渴望。这位公民(指华盛顿总统)为人谨慎、公正、节制、坚韧,长期以来他以一系列伟大的行动,领导着一个为共同美德所鼓舞的、为共同强烈的爱国心所激励的和热爱自由的民族,

John Adams
约翰·亚当斯(1735-1826)
2nd President of the United States (1797-1801)

of his fellow-citizens, commanded the highest praises of foreign nations, and secured immortal glory with posterity.

In that retirement which is his voluntary choice may he long live to enjoy the delicious recollection of his services, the gratitude of mankind, the happy fruits of them to himself and the world, which are daily increasing, and that splendid prospect of the future fortunes of this country which is opening from year to year. His name may be still a rampart, and the knowledge that he lives a bulwark, against all open or secret enemies of his country's peace. This example has been recommended to the imitation of his successors by both Houses of Congress and by the voice of the legislatures and the people throughout the nation.

On this subject it might become me better to be silent or to speak with diffidence; but as something may be expected, the occasion, I hope, will be admitted as an apology if I venture to say that if a preference, upon principle, of a free republican government, formed upon long and serious reflection, after a diligent and impartial inquiry after truth; if an attachment to the Constitution of the United States, and a conscientious determination to support it until it shall be altered by the judgments and wishes of the people, expressed in the mode prescribed in it; if a respectful attention to the constitutions of the individual States and a constant caution and delicacy toward the State governments; if an equal and impartial regard to the rights, interest, honor, and happiness of all the States

走向独立、维护和平、增加财富和创造空前的繁荣昌盛。他值得他的人民对他表示感激,他博得了世界各国的高度赞扬,他必将名垂千古。

他自愿选择了隐退。愿他在隐退后颐养天年,并幸福地享受回忆他的供职生涯之乐,享受人类对他的感激,享受他所作出的奉献给他本人和全世界带来的与日俱增的幸福果实,以及享受这个国家的未来命运决定的、正在一年年逐步展开的光明前景。他的名字仍将是一道防线,他的长寿将是一座堡垒,抵御着任何危害美国和平公开的或隐蔽的敌人。他的这一举动已得到国会两院、各州立法机构和全国人民的一致推荐,并将成为继任者效法的榜样(指华盛顿拒绝再次连任,为后来的总统树立了榜样)!

在这个问题上,我也许保持沉默或说话谨慎些为好。不过,如同各位期待的那样,我希望能够利用这个场合为我的斗胆直言作辩护。我认为,人们经过长期认真的考虑,经过孜孜不倦和不偏不倚地探求真理,根据原则作出了这个选择,应对自由的共和政体产生热爱之情;对合众国宪法的热爱和衷心的坚决拥护,直到人民根据判断和意愿对宪法进行修订;尊重各州宪法,时时小心谨慎地对待和关心各州政府;平等公正地对待

in the Union, without preference or regard to a northern or southern, an eastern or western, position, their various political opinions on unessential points or their personal attachments; if a love of virtuous men of all parties and denominations; if a love of science and letters and a wish to patronize every rational effort to encourage schools, colleges, universities, academies, and every institution for propagating knowledge, virtue, and religion among all classes of the people, not only for their benign influence on the happiness of life in all its stages and classes, and of society in all its forms, but as the only means of preserving our Constitution from its natural enemies, the spirit of sophistry, the spirit of party, the spirit of intrigue, the profligacy of corruption, and the pestilence of foreign influence, which is the angel of destruction to elective governments; if a love of equal laws, of justice, and humanity in the interior administration; if an inclination to improve agriculture, commerce, and manufacturers for necessity, convenience, and defense; if a spirit of equity and humanity toward the aboriginal nations of America, and a disposition to meliorate their condition by inclining them to be more friendly to us, and our citizens to be more friendly to them; if an inflexible determination to maintain peace and inviolable faith with all nations, and that system of neutrality and impartiality among the belligerent powers of Europe which has been adopted by this Government and so solemnly sanctioned by both Houses of Congress and applauded by the legislatures of the States and the public opinion, until it shall be otherwise ordained by Congress; if a personal esteem for the French nation, formed in a residence of seven years chiefly among them, and a sincere desire to preserve the friendship which has been so much for the honor and interest of both nations; if, while the conscious honor and integrity of the people of America and the internal sentiment of their own power and energies must

联邦各州的权利、利益、荣誉和幸福,不加偏袒,不分北方人、南方人、东部人或西部人,不分地位如何;不管他们在无关宏旨的问题上持何种政治观点及感情;爱护贤达之士,不论其政党和派别;热爱科学文化,愿意支持任何合理的努力,以鼓励学校、学院、大学、研究院和各个和向各阶层人民传播知识、美德和宗教的机构,不仅因为这些设施能对各个年龄、各个阶层和各种社团的幸福生活产生良好的影响,而且因为它们是维护宪法的唯一手段,使它免遭诡辩、党派、阴谋、腐败挥霍之风和外来影响的时疫这类天敌的侵害,而这些都是民选政府的祸星;在内政上热爱平等的法律、崇尚公正和奉行人道;赞成改进农业、商业和制造业,以便满足需要、提供便利和保障国防;对美洲原始土著部落持平等和人道主义精神,使他们对我们更友好,使我们的公民对他们也更友好,以便设法改善他们的境况;下定决心与各国维持和平,坚守不可违背的信义,在交战国之间坚持我国政府迄今奉行的、国会两院庄严批准的、各州议会和舆论一致赞成的中立和不偏不倚的立场,直至国会另作规定;我因有七年时间主要居住在法国而对法国民族怀有敬意,并衷心希望两国维持非常有益于双方荣誉和利益的友谊;美国人民强烈的荣誉感和

John Adams

约翰·亚当斯(1735-1826)
2nd President of the United States (1797-1801)

be preserved, an earnest endeavor to investigate every just cause and remove every colorable pretense of complaint; if an intention to pursue by amicable negotiation a reparation for the injuries that have been committed on the commerce of our fellow-citizens by whatever nation, and if success cannot be obtained, to lay the facts before the Legislature, that they may consider what further measures the honor and interest of the Government and its constituents demand; if a resolution to do justice as far as may depend upon me, at all times and to all nations, and maintain peace, friendship, and benevolence with all the world; if an unshaken confidence in the honor, spirit, and resources of the American people, on which I have so often hazarded my all and never been deceived; if elevated ideas of the high destinies of this country and of my own duties toward it, founded on a knowledge of the moral principles and intellectual improvements of the people deeply engraved on my mind in early life, and not obscured but exalted by experience and age; and, with humble reverence, I feel it to be my duty to add, if a veneration for the religion of a people who profess and call themselves Christians, and a fixed resolution to consider a decent respect for Christianity among the best recommendations for the public service, can enable me in any degree to comply with your wishes, it shall be my strenuous endeavor that this sagacious injunction of the two Houses shall not be without effect.

诚实正直之心,以及他们有关自己的权力和力量的内在情感固然应当加以维护,但同时应当对每一正当的事业竭力审议,以杜绝各种刻意渲染的抱怨借口;当公民们在商务活动中受到任何国家的侵犯时,首先愿意通过友好谈判寻求赔偿,假如谈判达不到目的,就将事实呈送立法机构,由它根据政府和当事人的荣誉和利益,考虑进一步的措施;我下定决心,只要我能做到,无论何时都公正地对待所有国家,与全世界一起来保持和平、友谊和仁爱;对美国人民的荣誉、精神和力量具有不可动摇的信心,对此我常常孤注一掷而且从未感到失望;对于我国命运和我对它应尽职责的崇高理想加以深刻领会,这种领会是建立在认识人民的道德原则和思想进步的认知基础上的,而且这一认识在我早年生活中就已刻骨铭心,而随着阅历和年龄的增加,不但没有淡忘,反而进一步得到升华;最后,我怀着谦卑而恭敬的心情,觉得有责任再补充一点,这就是,如果一个宣称信奉上帝并自称基督教徒的民族对宗教虔诚,加之在举荐最佳公职人选时坚定不移地适当考虑尊重基督教,对宗教的这种敬意使我得以最大限度满足大家的愿望。如果以上条件均能达到,我一定会奋发努力,使两院做出的这个深谋远虑的决断不会毫无效果。

With this great example before me, with the sense and spirit, the faith and honor, the duty and interest, of the same American people pledged to support the Constitution of the United States, I entertain no doubt of its continuance in all its energy, and my mind is prepared without hesitation to lay myself under the most solemn obligations to support it to the utmost of my power.

And may that Being who is supreme over all, the Patron of Order, the Fountain of Justice, and the Protector in all ages of the world of virtuous liberty, continue His blessing upon this nation and its Government and give it all possible success and duration consistent with the ends of His providence.

有了之前一个伟大的表率,有了同样誓愿支持美国宪法的美国人民,凭借他们的这种思想和精神、信仰和荣誉、责任和利益,我将毫不怀疑宪法将保持全部力量,我将毫不犹豫地献身于执行最神圣的义务,竭尽全力去支持这部宪法。

愿至高无上的上帝,秩序的守护神,正义的源泉,各个时代善良的自由世界的守卫者,继续保佑这个国家及其政府,并依照天意赐予它事事顺遂,永久长存。

Thomas Jefferson
托马斯·杰斐逊(1743-1826)
3rd President of the United States (1801-1809)

托马斯·杰斐逊:美国第3任总统(1801—1809),民主共和党(今日民主党之前身)创始人。他的当选,使美国政府第一次从一个政党转到另一个政党手中,标志着两党轮流执政的开始。从杰斐逊开始,美国总统均在首都华盛顿发表就职演说。

Thomas Jefferson
托马斯·杰斐逊(1743-1826)
3rd President of the United States (1801-1809)
Political Party: Democratic-Republican

The Essential Principles of Our Government
政府的基本原则

Friends and Fellow-citizens,

  Called upon to undertake the duties of the first executive office of our country, I avail myself of the presence of that portion of my fellow-citizens which is here assembled to express my grateful thanks for the favor with which they have been pleased to look toward me, to declare a sincere consciousness that the task is above my talents, and that I approach it with those anxious and awful presentiments which the greatness of the charge and the weakness of my powers so justly inspire. A rising nation,

朋友们、同胞们:

  我应召担任国家的最高行政长官,值此诸位同胞集会之时,我衷心感谢大家寄予我的厚爱,诚挚地说,我意识到这项任务非我能力所及,其责任之重大,本人能力之浅薄,自然使我就任时忧惧交加。一个沃野千里的新兴国家,带着丰富的工业产品跨海渡洋,同那些自恃强权、不顾公理的

spread over a wide and fruitful land, traversing all the seas with the rich productions of their industry, engaged in commerce with nations who feel power and forget right, advancing rapidly to destinies beyond the reach of mortal eye—when I contemplate these transcendent objects, and see the honor, the happiness, and the hopes of this beloved country committed to the issue and the auspices of this day, I shrink from the contemplation, and humble myself before the magnitude of the undertaking. Utterly, indeed, should I despair did not the presence of many whom I here see remind me that in the other high authorities provided by our Constitution I shall find resources of wisdom, of virtue, and of zeal on which to rely under all difficulties. To you, then, gentlemen, who are charged with the sovereign functions of legislation, and to those associated with you, I look with encouragement for that guidance and support which may enable us to steer with safety the vessel in which we are all embarked amidst the conflicting elements of a troubled world.

During the contest of opinion through which we have passed the animation of discussions and of exertions has sometimes worn an aspect which might impose on strangers unused to think freely and to speak and to write what they think; but this being now decided by the voice of the nation, announced according to the rules of the Constitution, all will, of course, arrange themselves under the will of the law, and unite in common efforts for the common good. All, too, will bear in mind this sacred principle, that though the will of the majority is in all cases to prevail, that will to be rightful must be reasonable; that the minority possess their equal rights, which equal law must protect, and to violate would be oppression. Let us, then, fellow-citizens, unite with one heart and one mind. Let us restore to social intercourse that harmony and affection without which liberty and even

国家进行贸易，向着世人无法预见的天命疾奔——当我思考这些重大的目标，当我想到这个我所热爱的国家，其荣誉、幸福和希望都系于这个问题和今天的盛典，我就不敢再想下去，并面对这宏图大业自惭形秽。确实，若不是在这里见到许多先生们在场，使我想起无论遇到什么困难，都可以向宪法规定的另一高级机构寻找智慧、美德和热忱的源泉，我一定会完全心灰意冷。因此，负有神圣的立法职责的先生们和各位有关人士，我鼓起勇气期望你们给予指引和支持，使我们能够在乱世纷争中同舟共济，安然航行。

在我们过去的意见交锋中，大家热烈讨论，各展所长，这种紧张气氛，有时会使不习惯于自由思想、不习惯于说出或写下自己想法的人感到不安；但如今，这场争论已由全国的民意作出决定，而且根据宪法的规定予以公布，大家当然会服从法律的意志，安排妥当，为共同的利益齐心协力。大家也会铭记这条神圣的原则，尽管在任何情况下，多数人的意志是起决定作用的，但这种意志必须合理才站得住脚；少数人享有同等权利，这种权利必须同样受到法律保护，如果侵犯，便是压迫。因

Thomas Jefferson
托马斯·杰斐逊(1743-1826)
3rd President of the United States (1801-1809)

life itself are but dreary things. And let us reflect that, having banished from our land that religious intolerance under which mankind so long bled and suffered, we have yet gained little if we countenance a political intolerance as despotic, as wicked, and capable of as bitter and bloody persecutions. During the throes and convulsions of the ancient world, during the agonizing spasms of infuriated man, seeking through blood and slaughter his long-lost liberty, it was not wonderful that the agitation of the billows should reach even this distant and peaceful shore; that this should be more felt and feared by some and less by others, and should divide opinions as to measures of safety. But every difference of opinion is not a difference of principle. We have called by different names brethren of the same principle. We are all Republicans, we are all Federalists. If there be any among us who would wish to dissolve this Union or to change its republican form, let them stand undisturbed as monuments of the safety with which error of opinion may be tolerated where reason is left free to combat it. I know, indeed, that some honest men fear that a republican government cannot be strong, that this Government is not strong enough; but would the honest patriot, in the full tide of successful experiment, abandon a government which has so far kept us free and firm on the theoretic and visionary fear that this Government, the world's best hope, may by possibility want energy to preserve itself? I trust not. I believe this, on the contrary, the strongest Government on earth. I believe it the only one where every man, at the call of the law, would fly to the standard of the law, and would meet invasions of the public order as his own personal concern. Sometimes it is said that man cannot be trusted with the government of himself. Can he, then, be trusted with the government of others? Or have we found

此,公民们,让我们同心同德地团结起来。让我们在社会交往中和睦如初、恢复友爱,如果没有这些,自由,甚至生活本身都会索然寡味。让我们再想一想,我们已经将长期以来造成人类流血、受苦的宗教信仰上的不宽容现象逐出国土,如果我们鼓励某种政治上的不宽容,其专横、邪恶和可能造成的残酷、血腥迫害均与此相仿,那么我们必将无所收获。当旧世界经历阵痛和骚动,当愤怒的人挣扎着想通过流血、杀戮来寻求失去已久的自由,那波涛般的激情甚至也会冲击这片遥远而宁静的海岸。对此,人们的感触和忧患不会一样,因而对安全措施的意见就出现了分歧,这些都不足为奇。但是,各种意见分歧并不都是原则分歧。我们以不同的名字呼唤同一原则的兄弟。我们都是共和党人,我们都是联邦党人。如果我们当中有人想解散这个联邦,或者想改变它的共和体制,那就让他们不受干扰作为平安的纪念碑竖立在那儿吧,因为有了平安,错误的意见就可得到宽容,理性就得以自由地与之抗争。诚然,我知道,有些正直人士担心共和制政府无法成为强有力的政府,担心我们这个政府不够坚强;但是,在实验取得最成功的时候,一个诚实的爱国者,难道会因为一种假设的和幻想的恐惧,就以为这个被世界寄予最大希

angels in the forms of kings to govern him? Let history answer this question.

Let us, then, with courage and confidence pursue our own Federal and Republican principles, our attachment to union and representative government. Kindly separated by nature and a wide ocean from the exterminating havoc of one quarter of the globe; too high-minded to endure the degradations of the others; possessing a chosen country, with room enough for our descendants to the thousandth and thousandth generation; entertaining a due sense of our equal right to the use of our own faculties, to the acquisitions of our own industry, to honor and confidence from our fellow-citizens, resulting not from birth, but from our actions and their sense of them; enlightened by a benign religion, professed, indeed, and practiced in various forms, yet all of them inculcating honesty, truth, temperance, gratitude, and the love of man; acknowledging and adoring an overruling Providence, which by all its dispensations proves that it delights in the happiness of man here and his greater happiness hereafter—with all these blessings, what more is necessary to make us a happy and a prosperous people? Still one thing more, fellow-citizens—a

望的政府可能需要力量才得以自存，因而就放弃这个迄今带给我们自由和坚定的政府吗？我相信不会。相反，我相信这是世界上最坚强的政府。我相信唯有在这种政府的治理下，每个人才会响应法律的号召，奔向法律的旗帜下，像对待切身利益那样，迎击侵犯公共秩序的举动。有时我们听到一种说法：不能让人们自己管理自己。那么，能让别人去管理他吗？或者，我们在统治人民的君王名单中发现了天使吗？这个问题让历史来回答吧。

因此，让我们以勇气和信心，追求我们自己的联邦的与共和党的原则，拥戴联邦与代议制政府。我们由于自然环境和大洋的阻隔，幸免于地球上四分之一地区发生的那场毁灭性浩劫；我们品格高尚，不能容忍他人的堕落；我们天赐良邦，其幅员足以容纳子孙万代；我们充分认识到在发挥个人才干、以勤劳换取收入、受到同胞的尊敬与信赖上，大家享有平等的权利，但这种尊敬和信赖不是出于门第，而是出于我们的行为和同胞的评判；我们受到仁慈的宗教的启迪，尽管教派不同，形式各异，但它们都教人以正直、忠诚、节制、恩义和仁爱；我们承认和崇拜全能的上帝，而天意表明，他乐于使这里的人们得到幸福，今后还将得到更多的幸

Thomas Jefferson
托马斯·杰斐逊(1743-1826)
3rd President of the United States (1801-1809)

wise and frugal Government, which shall restrain men from injuring one another, shall leave them otherwise free to regulate their own pursuits of industry and improvement, and shall not take from the mouth of labor the bread it has earned. This is the sum of good government, and this is necessary to close the circle of our felicities.

About to enter, fellow-citizens, on the exercise of duties which comprehend everything dear and valuable to you, it is proper you should understand what I deem the essential principles of our Government, and consequently those which ought to shape its Administration. I will compress them within the narrowest compass they will bear, stating the general principle, but not all its limitations. Equal and exact justice to all men, of whatever state or persuasion, religious or political; peace, commerce, and honest friendship with all nations, entangling alliances with none; the support of the State governments in all their rights, as the most competent administrations for our domestic concerns and the surest bulwarks against anti-republican tendencies; the preservation of the General Government in its whole constitutional vigor, as the sheet anchor of our peace at home and safety abroad; a jealous care of the right of election by the people — a mild and safe corrective of abuses which are lopped by the sword of revolution where peaceable remedies are unprovided; absolute acquiescence in the decisions of the majority, the vital principle of republics, from which is no appeal but to force, the vital principle and immediate parent of despotism; a well-disciplined militia, our best reliance in peace and for the first moments of war till regulars may relieve them; the supremacy of the civil over the military authority; economy in the public expense, that labor may

福——我们有了这些福祉,还需要什么才能够使我们成为快乐而兴旺的民族呢?公民们,我们还需要一样,那就是贤明而节俭的政府,它会制止人们相互伤害,使他们自由地管理自己的实业和进步活动,它不会侵夺人们的劳动果实。这就是良好政府的要旨,这也是我们达到幸福圆满之必需。

公民们,我即将履行职责,这些职责包括你们所珍爱的一切,因此,你们应当了解我所认为的政府基本原则是什么,确定其行政依据的原则又是什么。我将尽量扼要地加以叙述,只讲一般原则,不讲其种种限制。实行人人平等和真正的公平,而不论其宗教或政治上的地位或派别;同所有国家和平相处、商务往来、真诚友好,而不与任何国家结盟,维护各州政府的一切权利,将它们作为我国最有权能的内政机构和抵御反共和趋势的最可靠屏障;维持全国政府在宪制上的全部活力,将其作为国内安定和国际安全的最后依靠;忠实地维护人民的选举权——将它作为一种温和而稳妥的矫正手段,对革命留下的、尚无和平补救办法的种种弊端予以矫正;绝对同意多数人的决定,因为这是共和制的主要原则,反之,不诉诸舆论而诉诸武力乃是专制的主要原则和直接根源;建立一支训练有素的民兵,作为和

be lightly burthened; the honest payment of our debts and sacred preservation of the public faith; encouragement of agriculture, and of commerce as its handmaid; the diffusion of information and arraignment of all abuses at the bar of the public reason; freedom of religion; freedom of the press, and freedom of person under the protection of the habeas corpus, and trial by juries impartially selected. These principles form the bright constellation which has gone before us and guided our steps through an age of revolution and reformation. The wisdom of our sages and blood of our heroes have been devoted to their attainment. They should be the creed of our political faith, the text of civic instruction, the touchstone by which to try the services of those we trust; and should we wander from them in moments of error or of alarm, let us hasten to retrace our steps and to regain the road which alone leads to peace, liberty, and safety.

I repair, then, fellow-citizens, to the post you have assigned me. With experience enough in subordinate offices to have seen the difficulties of this the greatest of all, I have learnt to expect that it will rarely fall to the lot of imperfect man to retire from this station with the reputation and the favor which bring him into it. Without pretensions to that high confidence you reposed in our first and greatest revolutionary character, whose preeminent services had entitled him to the first place in his country's love and destined for him the fairest page in the volume of faithful history, I ask so much confidence only as may give firmness and effect to the legal administration of your affairs. I shall often go wrong through defect of judgment. When right, I

平时期和战争初期的最好依靠，直到正规军来接替；实行文职权高于军职权；节约政府开支，减轻劳工负担；如实地偿还债务，庄严地维护政府信誉；鼓励农业，辅之以商业；传播信息，以公众理智为准绳补偏救弊；实行宗教自由；实行出版自由和人身自由，根据人身保护法和由公正选出陪审团进行审判来保证人身自由。这些原则构成了明亮的星座，它在我们的前方照耀，指引我们经历了革命和改革时期。先哲的智慧和英雄的鲜血都曾为实现这些原则作出过奉献，这些原则应当是我们的政治信条，公民教育的课本，检验我们所信赖的人的工作的试金石；如果我们因一时错误或惊恐而背离这些原则，那就让我们赶紧回头，重返这唯一通向和平、自由和安全的大道。

各位公民，我即将担任你们委派给我的职务。根据我以往担任过的许多较低职务的经验，我已经意识到这是最艰巨的职务，因此，我能够预期，当一个并非尽善尽美的人从这个职位卸任时，很少能像就任时那样深孚众望。我不敢奢望大家如同信任我们第一位最伟大的革命元勋那样对我高度信任，因为他的卓著勋劳使他最有资格受到全国的爱戴，使他在忠实的史书中占有最辉煌的一页。我只要

Thomas Jefferson
托马斯·杰斐逊(1743-1826)
3rd President of the United States (1801-1809)

shall often be thought wrong by those whose positions will not command a view of the whole ground. I ask your indulgence for my own errors, which will never be intentional, and your support against the errors of others, who may condemn what they would not if seen in all its parts. The approbation implied by your suffrage is a great consolation to me for the past, and my future solicitude will be to retain the good opinion of those who have bestowed it in advance, to conciliate that of others by doing them all the good in my power, and to be instrumental to the happiness and freedom of all.

Relying, then, on the patronage of your good will, I advance with obedience to the work, ready to retire from it whenever you become sensible how much better choice it is in your power to make. And may that Infinite Power which rules the destinies of the universe lead our councils to what is best, and give them a favorable issue for your peace and prosperity.

求大家给我相当的信任,使我足以坚定地、有效地依法管理大家的事务。由于判断有误,我会常常犯错误。即使我是正确的,那些不是站在统筹全局的立场上看问题的人,也会常常认为我是错误的。我请求你们宽容我自己犯的错误,而这些错误绝非故意;我也请求你们支持我反对别人的错误,而这些人如果通盘考虑,也是绝不会犯的。从投票结果来看,大家对我的过去甚为嘉许,这是我莫大的安慰。今后我所渴望的是,力求赐予我好评的各位能保持这种好评,在我职权范围内为其他各位效劳以博得他们的好评,并为所有同胞们的幸福和自由而尽力。

现在,我仰承各位的好意,恭顺地就任此职,一旦你们觉得需要作出你们有权作出的更好的选择,我便准备辞去此职。愿主宰天地万物命运的上帝引导我们的机构臻于完善,并为大家的和平与昌盛,赐给它一个值得赞许的结果。

詹姆斯·麦迪逊:美国第4任总统(1809—1817),"合众国宪法之父"。任内遭遇英美之战,英军一度攻占并焚烧白宫,但他坚定地领导美国人民取得了最终的胜利,极大地巩固了这个新兴国家的地位。

James Madison
詹姆斯·麦迪逊(1751-1836)
4th President of the United States (1809-1817)
Political Party: Democratic-Republican

To Cultivate Peace by Observing Justice
坚守正义　维护和平

Unwilling to depart from examples of the most revered authority, I avail myself of the occasion now presented to express the profound impression made on me by the call of my country to the station to the duties of which I am about to pledge myself by the most solemn of sanctions. So distinguished a mark of confidence, proceeding from the deliberate and tranquil suffrage of a free and virtuous nation, would under any circumstances have commanded my gratitude and devotion, as well as filled me with an awful sense of the trust to be assumed. Under the various

我不愿违背最受人尊敬的前任总统所树立的榜样,我要借此机会表达当我接受国家召唤,即将在庄严神圣的仪式下宣誓就职时的深切感受。一个自由、公正的国家,在审慎而平静的选举中对本人表现了极大的信心,这在任何情况下都将激起我的感激之情和献身之心,同时也使我心中充满了人民对我的信赖。由于

James Madison
詹姆斯·麦迪逊(1751-1836)
4th President of the United States (1809-1817)

circumstances which give peculiar solemnity to the existing period, I feel that both the honor and the responsibility allotted to me are inexpressibly enhanced.

The present situation of the world is indeed without a parallel and that of our own country full of difficulties. The pressure of these, too, is the more severely felt because they have fallen upon us at a moment when the national prosperity being at a height not before attained, the contrast resulting from the change has been rendered the more striking. Under the benign influence of our republican institutions, and the maintenance of peace with all nations whilst so many of them were engaged in bloody and wasteful wars, the fruits of a just policy were enjoyed in an unrivaled growth of our faculties and resources. Proofs of this were seen in the improvements of agriculture, in the successful enterprises of commerce, in the progress of manufacturers and useful arts, in the increase of the public revenue and the use made of it in reducing the public debt, and in the valuable works and establishments everywhere multiplying over the face of our land.

It is a precious reflection that the transition from this prosperous condition of our country to the scene which has for some time been distressing us is not chargeable on any unwarrantable views, nor, as I trust, on any involuntary errors in the public councils. Indulging no passions which trespass on the rights or the repose of other nations, it has been the true glory of the United States to cultivate peace by observing justice, and to entitle themselves to the respect of the nations at war by fulfilling their neutral obligations with the most scrupulous impartiality. If there be candor in the world, the truth of these assertions will not be questioned; posterity at least will do justice to them.

各种情况都使此时此刻变得格外庄严,我感到给予我的荣誉和责任都难以形容地增加了。

目前的国际形势确实是前所未有,而国内形势又困难重重。由于这种形势是在国家达到空前繁荣时降临的,因此,这一变化形成了强烈的对照,更使人感受到严峻的压力。我们的共和制发挥了良好的作用,当许多国家处在流血、损耗性战争时,我们坚持与各国和平交往的正确的政策结出了硕果,我们的力量和资源都得到了极大的发展。诸如农业的改进、商业的成功、制造业和工艺的进步、国库收入的增加、公债数额的减少、越来越多的有价值的工程设施遍及全国各地等等,都是证明。

难能可贵的是,我们要认识到,我国之所以从繁荣景象转变为一段时期以来令人沮丧的情景,不应当归咎于政府政策上的失误,而且我认为,这绝非政府本意。美国丝毫不想侵犯其他国家的权利或安宁,美国的真正光荣是坚守正义、维护和平,对交战的国家严格奉行不偏不倚的态度,尽到中立国的责任,从而有资格赢得这些国家的尊重。如果世界上存在公理,这些论断的真实性就不容置疑,至少我们的子孙后代会有公断。

This unexceptionable course could not avail against the injustice and violence of the belligerent powers. In their rage against each other, or impelled by more direct motives, principles of retaliation have been introduced equally contrary to universal reason and acknowledged law. How long their arbitrary edicts will be continued in spite of the demonstrations that not even a pretext for them has been given by the United States, and of the fair and liberal attempt to induce a revocation of them, cannot be anticipated. Assuring myself that under every vicissitude the determined spirit and united councils of the nation will be safeguards to its honor and its essential interests, I repair to the post assigned me with no other discouragement than what springs from my own inadequacy to its high duties. If I do not sink under the weight of this deep conviction it is because I find some support in a consciousness of the purposes and a confidence in the principles which I bring with me into this arduous service.

To cherish peace and friendly intercourse with all nations having correspondent dispositions; to maintain sincere neutrality toward belligerent nations; to prefer in all cases amicable discussion and reasonable accommodation of differences to a decision of them by an appeal to arms; to exclude foreign intrigues and foreign partialities, so degrading to all countries and so baneful to free ones; to foster a spirit of independence too just to invade the rights of others, too proud to surrender our own, too liberal to indulge unworthy prejudices ourselves and too elevated not to look down upon them in others; to hold the union of the States as the basis of their peace and happiness; to support the Constitution, which is the cement of the Union, as well

这一无可指责的方针未能制止那些好战国家的不公正之举和暴力行为。它们在互相迁怒的过程中，或是迫于更直接的动机，采取了完全违背普通理性和公认法则的报复原则。我们无法预知这些国家专断的敕令还将维持多久，尽管事实证明美国丝毫没有授人以借口，而且为取消这些法令作出了公正而宽大的努力。我相信，无论风云如何变化，国家的坚定精神和团结一致将是其荣誉和基本利益的保证。因此，在我即将就任委派给我的职务时，除了使我担心的是如何跨越本人的能力不足与崇高的责任之间的鸿沟。如果说我并没有在这种深刻的认识的压力下消沉，那是因为我在执行这项艰巨任务时，意识到了一些目标并深信某些原则，因而找到了支持。

珍惜与所有志同道合的国家的和平友好往来；对交战的国家保持真挚的中立；在任何情况下，以友善的讨论和通情达理的调停，而不是以诉诸武力来解决分歧；在外交上摒弃阴谋和偏见，那些对任何国家来说都是卑下可鄙的，对自由国家则更是危害匪浅，故予以摒弃；倡导一种独立精神，它必须主持公道而不侵犯他人利益，必须自重而不自暴自弃，必须信奉自由而不沉溺于自身的毫无价值的偏见，必须

James Madison
詹姆斯·麦迪逊(1751-1836)
4th President of the United States (1809-1817)

in its limitations as in its authorities; to respect the rights and authorities reserved to the States and to the people as equally incorporated with and essential to the success of the general system; to avoid the slightest interference with the right of conscience or the functions of religion, so wisely exempted from civil jurisdiction; to preserve in their full energy the other salutary provisions in behalf of private and personal rights, and of the freedom of the press; to observe economy in public expenditures; to liberate the public resources by an honorable discharge of the public debts; to keep within the requisite limits a standing military force, always remembering that an armed and trained militia is the firmest bulwark of republics—that without standing armies their liberty can never be in danger, nor with large ones safe; to promote by authorized means improvements friendly to agriculture, to manufactures, and to external as well as internal commerce; to favor in like manner the advancement of science and the diffusion of information as the best aliment to true liberty; to carry on the benevolent plans which have been so meritoriously applied to the conversion of our aboriginal neighbors from the degradation and wretchedness of savage life to a participation of the improvements of which the human mind and manners are susceptible in a civilized state—as far as sentiments and intentions such as these can aid the fulfillment of my duty, they will be a resource which cannot fail me.

奋发向上而不轻视他人的偏见;以合众国的团结作为和平幸福的基础;支持使联邦得以巩固的宪法,遵守宪法的规定和拥护宪法的权威;尊重各州保留的权利和权力,以及同样作为联邦组成部分的人民所保留的权利和权力,因为这是整个制度取得成功所必不可少的;丝毫不要涉及个人信仰或宗教活动的权利,以便明智地避免卷入民事管辖的范围;维持关于私人权利、人身权利和出版自由的其他有益条款的全部效力;对政府的开支要厉行节约;以清偿公债为荣,调动公共资源;在必要范围内保持一支常备武装,时刻牢记一支训练有素的武装民兵是所有共和国的最坚强堡垒——并且要记住,没有常备部队,自由绝不至于处于危险的境地,而庞大的武装则并不意味着安全;通过合法手段促进有利于农业、制造业和国内外贸易的各项改进措施;以同样方式促进科学发展和知识普及,将其作为真正自由的最佳滋养;实施慈善计划,而值得称道的是,这些计划已被用于转化我国的土著居民,使他们摆脱野蛮生活的低级和悲惨的状态,从而参与文明国度中人类思想和举止的各种改进——上述这些想法和打算能够帮助我完成任务,就此而言,它们将成为我取之不竭的源泉。

It is my good fortune, moreover, to have the path in which I am to tread lighted by examples of illustrious services successfully rendered in the most trying difficulties by those who have marched before me. Of those of my immediate predecessor it might least become me here to speak. I may, however, be pardoned for not suppressing the sympathy with which my heart is full in the rich reward he enjoys in the benedictions of a beloved country, gratefully bestowed or exalted talents zealously devoted through a long career to the advancement of its highest interest and happiness.

But the source to which I look or the aids which alone can supply my deficiencies is in the well-tried intelligence and virtue of my fellow-citizens, and in the counsels of those representing them in the other departments associated in the care of the national interests. In these my confidence will under every difficulty be best placed, next to that which we have all been encouraged to feel in the guardianship and guidance of that Almighty Being whose power regulates the destiny of nations, whose blessings have been so conspicuously dispensed to this rising Republic, and to whom we are bound to address our devout gratitude for the past, as well as our fervent supplications and best hopes for the future.

另外，我很幸运，我的前任们已克服了极大的困难，成功地树立了杰出的服务典范，照亮了我即将奔赴的道路。至于刚刚卸任的总统的情况，由我在此评说也许极不适当。但是，你们也许可以宽恕我表达出内心的感受：他从一个可爱的国家的赐福中得到了丰厚的奖赏，在漫长的人生道路上，他以他的高贵才能，满腔热忱地为促进国家的最高利益和幸福作出了奉献。

但是，我所寻求的力量源泉，或者说足以弥补本人不足的，在于公民们久经磨炼的才智和美德，在于公民们的代表者提出的各种意见，这些人遍布各个部门，关心着国家利益。不论遇到什么困难，有了这些，我就拥有最大的信心。更重要的是，我们都感到全能的上帝在护佑和指引着我们，它的力量驾驭着各民族的命运，它的祝福赐予这个新兴的共和国更是世所瞩目，我们必须为过去向它表示虔诚的感谢，为未来向它表示热忱的祈祷和最美好的希望。

Andrew Jackson
安德鲁·杰克逊(1767-1845)
7th President of the United States (1829-1837)

安德鲁·杰克逊:美国第7任总统(1829—1837),第一位"小木屋"出生的总统。曾在新奥尔良大败英军,为美国取得第二次对英战争的胜利奠定了基础。任期内粉碎南卡罗来纳州脱离联邦的阴谋,强化了总统制。

Andrew Jackson
安德鲁·杰克逊(1767-1845)
7th President of the United States (1829-1837)
Political Party: Democratic-Republican and Democratic

Duties of a President
总统职责

Fellow-Citizens:

About to undertake the arduous duties that I have been appointed to perform by the choice of a free people, I avail myself of this customary and solemn occasion to express the gratitude which their confidence inspires and to acknowledge the accountability which my situation enjoins. While the magnitude of their interests convinces me that no thanks can be adequate to the honor they have conferred, it admonishes me that the best return I can make is the zealous dedication of my humble abilities to their service and their good.

同胞们:

在我即将承担一个自由的民族选择挑选所委派于我的艰巨职责时,我谨利用这一约定俗成的庄严场合来表达你们的信任在我心中激起的感激之情,并接受我的职务所负有的责任。你们的极大关注使我深信,任何感谢之辞都不足以报答你们所授予我的荣誉,同时又告诫我,我所能作出的最好的报答,就是将我微薄的能力热忱地奉献给为你们谋福利尽义务的事业。

As the instrument of the Federal Constitution it will devolve on me for a stated period to execute the laws of the United States, to superintend their foreign and their confederate relations, to manage their revenue, to command their forces, and, by communications to the Legislature, to watch over and to promote their interests generally. And the principles of action by which I shall endeavor to accomplish this circle of duties it is now proper for me briefly to explain.

In administering the laws of Congress I shall keep steadily in view the limitations as well as the extent of the Executive power trusting thereby to discharge the functions of my office without transcending its authority. With foreign nations it will be my study to preserve peace and to cultivate friendship on fair and honorable terms, and in the adjustment of any differences that may exist or arise to exhibit the forbearance becoming a powerful nation rather than the sensibility belonging to a gallant people.

In such measures as I may be called on to pursue in regard to the rights of the separate States I hope to be animated by a proper respect for those sovereign members of our Union, taking care not to confound the powers they have reserved to themselves with those they have granted to the Confederacy.

The management of the public revenue—that searching operation in all governments—is among the most delicate and important trusts in ours, and it will, of course, demand no inconsiderable share of my official solicitude. Under every aspect in which it can be considered it would appear that advantage must result from the observance of a strict and faithful economy. This I shall aim at the more anxiously both because it will facilitate the extinguishment of the national debt, the unnecessary duration of which is incompatible with real independence, and because it will

根据联邦宪法的规定,在一段规定的时期内,执行合众国的法律,主管外交及联邦各州关系,管理税收,指挥武装部队,通过向立法机构传达意见,普遍保护并促进美国各项利益等职责将移交给我。现在由我简要地解释一下我将努力完成这一系列职责的行动准则是必要的。

在实施国会的法律时,我将始终铭记总统权力的限制及范围,希望借以执行我的职能而不越权。在与外交方面,我将致力于研究调停各种可能存在和可能产生的争端,更多地表现出一个大国的宽容大度而不只是一个勇敢的民族所具有的敏感,在公正和体面的条件下维护和平及缔结邦交。

在我出于需要可能被要求执行的有关各州权利的措施里,我希望对我们合众国各个自主州的适当尊敬将能激励我工作,我将小心翼翼绝不混淆他们为自己保留的权利和他们赋予联邦政府的权力。

国家税收的管理——在所有的政府中这都是一件棘手的工作——是我们政府中最微妙和最重要的职责之一,我理所当然要予以足够的重视和关注。从各个方面来考虑,厉行节约看来将大有裨益。我之所以急切地希望能达到这个目标,是因为它既有利于偿清国债,而对此作不必要的拖延同真正的独立不相

Andrew Jackson

安德鲁·杰克逊(1767-1845)
7th President of the United States (1829-1837)

counteract that tendency to public and private profligacy which a profuse expenditure of money by the Government is but too apt to engender. Powerful auxiliaries to the attainment of this desirable end are to be found in the regulations provided by the wisdom of Congress for the specific appropriation of public money and the prompt accountability of public officers.

With regard to a proper selection of the subjects of impost with a view to revenue, it would seem to me that the spirit of equity, caution and compromise in which the Constitution was formed requires that the great interests of agriculture, commerce, and manufactures should be equally favored, and that perhaps the only exception to this rule should consist in the peculiar encouragement of any products of either of them that may be found essential to our national independence.

Internal improvement and the diffusion of knowledge, so far as they can be promoted by the constitutional acts of the Federal Government, are of high importance.

Considering standing armies as dangerous to free governments in time of peace, I shall not seek to enlarge our present establishment, nor disregard that salutary lesson of political experience which teaches that the military should be held subordinate to the civil power. The gradual increase of our Navy, whose flag has displayed in distant climes our skill in navigation and our fame in arms; the preservation of our forts, arsenals, and dockyards, and the introduction of progressive improvements in the discipline and science of both branches of our military service are so plainly prescribed by prudence that I should be excused for omitting their mention sooner than for enlarging on their importance. But the bulwark of our defense is the national militia, which in the present state of our intelligence and population must render us invincible. As long as our

容的,也由于它将能抵制政府和个人的恣意浪费的趋势,而政府的庞大开支是极易造成这种浪费的风气。国会明智地制定了关于公款的专款专用和政府官员欠账偿付期限责任的规定,这将大大有助于达到这一理想的目标。

至于旨在充实国家收入的纳税对象的适当选择,我认为制定宪法本着公正、谨慎和互让的精神,要求农业、商业和制造业的巨大利益应当受到同样的关照。也许这一原则唯一的例外在于,对其中任何一种与民族独立必不可缺的产品给以特殊的鼓励。

国内的进步以及知识的传播是极其重要的,它们将受到联邦政府宪法条例的最大的鼓励。

考虑到常备军在和平时期对自由政府构成的威胁,我将不寻求扩大现在的编制,我也不会无视政治经验提供的有益教训,即军方必须隶属于文官政府。我国海军要逐步增强,让它的战旗在遥远的海域飘扬,显示出我们航海的技术和军事的声望;我们的要塞、军火库和码头要得到维护,我们的两个兵种在训练和技术上要采用先进的手段等等,这些都有审慎的明文规定,恕我不在此絮谈其重要性。但是我们的国防堡垒是全国的民兵,在我国目前的知

Government is administered for the good of the people, and is regulated by their will; as long as it secures to us the rights of person and of property, liberty of conscience and of the press, it will be worth defending; and so long as it is worth defending a patriotic militia will cover it with an impenetrable aegis. Partial injuries and occasional mortifications we may be subjected to, but a million of armed freemen, possessed of the means of war, can never be conquered by a foreign foe. To any just system, therefore, calculated to strengthen this natural safeguard of the country I shall cheerfully lend all the aid in my power.

It will be my sincere and constant desire to observe toward the Indian tribes within our limits a just and liberal policy, and to give that humane and considerate attention to their rights and their wants which is consistent with the habits of our Government and the feelings of our people.

The recent demonstration of public sentiment inscribes on the list of Executive duties, in characters too legible to be overlooked, the task of reform, which will require particularly the correction of those abuses that have brought the patronage of the Federal Government into conflict with the freedom of elections, and the counteraction of those causes which have disturbed the rightful course of appointment and have placed or continued power in unfaithful or incompetent hands.

In the performance of a task thus generally delineated I shall endeavor to select men whose diligence and talents will insure in their respective stations able and faithful cooperation, depending for the advancement of the public

识水平和人口的状况下,它一定会使我们坚不可摧。只要我们的政府为民众谋福利,按他们的意志进行管理;只要它保障我们人身和财产的权利,保护信仰自由和出版自由,它定将值得捍卫;只要它值得捍卫,一支爱国的民兵将以坚不可摧的盾牌来护卫它。我们可能会遭受部分的伤害和偶尔的屈辱,但是成百万掌握作战方法的武装的自由人决不会被外国敌人所征服。因此,对任何以加强国家的这个天然屏障为目标的合理制度,我都会在我能力之内乐于尽力给以支持。

对我们境内的印第安部落,我真诚地永久希望遵循一项公正和宽容的政策,我们将对他们的权利和要求给予人道的和周到的考虑,而这种权利和要求是同我国政府的习惯和人民的感情相一致的。

最近公众强烈呼吁进行改革,从而使这一任务列入行政任务表里了,字字清晰,不容忽视。这项任务特别要求纠正那些使联邦政府的保护同自由选举发生冲突的滥用职权的弊端,并抵制那些扰乱任命的合法途径和将权力交给或继续留在不忠实和不称职的人的手中的情况。

在执行上述任务时,我将努力任用这样一些人。他们的勤勉和才干将确保他们在各自的岗位上有效和忠实地

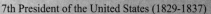

service more on the integrity and zeal of the public officers than on their numbers.

A diffidence, perhaps too just, in my own qualifications will teach me to look with reverence to the examples of public virtue left by my illustrious predecessors, and with veneration to the lights that flow from the mind that founded and the mind that reformed our system. The same diffidence induces me to hope for instruction and aid from the coordinate branches of the Government, and for the indulgence and support of my fellow-citizens generally.

And a firm reliance on the goodness of that Power whose providence mercifully protected our national infancy, and has since upheld our liberties in various vicissitudes, encourages me to offer up my ardent supplications that He will continue to make our beloved country the object of His divine care and gracious benediction.

进行合作,为了推进政府工作,我将更多地仰赖政府官员的廉正和热忱,而不是他们的数量。

我对自己担任这一职务的资质缺乏自信,这样说也许再恰当不过,这使我懂得,我要遵从各位杰出前任的榜样,敬仰他们留下的公共美德,景慕他们的光辉思想,因为是他们创立和改造了我们国家的制度,也正是由于缺乏自信,才使我尤为期望得到政府其他平级部门的指导和帮助,得到广大公民同胞的体谅和支持。

在我们的国家尚处于襁褓之中时,上帝即给予了仁慈的保护;在后来的各种风云变幻中,上帝又一直维护着我们的自由,因而我对上帝的仁慈抱有坚定的信念,这使我有勇气热烈地祈求上帝继续庇佑我们可爱的国家,赐予我国美好的祝福。

亚伯拉罕·林肯:美国第16任总统(1861—1865),美国人心目中最伟大的总统之一,曾领导人民投入南北战争,挽救了联邦,重新统一了美国。1865年遇刺。本篇深明大义,苦口婆心地对"不满意的同胞们"进行了规劝。由于内战迫在眉睫,就职仪式首次动用军队进行了保护。

Abraham Lincoln
亚伯拉罕·林肯(1809-1865)
16th President of the United States (1861-1865)
Political Party: Whig (1832-1854)
Republican (1854-1864)
National Union (1864-1865)

The Union and the Government
联邦和政府

Fellow-Citizens of the United States:

In compliance with a custom as old as the Government itself, I appear before you to address you briefly and to take in your presence the oath prescribed by the Constitution of the United States to be taken by the President before he enters on the execution of this office.

I do not consider it necessary at present for me to discuss those matters of administration about which there is no special anxiety or excitement.

美国同胞们:

按照一个和我们的政府一样古老的习惯,我现在来到诸位的面前,简单地讲几句话,并在你们的面前,遵照合众国宪法一个总统在他"到职执事之前"必须进行宣誓的仪式的规定,在大家面前宣誓。

我认为没有必要在这里来讨论并不特别令人忧虑和不安的行政方面的问题。

Abraham Lincoln
亚伯拉罕·林肯(1809-1865)
16th President of the United States (1861-1865)

Apprehension seems to exist among the people of the Southern States that by the accession of a Republican Administration their property and their peace and personal security are to be endangered. There has never been any reasonable cause for such apprehension. Indeed, the most ample evidence to the contrary has all the while existed and been open to their inspection. It is found in nearly all the published speeches of him who now addresses you. I do but quote from one of those speeches when I declare that—I have no purpose, directly or indirectly, to interfere with the institution of slavery in the States where it exists. I believe I have no lawful right to do so, and I have no inclination to do so.

Those who nominated and elected me did so with full knowledge that I had made this and many similar declarations and had never recanted them; and more than this, they placed in the platform for my acceptance, and as a law to themselves and to me, the clear and emphatic resolution which I now read:

Resolved: That the maintenance inviolate of the rights of the States, and especially the right of each State to order and control its own domestic institutions according to its own judgment exclusively, is essential to that balance of power on which the perfection and endurance of our political fabric depend; and we denounce the lawless invasion by armed force of the soil of any State or Territory, no matter what pretext, as among the gravest of crimes.

在南方各州人民中似乎存在着一种恐惧心理。他们认为,随着共和党政府的执政,他们的财产,他们的和平生活和人身安全都将遭到危险。这种恐惧是从来没有任何事实根据的。说实在的,大量相反的证据倒是一直存在,并随时可以供他们检查的。那种证据几乎在现在对你们讲话的这个人公开发表的每一篇演说中都能找到。这里我只想引用其中的一篇,在其中一篇演说中我曾说,"我完全无意,对已经存在奴隶制的各州的这一制度进行直接或间接的干涉。我深信我根本没有合法权利那样做,而且我无此意图。"

那些提名我并选举我的人都完全知道,我曾明确这么讲过,并且还讲过许多类似的话,而且从来也没有收回过我已讲过的这些话。不仅如此,他们还在纲领中,写进了对他们和对我来说,都具有法律效力的一项清楚明白、不容含糊的决议让我接受。这里我来对大家谈谈这一决议:

决议:"保持各州的各种权利不受侵犯,特别是各州完全凭自己的决断来安排和控制本州内部各种制度的权利不受侵犯,这种权力平衡是必要的,能保证我们的政体尽善尽美和持久长远;我们谴责使用武装力量非法入侵任何一个州或准州的土地,这种入侵不论使用什么借口,都是最严重的罪行。"

I now reiterate these sentiments, and in doing so I only press upon the public attention the most conclusive evidence of which the case is susceptible that the property, peace, and security of no section are to be in any wise endangered by the now incoming Administration. I add, too, that all the protection which, consistently with the Constitution and the laws, can be given will be cheerfully given to all the States when lawfully demanded, for whatever cause—as cheerfully to one section as to another.

There is much controversy about the delivering up of fugitives from service or labor. The clause I now read is as plainly written in the Constitution as any other of its provisions:

No person held to service or labor in one State, under the laws thereof, escaping into another, shall in consequence of any law or regulation therein be discharged from such service or labor, but shall be delivered up on claim of the party to whom such service or labor may be due.

It is scarcely questioned that this provision was intended by those who made it for the reclaiming of what we call fugitive slaves; and the intention of the lawgiver is the law. All members of Congress swear their support to the whole Constitution—to this provision as much as to any other. To the proposition, then, that slaves whose cases come within the terms of this clause "shall be delivered up" their oaths are unanimous. Now, if they would make the effort in good temper, could they not with nearly equal unanimity frame and pass a law by means of which to keep

我现在重申这些观点:而在这样做的时候,我只想提请公众注意,最能对这一点提出确切证据的那就是全国任何一个地方的财产、和平生活和人身安全决不会在任何情况下,由于即将上任的政府而遭到危险。这里我还要补充说,各州只要符合宪法和法律规定,合法地提出保护要求,政府便一定会乐于给予保护,不管是出于什么原因——而且对任何一个地方都一视同仁。

有一个争论得很多的问题是,关于逃避服务或引渡从劳役中逃走的人的问题。我现在要宣读的条文,也和任何有关其他问题的条款一样,明明白白写在宪法之中:

"凡根据一个州的法律应在该州服务或从事劳役的人,如逃到另一州,一律不得按照这一州的法律或条例,使其解除该项服务或劳役,而必须按照有权享有该项服务或劳役当事人的要求,将其引渡。"

毫无疑问,按照制定这一条款人的意图,此项规定实际指的就是,对我们所说的逃亡奴隶有权索回;而法律制定人的这一意图实际已成为法律。国会的所有议员都曾宣誓遵守宪法中的一切条款——对这一条和其他各条并无两样。因此,关于适合这一条款规定的奴隶应"将其引渡"这一点,他们的誓言是完全一致的。

Abraham Lincoln
亚伯拉罕·林肯(1809-1865)
16th President of the United States (1861-1865)

good that unanimous oath?

There is some difference of opinion whether this clause should be enforced by national or by State authority, but surely that difference is not a very material one. If the slave is to be surrendered, it can be of but little consequence to him or to others by which authority it is done. And should anyone in any case be content that his oath shall go unkept on a merely unsubstantial controversy as to how it shall be kept?

Again: In any law upon this subject ought not all the safeguards of liberty known in civilized and humane jurisprudence to be introduced, so that a free man be not in any case surrendered as a slave? And might it not be well at the same time to provide by law for the enforcement of that clause in the Constitution which guarantees that "the citizens of each State shall be entitled to all privileges and immunities of citizens in the several States"?

I take the official oath today with no mental reservations and with no purpose to construe the Constitution or laws by any hypercritical rules; and while I do not choose now to specify particular acts of Congress as proper to be enforced, I do suggest that it will be much safer for all, both in official and private stations, to conform to and abide by all those acts which stand unrepealed than

那么现在如果他们心平气和地作一番努力,他们难道不能以几乎同样完全一致的誓言,制定一项法律,以使他们的共同誓言得以实施吗?

究竟这一条款应该由国家当局,还是由州当局来执行,大家的意见还不完全一致;但可以肯定地说,这种分歧并不是什么十分重要的问题。只要奴隶能被交还,那究竟由哪一个当局来交还,对奴隶或对别的人来说,没有什么差别。任何人,在任何情况下,会因为应以何种方式来实现他的誓言这样一个无关紧要的争执,而愿意违背自己的誓言吗?

另外,在任何有关这一问题的法律中,应不应该把文明和人道法学中关于自由的各项保证都写上,以防止在任何情况下使一个自由人被作为奴隶交出吗?同时,宪法中还有一条规定,明确保证"每一州的公民都享有其他各州公民所享有公民的一切特权和豁免权",我们用法律保证使这一条文得以执行,那不是更好吗?

我今天在这里正式宣誓,思想上绝无任何保留,也决无意以任何过于挑剔的标准来解释宪法或法律条文。我现在虽不打算详细指出国会的哪些法令必须要遵照执行,但我建议,我们大家,不论以个人身份还是以公职人员的身

to violate any of them trusting to find impunity in having them held to be unconstitutional.

It is seventy-two years since the first inauguration of a President under our National Constitution. During that period fifteen different and greatly distinguished citizens have in succession administered the executive branch of the Government. They have conducted it through many perils, and generally with great success. Yet, with all this scope of precedent, I now enter upon the same task for the brief constitutional term of four years under great and peculiar difficulty. A disruption of the Federal Union, heretofore only menaced, is now formidably attempted.

I hold that in contemplation of universal law and of the Constitution the Union of these States is perpetual. Perpetuity is implied, if not expressed, in the fundamental law of all national governments. It is safe to assert that no government proper ever had a provision in its organic law for its own termination. Continue to execute all the express provisions of our National Constitution, and the Union will endure forever, it being impossible to destroy it except by some action not provided for in the instrument itself.

Again: If the United States be not a government proper, but an association of States in the nature of contract merely, can it, as a contract, be peaceably unmade by less than all the parties who made it? One party to a contract

份，为了有更多的安全，我们最好服从并遵守现在还没有废除的一切法令，而不要轻易相信可以指之为不合宪法，便可以逃脱罪责，而对其公然违反。

自从第一任总统根据国家宪法宣誓就职以来，七十二年已经过去了。在这期间，十五位十分杰出的公民相继主持过政府的行政部门。他们引导着它度过了许多艰难险阻，基本上都获得极大的成功。然而，尽管有这么多可供参考的先例，我现在将在宪法所规定的短短四年任期中来担任这同一任务，却面临着巨大的非同一般的困难。在此以前，分裂联邦只是受到了威胁，而现在却是已出现力图分裂它的可怕行动了。

从一般法律和我们的宪法来仔细考虑，我坚信，我们各州组成的联邦是永久性的。在一切国民政府的根本大法中永久性这一点，虽不一定写明，却是不言而喻的。我们完全可以肯定说，没有一个名副其实的政府会在自己的根本法中定出一条，规定自己完结的期限。继续执行我国宪法明文规定的各项条文，联邦便将永远存在下去——除了采取并未见之于宪法的行动，谁也不可能毁灭掉联邦。

还有，就算合众国并不是个名副其实的政府，而只是依靠契约成立的一个各州的联合体，那既有契约的约束，若

Abraham Lincoln
亚伯拉罕·林肯(1809-1865)
16th President of the United States (1861-1865)

may violate it—break it, so to speak—but does it not require all to lawfully rescind it?

Descending from these general principles, we find the proposition that in legal contemplation the Union is perpetual confirmed by the history of the Union itself. The Union is much older than the Constitution. It was formed, in fact, by the Articles of Association in 1774. It was matured and continued by the Declaration of Independence in 1776. It was further matured, and the faith of all the then thirteen States expressly plighted and engaged that it should be perpetual, by the Articles of Confederation in 1778. And finally, in 1787, one of the declared objects for ordaining and establishing the Constitution was "to form a more perfect Union."

But if destruction of the Union by one or by a part only of the States be lawfully possible, the Union is less perfect than before the Constitution, having lost the vital element of perpetuity.

It follows from these views that no State upon its own mere motion can lawfully get out of the Union; that resolves and ordinances to that effect are legally void, and that acts of violence within any State or States against the authority of the United States are insurrectionary or revolutionary, according to circumstances.

I therefore consider that in view of the Constitution and

非参加这一契约的各方一致同意,我们能说取消就把它取消吗?参加订立契约的一方可以违约,或者说毁约;但如果合法地取消这一契约,岂能不需要大家一致同意吗?

从这些总原则出发,我们发现,从法学观点来看,联邦具有永久性质的提法,是为联邦自身的历史所证实的。联邦本身比宪法更为早得多。事实上,它是由1774年签订的《联合条款》建立的。到1776年的《独立宣言》才使它进一步成熟和延续下来。然后,通过1778年的《邦联条款》使它更加成熟,当时参加的十三个州便已明确保证要使邦联永久存在下去。最后,在1787年制定的宪法公开宣布的目的之一,便是"组建一个更为完美的联邦"。

但是,如果任何一个州,或几个州也可以合法地把联邦给取消掉,这个联邦可是比它在宪法制定以前还更不完美了,因为它已失去了它的一个至关重要因素——永久性。

从这些观点我们可以认定,任何一个州,都不可能仅凭自己动议,便能合法地退出联邦——而任何以此为目的的决议和法令在法律上都是无效的;至于任何一州或几州的反对合众国当局的暴力行为,都可以依据具体情况视为叛乱或革命行为。

因此我认为,从宪法和法

the laws the Union is unbroken, and to the extent of my ability, I shall take care, as the Constitution itself expressly enjoins upon me, that the laws of the Union be faithfully executed in all the States. Doing this I deem to be only a simple duty on my part, and I shall perform it so far as practicable unless my rightful masters, the American people, shall withhold the requisite means or in some authoritative manner direct the contrary. I trust this will not be regarded as a menace, but only as the declared purpose of the Union that it will constitutionally defend and maintain itself.

In doing this there needs to be no bloodshed or violence, and there shall be none unless it be forced upon the national authority. The power confided to me will be used to hold, occupy, and possess the property and places belonging to the Government and to collect the duties and imposts; but beyond what may be necessary for these objects, there will be no invasion, no using of force against or among the people anywhere. Where hostility to the United States in any interior locality shall be so great and universal as to prevent competent resident citizens from holding the Federal offices, there will be no attempt to force obnoxious strangers among the people for that object. While the strict legal right may exist in the Government to enforce the exercise of these offices, the attempt to do so would be so irritating and so nearly impracticable withal that I deem it better to forego for the time the uses of such offices.

律的角度来看，联邦是不容分裂的，我也将竭尽全力，按照宪法明确赋予我的责任，坚决负责让联邦的一切法令在所有各州得以贯彻执行。这样做，我认为只是履行我应尽的简单职责；只要是可行的，我就一定要履行它，除非我的合法主人——美国人民，限制必要的手段，或行使他们的权威，命令我采取相反的行动。我相信我这决不会被看成是一种恫吓，而只会被看作实现联邦已公开宣布的目的，它必将按照宪法保卫和维持它自己的存在。

要做到这一点并不需要流血或使用暴力，除非有人把它强加于国家当局，否则便绝不会发生那种情况。赋予我的权力将被用来执掌、使用和保有属于政府的一切财产和土地，征收各种税款和关税；但除了为了这些目的所必须进行的工作外，决不会有什么入侵问题——决不会在任何地方用暴力去反对或离间任何地区的人民。在国内任何地方，即使对联邦政府的敌对情绪已十分严重和普遍，以致妨害有能力的当地公民执行联邦职务的时候，政府也决不会强制派进令人反感的外来人去担任这些职务。尽管按严格的法律规定，政府有权强制履行这些职责，但一定要那样做，必然引起极大的愤怒，也几乎是行不通的，所以我认为最好还是暂时先把这些职责放一放。

Abraham Lincoln
亚伯拉罕·林肯(1809-1865)
16th President of the United States (1861-1865)

The mails, unless repelled, will continue to be furnished in all parts of the Union. So far as possible the people everywhere shall have that sense of perfect security which is most favorable to calm thought and reflection. The course here indicated will be followed unless current events and experience shall show a modification or change to be proper, and in every case and exigency my best discretion will be exercised, according to circumstances actually existing and with a view and a hope of a peaceful solution of the national troubles and the restoration of fraternal sympathies and affections.

That there are persons in one section or another who seek to destroy the Union at all events and are glad of any pretext to do it I will neither affirm nor deny; but if there be such, I need address no word to them. To those, however, who really love the Union may I not speak?

Before entering upon so grave a matter as the destruction of our national fabric, with all its benefits, its memories, and its hopes, would it not be wise to ascertain precisely why we do it? Will you hazard so desperate a step while there is any possibility that any portion of the ills you fly from have no real existence? Will you, while the certain ills you fly to are greater than all the real ones you fly from, will you risk the commission of so fearful a mistake?

All profess to be content in the Union if all constitutional rights can be maintained. Is it true, then, that any right plainly written in the Constitution has been

邮政,除非遭到拒收,仍将在联邦全境运作。在可能的情况下,一定要让各地人民,都享有完善的安全感,这十分有利于冷静思索和反思。我在这里所讲的这些方针必将奉行,除非当前事态和实际经验表明修改或改变方针是合适的。对任何一个事件和紧急问题,我一定会根据当时出现的具体形势谨慎从事,期望以和平手段解决国内纠纷,力图恢复兄弟爱、手足情。

至于说某些地方总有些人不顾一切一心想破坏联邦,并不惜以任何借口图谋不轨,我不打算肯定或否定;如果确有这样一些人,我不必要再对他们讲什么。但对那些真正热爱联邦的人,我不可以讲几句吗?

在我们着手研究有关我们国家组织和它的利益、记忆和希望这样重大事情之前,难道明智的做法不是先仔细研究一下那样做究竟是为了什么?当事实上极有可能你企图逃避的祸害并不存在的时候,你还会不顾一切走出冒险的一步吗?或者你要逃避的灾祸虽确实存在,而在你逃往的地方却有更大的灾祸在等着你;那你会往那里逃吗?你会冒险犯下如此可怕的一个错误吗?

大家都说,如果宪法中所规定的一切权利都确实得到执行,那人们都会承认处于联

denied? I think not. Happily, the human mind is so constituted that no party can reach to the audacity of doing this. Think, if you can, of a single instance in which a plainly written provision of the Constitution has ever been denied. If by the mere force of numbers a majority should deprive a minority of any clearly written constitutional right, it might in a moral point of view justify revolution; certainly would if such right were a vital one. But such is not our case. All the vital rights of minorities and of individuals are so plainly assured to them by affirmations and negations, guaranties and prohibitions, in the Constitution that controversies never arise concerning them. But no organic law can ever be framed with a provision specifically applicable to every question which may occur in practical administration. No foresight can anticipate nor any document of reasonable length contain express provisions for all possible questions. Shall fugitives from labor be surrendered by national or by State authority? The Constitution does not expressly say. May Congress prohibit slavery in the Territories? The Constitution does not expressly say. Must Congress protect slavery in the Territories? The Constitution does not expressly say.

邦之中是满意的。那么，真有什么如宪法中明文规定的权利被否定了吗？我想没有。很幸运，人的头脑是如此的一致，没有哪一方敢于如此冒天下之大不韪。如果可能，请你们讲出哪怕是一个例子来，说明有什么宪法中明文规定的条款是没有得到执行的。如果多数派完全靠人数上的优势，剥夺掉少数派宪法上明文规定的权利，这件事从道义的角度来看，也许可以说革命是正当的——如果被剥夺的是极为重要的权利，那革命就肯定无疑是合理行动。但我们的情况却并非如此。少数派和个人的一切重要权利，在宪法中，通过肯定和否定、保证和禁令都一一向他们作了明确保证，以至关于这类问题，从来也没有引起过争论。但是，在制定基本法时却不可能对实际工作中出现的任何问题，都一一写下可以立即加以应用的条文。再高明的预见也不可能料定未来的一切，任何长度适当的文件也不可能包容下针对一切可能发生的问题的条文。逃避劳役的人到底应该由联邦政府交还还是由州政府交还呢？宪法上没有具体规定。国会可以在准州禁止奴隶制吗？宪法没有具体规定。国会必须保护准州的奴隶制吗？宪法也没有具体规定。

Abraham Lincoln
亚伯拉罕·林肯(1809-1865)
16th President of the United States (1861-1865)

From questions of this class spring all our constitutional controversies and we divide upon them into majorities and minorities. If the minority will not acquiesce, the majority must, or the Government must cease. There is no other alternative, for continuing the Government is acquiescence on one side or the other. If a minority in such case will secede rather than acquiesce, they make a precedent which in turn will divide and ruin them, for a minority of their own will secede from them whenever a majority refuses to be controlled by such minority. For instance, why may not any portion of a new confederacy a year or two hence arbitrarily secede again, precisely as portions of the present Union now claim to secede from it? All who cherish disunion sentiments are now being educated to the exact temper of doing this.

Is there such perfect identity of interests among the States to compose a new union as to produce harmony only and prevent renewed secession?

Plainly the central idea of secession is the essence of anarchy. A majority held in restraint by constitutional checks and limitations, and always changing easily with deliberate changes of popular opinions and sentiments, is the only true sovereign of a free people. Whoever rejects it does of necessity fly to anarchy or to despotism. Unanimity is impossible. The rule of a minority, as a permanent arrangement, is wholly inadmissible; so that, rejecting the majority principle, anarchy or despotism in some form is all

从这类问题中引出了我们对宪法问题的争端,并因这类问题使我们分成了多数派和少数派。如果少数派不肯服从,多数派便必须服从,否则政府便只好停止工作了。再没有任何别的路可走,要让政府继续行使职权,便必须要这一方或那一方服从。在这种情况下,如果一个少数派宁可脱离也决不默认,那他们也就开创将来必会使他们分裂和毁灭的先例,因为,当多数派拒绝接受这样一个少数派的控制的时候,他们中的少数派便必会从他们之中再脱离出去。比如说,一个新的联盟的任何一部分,在一两年之后,为什么就不会像现在的联邦中的一些部分坚决要脱离出去一样,执意要从那个新联盟中脱离出去?所有怀着分裂联邦思想的人现在都正接受着分裂思想的教育。

难道要组成一个新联邦的州,它们的利益竟会是那样完全一致,它们只会有和谐,而不会再出现脱离行动吗?

非常清楚,退出联邦的中心思想实质就是无政府主义。一个受着宪法的检验和限制的约束,总是随着大众意见和情绪的慎重变化而及时改变的多数派,是自由人民的唯一真正的统治者。谁要想排斥他们,便必然走向无政府主义或专制主义。完全一致是根本不可能的,把少数派的统治

that is left.

I do not forget the position assumed by some that constitutional questions are to be decided by the Supreme Court, nor do I deny that such decisions must be binding in any case upon the parties to a suit as to the object of that suit, while they are also entitled to very high respect and consideration in all parallel cases by all other departments of the Government. And while it is obviously possible that such decision may be erroneous in any given case, still the evil effect following it, being limited to that particular case, with the chance that it may be overruled and never become a precedent for other cases, can better be borne than could the evils of a different practice. At the same time, the candid citizen must confess that if the policy of the Government upon vital questions affecting the whole people is to be irrevocably fixed by decisions of the Supreme Court, the instant they are made in ordinary litigation between parties in personal actions the people will have ceased to be their own rulers, having to that extent practically resigned their Government into the hands of that eminent tribunal. Nor is there in this view any assault upon the court or the judges. It is a duty from which they may not shrink to decide cases properly brought before them, and it is no fault of theirs if others seek to turn their decisions to political purposes.

One section of our country believes slavery is right and ought to be extended, while the other believes it is wrong

作为一种长期安排是完全不能接受的,所以,一旦排斥了多数原则,剩下的便只有某种形式的无政府主义或某专制主义了。

我没有忘记某些人的设想,认为宪法问题应该由最高法院来裁决。我也不否认这种裁决,在任何情况下,对诉讼各方,以及诉讼目的,完全具有约束力,而且在类似的情况中,应受到政府的一切其他部门高度的尊重和重视。尽管非常明显,这类裁决在某一特定案例中都很可能会是错误的,然而,这样随之而来的恶果总只限于该特定案件,同时裁决还有机会被驳回,不至于成为以后判案的先例,那这种过失比起其他的过失来当然更让人容易忍受。同时,正直的公民必须承认,如果政府有关全体人民利益的重大问题的政策,都由最高法院裁决,那么个人之间的一般诉讼一经裁决,人民便不再是自己的主人,因为到了那种程度,人民实际上将他们的政府交给那个高于一切的法庭了。我这样说,决无意对法院或法官表示不满。一件案子按正常程序送到他们面前,对它作出正当裁决,是他们的不可推卸的责任;如果别的人硬要把他们的判决用来达到政治目的,那并不是他们的过错。

我国有一部分地区相信奴隶制是正确的,应该扩展,

Abraham Lincoln
亚伯拉罕·林肯(1809-1865)
16th President of the United States (1861-1865)

and ought not to be extended. This is the only substantial dispute. The fugitive-slave clause of the Constitution and the law for the suppression of the foreign slave trade are each as well enforced, perhaps, as any law can ever be in a community where the moral sense of the people imperfectly supports the law itself. The great body of the people abide by the dry legal obligation in both cases, and a few break over in each. This, I think, cannot be perfectly cured, and it would be worse in both cases after the separation of the sections than before. The foreign slave trade, now imperfectly suppressed, would be ultimately revived without restriction in one section, while fugitive slaves, now only partially surrendered, would not be surrendered at all by the other.

Physically speaking, we cannot separate. We cannot remove our respective sections from each other nor build an impassable wall between them. A husband and wife may be divorced and go out of the presence and beyond the reach of each other, but the different parts of our country cannot do this. They cannot but remain face to face, and intercourse, either amicable or hostile, must continue between them. Is it possible, then, to make that intercourse more advantageous or more satisfactory after separation than before? Can aliens make treaties easier than friends can make laws? Can treaties be more faithfully enforced between aliens than laws can among friends? Suppose you go to war, you cannot fight always; and when, after much loss on both sides and no gain on either, you cease fighting, the identical old questions, as to terms

而另一部分地区又相信它是错误的,不应该扩展。这是唯一的实质性的争执,宪法中有关逃亡奴隶的条款,以及制止对外奴隶贸易的法律,在一个人民的道德观念并不支持该法的社会里,它们的执行情况也许不亚于任何一项法律所能达到的程度。在两种情况下,绝大多数的人都遵守枯燥乏味的法律义务,但又都有少数人不听那一套。关于这一点,我想,要彻底解决是根本不可能的;如果硬把两个地区分离,以后情况只会更坏。外籍奴隶贩卖现在并未能完全加以禁止,之后将会在一个地区不受限制地恢复起来;对于逃亡奴隶,在另一个地区,现在送回的只是一部分,将来会完全不肯交出来了。

就自然条件而言,我们是不能分离的。我们决不能把我们的各个地区相互搬开,也不可能在它们之间修建起一道无法逾越的高墙。一对夫妻可以离婚,各走各的路,彼此再不见面。但我们国家的各部分无法这么做。他们只能面对面相处,友好也罢,仇视也罢,他们仍必须彼此交往。我们难道能有任何办法使得这种交往在分离之后,比分离之前更为有利,更为令人满意吗?难道在外人之间订立条约,比在朋友之间制定法律还更为容易吗?难道在外

of intercourse, are again upon you.

　　This country, with its institutions, belongs to the people who inhabit it. Whenever they shall grow weary of the existing Government, they can exercise their constitutional right of amending it or their revolutionary right to dismember or overthrow it. I cannot be ignorant of the fact that many worthy and patriotic citizens are desirous of having the National Constitution amended. While I make no recommendation of amendments, I fully recognize the rightful authority of the people over the whole subject, to be exercised in either of the modes prescribed in the instrument itself; and I should, under existing circumstances, favor rather than oppose a fair opportunity being afforded the people to act upon it. I will venture to add that to me the convention mode seems preferable, in that it allows amendments to originate with the people themselves, instead of only permitting them to take or reject propositions originated by others, not especially chosen for the purpose, and which might not be precisely such as they would wish to either accept or refuse. I understand a proposed amendment to the Constitution—which amendment, however, I have not seen—has passed Congress, to the effect that the Federal Government shall never interfere with the domestic institutions of the States, including that of persons held to service. To avoid misconstruction of what I have said, I depart from my purpose not to speak of particular amendments so far as to

人之间履行条约，比在朋友之间按法律办事还更忠实吗？就算你们决定诉诸战争，你们总不能永远打下去吧。最后当两败俱伤而双方都一无所获时，你们停止战斗，那时依照什么条件相互交往，这同一个老问题仍会照样摆在你们面前了。

　　这个国家，连同它的各种机构，都属于居住在这里的人民。任何时候，他们对现存政府感到厌倦了，他们可以行使他们的宪法权利，改革这个政府，或者行使他们的革命权利解散它或者推翻它。我当然知道，现在就有许多尊贵的、爱国的公民急于想修订我们的宪法。尽管我自己不会那么建议，我却也完全承认他们在这个问题上的合法权利，承认他们可以按照宪法所规定的两种方式中的任何一种来行使这种权利；而且，在目前情况下，我不但不反对，反而倒是赞成给人民一个公正的机会让他们去行动。我还不禁要补充一点，在我看来，采取举行会议的方式似乎更好一些，这样可以使修订方案完全由人民自己提出，而不是只让他们去接受或拒绝一些并非特别并非为人民的意图而选出的一些人提出的方案，因为也可能那些方案恰恰并不是他们愿意接受或拒绝的。我了解到现在已有人提出一项宪法修正案——这修正案

Abraham Lincoln
亚伯拉罕·林肯(1809-1865)
16th President of the United States (1861-1865)

say that, holding such a provision to now be implied constitutional law, I have no objection to its being made express and irrevocable.

The Chief Magistrate derives all his authority from the people, and they have referred none upon him to fix terms for the separation of the States. The people themselves can do this if also they choose, but the Executive as such has nothing to do with it. His duty is to administer the present Government as it came to his hands and to transmit it unimpaired by him to his successor.

Why should there not be a patient confidence in the ultimate justice of the people? Is there any better or equal hope in the world? In our present differences, is either party without faith of being in the right? If the Almighty Ruler of Nations, with His eternal truth and justice, be on your side of the North, or on yours of the South, that truth and that justice will surely prevail by the judgment of this great tribunal of the American people.

By the frame of the Government under which we live this same people have wisely given their public servants but little power for mischief, and have with equal wisdom provided for the return of that little to their own hands at very short intervals. While the people retain their virtue

我并没有看到,但在国会中已经通过了,大意说,联邦政府将永远不再干涉各州内部制度,包括那些应服劳役者的问题。为了使我讲的话不致被误解,我现在改变我不谈具体修正案这一原来的打算,明确声明,这样一个条款,既然现在可能列入宪法,我不反对使它成为明确而不可改动的条文。

合众国总统的一切权威都来之于人民,人民并没有授予他规定条件让各州脱离出去的权力。人民自己如果要那样干,那自然也是可以的。可是现在的行政当局不能这样做。他的职责,是按照他接任时的样子管理这个政府,然后,毫无损伤地再移交给他的继任者。

我们为什么不能耐心地坚决相信人民的最终的公道呢?难道在整个世界上还有什么更好的或与之等同的希望吗?在我们今天的分歧中,难道双方不都是认为自己正确吗?如果各国的全能统治者,以他永恒的真理和公正,站在你们北方一边,或你们南方一边,那么,依照美国人民这一伟大法官的判决,真理和公正必将胜利。

按照目前我们生活下的政府的构架,我国人民十分明智,授予他们的公仆胡作非为的权力微乎其微;而且同样还十分明智地规定,即使那点微

and vigilance no Administration by any extreme of wickedness or folly can very seriously injure the Government in the short space of four years.

My countrymen, one and all, think calmly and well upon this whole subject. Nothing valuable can be lost by taking time. If there be an object to hurry any of you in hot haste to a step which you would never take deliberately, that object will be frustrated by taking time; but no good object can be frustrated by it. Such of you as are now dissatisfied still have the old Constitution unimpaired, and, on the sensitive point, the laws of your own framing under it; while the new Administration will have no immediate power, if it would, to change either. If it were admitted that you who are dissatisfied hold the right side in the dispute, there still is no single good reason for precipitate action. Intelligence, patriotism, Christianity, and a firm reliance on Him who has never yet forsaken this favored land are still competent to adjust in the best way all our present difficulty.

In your hands, my dissatisfied fellow-countrymen, and not in mine, is the momentous issue of civil war. The Government will not assail you. You can have no conflict

乎其微的权力，经过很短一段时间后，就必须收回到他们自己手中。由于人民保持他们的正直和警惕，任何行政当局，在短短的四年之中，也不可能用极其恶劣或愚蠢的行为对这个政府造成严重的损害。

我的同胞们，请大家对这整个问题平心静气地好好想一想，真正有价值的东西是不会因从容对待而丧失的。如果有个目标使你迫不及待地要取得它，你采取的步骤是在审慎考虑的情况下不会采取的，那个目标的确可能会由于你的从容不迫而达不到，但一个真正好的目标是不会因为时间而落空的。你们中现在感到不满的人，仍然必须遵守原封未动的老宪法，而且在敏感的问题上，你们仍然有根据宪法制定的各项法律；而对此二者，新政府即使想要加以改变，它自身也无此直接权力。即使承认那些心怀不满的人在这一争执中站在正确的一边，那也丝毫没有正当的理由要采取鲁莽行动。明智、爱国精神、基督教教义，以及对从未抛弃过这片得天独厚的土地的上帝的依赖，拥有这些我们仍然完全能以最理想的方式来解决当前的一切困难。

决定内战这个重大问题的是你们，心怀不满的同胞们，而并非由我决定。政府决不会攻击你们。只要你们自

Abraham Lincoln
亚伯拉罕·林肯(1809-1865)
16th President of the United States (1861-1865)

without being yourselves the aggressors. You have no oath registered in heaven to destroy the Government, while I shall have the most solemn one to "preserve, protect, and defend it."

I am loath to close. We are not enemies, but friends. We must not be enemies. Though passion may have strained it must not break our bonds of affection. The mystic chords of memory, stretching from every battlefield and patriot grave to every living heart and house all over this broad land, will yet swell the chorus of the Union, when again touched, as surely they will be, by the better angels of our nature.

己不当侵略者,就不会发生冲突。你们并没有对天发誓必须毁灭这个政府,而我却曾无比庄严地宣誓,一定要"保持、保护和保卫"这个政府。

我真不想就此结束我的讲话,我们不是敌人,而是朋友。我们决不能成为敌人。尽管目前的情绪有些紧张,但决不能容许它使我们之间的亲密情感纽带破裂。回忆的神秘琴弦,在整个这片辽阔的土地上,从每一个战场,每一个爱国志士的坟墓,延伸到每一颗跳动的心和每一个家庭,它有一天会被我们的良知所触动,再次奏出联邦合唱曲。

亚伯拉罕·林肯:美国第16任总统(1861—1865)。本篇发表于内战即将结束、百废待举之时,对医治战争创伤、保持公平公正进行了展望,堪称就职演说中的名篇。

Abraham Lincoln
亚伯拉罕·林肯(1809-1865)
16th President of the United States (1861-1865)
Political Party: Whig (1832-1854)
Republican (1854-1864)
National Union (1864-1865)

War and the Almighty's Purpose
战争和上帝旨意

Fellow-Countrymen:

At this second appearing to take the oath of the presidential office there is less occasion for an extended address than there was at the first. Then a statement somewhat in detail of a course to be pursued seemed fitting and proper. Now, at the expiration of four years, during which public declarations have been constantly called forth on every point and phase of his great contest which still absorbs the attention and engrosses the energies of the nation, little that is new could be presented. The progress of our arms, upon which all else chiefly depends, is as well

同胞们:

在第二次宣誓就任总统时,我不必像第一次那样发表长篇演说。那时,对于将要执行的方针作出比较详尽的说明似乎是恰当而适宜的。现在,四年任期已满,对于这场仍然吸引着全国关注并占用了全国力量的重大斗争的每一个重要关头和方面,这四年间已不断地发布公告,因此我没有什么新情况可以奉告。

Abraham Lincoln
亚伯拉罕·林肯(1809-1865)
16th President of the United States (1861-1865)

known to the public as to myself, and it is, I trust, reasonably satisfactory and encouraging to all. With high hope for the future, no prediction in regard to it is ventured.

On the occasion corresponding to this four years ago all thoughts were anxiously directed to an impending civil war. All dreaded it; all sought to avert it. While the inaugural address was being delivered from this place, devoted altogether to saving the Union without war, insurgent agents were in the city seeking to destroy it without war—seeking to dissolve the Union and divide effects by negotiation. Both parties deprecated war, but one of them would make war rather than let the nation survive, and the other would accept war rather than let it perish, and the war came.

One-eighth of the whole population were colored slaves, not distributed generally over the Union, but localized in the southern part of it. Their slaves constituted a peculiar and powerful interest. All knew that this interest was somehow the cause of the war. To strengthen, perpetuate, and extend this interest was the object for which the insurgents would rend the union even by war, while the Government claimed no right to do more than to restrict the territorial enlargement of it. Neither party expected for the war the magnitude or the duration, which it has already attained. Neither anticipated that the cause of the conflict might cease with or even before the conflict itself should cease. Each looked for an easier triumph, and a result less fundamental and astounding. Both read the same Bible and pray to the same God, and each invokes

我们军队的进展是其他一切的主要依靠，公众和我一样都清楚地了解军队进展的情况，我深信，大家对之都是感到满意和鼓舞的，我们虽对未来抱有极大的希望，却不敢作出任何预测。

四年前在与此同一场合里，同胞们的思想都焦急地集中在日益迫近的内战上，大家都害怕内战，都想避免内战。当我在这个地方发表就职演说，竭尽全力想不经过战争来拯救联邦时，叛乱分子却在这个城市里图谋不经过战争来毁灭联邦——企图以谈判方式解散并分割联邦。双方都表示反对战争，但一方宁愿发动战争而不惜牺牲国家，另一方则宁可接受战争也不肯让国家灭亡，于是战争就爆发了。

我国全部人口的八分之一是黑人奴隶，他们并不是遍布于联邦各地，而是集中在联邦南部。这些奴隶构成了一种特殊的、重大的利益。大家都知道，这种利益由于某种原因竟成了这次战争的根源。叛乱者的目的是加强、保持和扩大这种利益，为此他们不惜用战争来分裂联邦，而政府却只是宣布限制享有这种利益的地区的扩大。双方都没有料到战争竟会达到如此规模，历时如此长久。双方也没有预期冲突的根源会随着冲突本身而消除，甚至会提前消除。

His aid against the other. It may seem strange that any men should dare to ask a just God's assistance in wringing their bread from the sweat of other men's faces, but let us judge not, that we be not judged. That of neither has been answered fully. The Almighty has His own purposes. "Woe unto the world because of offenses; for it must need be that offenses come, but woe to that man by whom the offense comet." If we shall suppose that American slavery is one of those offenses which, in the providence of God, must needs come, but which, having continued through His appointed time, He now wills to remove, and that He gives to both North and South this terrible war as the woe due to those by whom the offense came, shall we discern there in any departure from those divine attributes which the believers in a living God always ascribe to Him? Fondly do we hope, fervently do we pray that this mighty scourge of war may speedily pass away? Yet, if God wills that it continue until all the wealth piled by the bondsman's two hundred and fifty years of unrequited toil shall be sunk, and until every drop of blood drawn with the lash shall be paid by another drawn with the sword, as was said three thousand years ago so still it must be said "The judgments of the Lord are true and righteous altogether."

　　With malice toward none, with charity for all, with

Abraham Lincoln
亚伯拉罕·林肯(1809-1865)
16th President of the United States (1861-1865)

firmness in the right as God gives us to see the might, let us strive on to finish the work we are in, to bind up the nation's wounds, to care for him who shall have borne the battle and for his widow and his orphan, to do all which may achieve and cherish a just and lasting peace among ourselves and with all nations.

对一切人心存宽厚,坚持正义,因为上帝使我们看到了正义,让我们继续努力完成正在从事的事业,包扎好国家的创伤,关心那些肩负战争重任的人,照顾他们的遗孀孤儿,去做能在我们自己中间和与一切国家缔造并保持公正持久和平的一切事情。

尤利西斯·S.格兰特：美国第18任总统(1869-1877)。内战中功劳显赫,被授予"五星上将"军衔；执政时丑闻迭出,被列为"最糟糕首脑"之一。

Ulysses S. Grant
尤利西斯·S. 格兰特(1822-1885)
18th President of the United States (1869-1877)
Political Party: Republican

The Greatest Good to the Greatest Number
为最大多数人谋最大利益

Citizens of the United States:

Your suffrages having elected me to the office of President of the United States, I have, in conformity to the Constitution of our country, taken the oath of office prescribed therein. I have taken this oath without mental reservation and with the determination to do to the best of my ability all that is required of me. The responsibilities of the position I feel, but accept them without fear. The office has come to me unsought; I commence its duties untrammeled. I bring to it a conscious desire and determination

美国公民们：

你们经投票选举我为合众国总统,依照我国宪法规定,我宣誓就职。我宣誓时毫无保留,决心为我的职责竭尽全力。我认识到总统应负的各项责任之重大,但无所畏惧地接受这些责任。对于这一职位我是不谋而得,因此我履行职责时也不受任何限制。我将以自觉的意愿和决心尽

Ulysses S. Grant
尤利西斯·S. 格兰特(1822-1885)
18th President of the United States (1869-1877)

to fill it to the best of my ability to the satisfaction of the people.

On all leading questions agitating the public mind I will always express my views to Congress and urge them according to my judgment, and when I think it advisable will exercise the constitutional privilege of interposing a veto to defeat measures which I oppose; but all laws will be faithfully executed, whether they meet my approval or not.

I shall on all subjects have a policy to recommend, but none to enforce against the will of the people. Laws are to govern all alike—those opposed as well as those who favor them. I know no method to secure the repeal of bad or obnoxious laws so effective as their stringent execution.

The country having just emerged from a great rebellion, many questions will come before it for settlement in the next four years which preceding Administrations have never had to deal with. In meeting these it is desirable that they should be approached calmly, without prejudice, hate, or sectional pride, remembering that the greatest good to the greatest number is the object to be attained.

This requires security of person, property, and free religious and political opinion in every part of our common country, without regard to local prejudice. All laws to secure these ends will receive my best efforts for their enforcement. A great debt has been contracted in securing to us and our posterity the Union. The payment of this, principal and interest, as well as the return to a specie basis as soon as it can be accomplished without material detriment to the debtor class or to the country at large, must be provided for. To protect the national honor, every dollar of Government indebtedness should be paid in gold, unless

力使全民满意。

对于困扰公众的一切重大问题，我将经常向国会陈述我的观点，并依我的判断敦促国会，而在适当时机，我将行使宪法给予我的特权，否决我所反对的议案，但所有法律均将得到切实的执行，不论我赞同与否。

我对每一事项都将提出一项方针，但执行任何方针均不得违反民意。法律约束所有的人，包括反对者和赞同者。我知道，即使是不适当的或引起反感的法律，一旦形成就要严格执行，难以废除。

这个国家刚脱离一场巨大的动乱，它在今后四年里有许多问题要加以解决。这些问题是以往历届政府所从未遇到的。面对这些问题，我们应该冷静对待，不怀偏见、仇恨和地区优越感，随时记住我们的目标是为最大多数人谋求最大的利益。

这就要求全国各地普遍地确保人身、财产的安全，宗教信仰与发表政见的自由，摒弃地域的偏见。我将全力履行旨在实现这些目标的一切法律。为了使我们与我们的后代保持联邦制度，国家背负了一笔巨额债务，偿还债款的本金和利息以及恢复硬币制度必须妥善安排，必须使债务人和国家不受物质损失。为了维护国家的荣誉，除非债约

otherwise expressly stipulated in the contract. Let it be understood that no repudiator of one farthing of our public debt will be trusted in public place, and it will go far toward strengthening a credit which ought to be the best in the world, and will ultimately enable us to replace the debt with bonds bearing less interest than we now pay. To this should be added a faithful collection of the revenue, a strict accountability to the Treasury for every dollar collected, and the greatest practicable retrenchment in expenditure in every department of Government.

When we compare the paying capacity of the country now, with the ten States in poverty from the effects of war, but soon to emerge, I trust, into greater prosperity than ever before, with its paying capacity twenty-five years ago, and calculate what it probably will be twenty-five years hence, who can doubt the feasibility of paying every dollar then with more ease than we now pay for useless luxuries? Why, it looks as though Providence had bestowed upon us a strong box in the precious metals locked up in the sterile mountains of the far West, and which we are now forging the key to unlock, to meet the very contingency that is now upon us.

Ultimately it may be necessary to insure the facilities to reach these riches and it may be necessary also that the General Government should give its aid to secure this access; but that should only be when a dollar of obligation to pay secures precisely the same sort of dollar to use now, and not before. Whilst the question of specie payments is in abeyance the prudent business man is careful about contracting debts payable in the distant future. The nation should follow the same rule. A prostrate commerce is to be

中另有规定,所有政府公债均应用黄金来偿还。应当明白,即使拒绝偿还公债中的一角钱,也会使政府不为公众所信任。我们必须进一步加强我们的信用制度,它应是世界上最可信赖的,以便能使我们以发行债券来代替借款,而支付较低的利息。为此,我们必须切实征税,财政部对征得的每一美元的使用均应严格核算,并实际地紧缩政府各部门的开支。

在衡量国家的偿还能力时,我们看到由于战争的结果,有10个州今天仍处于贫困之中。但我坚信,经济很快就会比过去任何时候都繁荣。把我们现在的偿付能力和25年前相比,并计算25年后的偿付能力,谁还会怀疑那时我们支付每一美元将比我们现在付款购买无益的奢侈品更加容易呢?这是肯定的,上苍赐给了我们一个坚固的金箱,它被深藏在遥远的西部荒山中,而现在我们正在打造一把开启金箱的钥匙,以应付当前的困境。

总之,为了获得这些宝藏,必须保证必要的手段,同时必须得到联邦政府的帮助。但是,必须保证偿还的每一美元与当前使用的美元等值,而不是以前的价值。以硬币偿付的问题尚未解决,谨慎的商人正小心地处理须经长期偿付的债务,国家也应当遵循这样的原则。我们将重建不景

Ulysses S. Grant
尤利西斯·S. 格兰特(1822-1885)
18th President of the United States (1869-1877)

rebuilt and all industries encouraged.

The young men of the country—those who from their age must be its rulers twenty-five years hence—have a peculiar interest in maintaining the national honor. A moment's reflection as to what will be our commanding influence among the nations of the earth in their day, if they are only true to themselves, should inspire them with national pride. All divisions—geographical, political, and religious—can join in this common sentiment. How the public debt is to be paid or specie payments resumed is not so important as that a plan should be adopted and acquiesced in. A united determination to do is worth more than divided counsels upon the method of doing. Legislation upon this subject may not be necessary now, or even advisable, but it will be when the civil law is more fully restored in all parts of the country and trade resumes its wonted channels.

It will be my endeavor to execute all laws in good faith, to collect all revenues assessed, and to have them properly accounted for and economically disbursed. I will to the best of my ability appoint to office those only who will carry out this design.

In regard to foreign policy, I would deal with nations as equitable law requires individuals to deal with each other, and I would protect the law-abiding citizen, whether of native or foreign birth, wherever his rights are jeopardized or the flag of our country floats. I would respect the rights of all nations, demanding equal respect for our own. If others depart from this rule in their dealings with us, we may be compelled to follow their precedent.

气的商业,振兴所有的工业。

美国青年——25年以后他们将成为国家的领导者——特别关心维护国家荣誉。如果说他们只对自己真诚,那么,稍许考虑一下我们对世界各国的重大影响,也应该激起他们的民族自豪感。一切部门——地理的、政治的和宗教的——都能以这种共同的情感团结起来。政府公债如何偿还,硬币如何支付等问题都不及采取和同意一项计划重要,关于行动的统一决心,比关于行动方法的有分歧的意见有价值。也许我们现在没有必要,也不适宜采取立法来完成这一计划。但是,当全国更全面地恢复实施民法,当贸易恢复常规时,就必须采取立法手段了。

我将真诚地致力于执行所有法律,课征一切应征税款,妥善安排,节省开支,我将尽力选拔称职者担任公职。

关于外交政策,我将像个人按照公正的法律彼此相处那样地对待各国。守法的公民,不论他出生在本土还是国外,只要是在我国国旗飘扬的地方,一旦他的权利受到危害,我就会予以保护。我将尊重各国的权益,并要求别国同样尊重我国的权益,如果他们在与我们的交往中背离了这一原则,我们将被迫援用他们做出的先例。

The proper treatment of the original occupants of this land—the Indians one deserving of careful study. I will favor any course toward them which tends to their civilization and ultimate citizenship.

The question of suffrage is one which is likely to agitate the public so long as a portion of the citizens of the nation are excluded from its privileges in any State. It seems to me very desirable that this question should be settled now, and I entertain the hope and express the desire that it may be by the ratification of the fifteenth article of amendment to the Constitution.

In conclusion I ask patient forbearance one toward another throughout the land, and a determined effort on the part of every citizen to do his share toward cementing a happy union; and I ask the prayers of the nation to Almighty God in behalf of this consummation.

如何妥善处置美洲大陆原来的居民——印第安人,需要认真加以研究。我将赞同一切有利于印第安人文化和基本公民权的方针。

选举权的问题受到公众的密切注意。在任何一州内,只要有部分公民被剥夺了选举权,就必定会使公众不满。我认为现在这个问题是非解决不可了。我希望并要求这个问题通过宪法第十五条修正案的批准获得解决。

总之,我希望在全国人民彼此宽容,决心各尽所能,建立一个幸福的联邦。我请求全国人民为实现这个伟大的目标而向全能的上帝祈祷。

Grover Cleveland
格罗佛·克利夫兰 (1837-1908)
22nd, 24th President of the United States (1885-1889,1893-1897)

格罗佛·克利夫兰：美国第22任（1885—1889）和24任（1893—1897）总统。任期内面临机构改革、关税纷争、工人罢工等难题，频频使用否决权，绰号"老否决"。克利夫兰的当选打破了共和党人连续执政24年的纪录。

Grover Cleveland
格罗佛·克利夫兰 (1837-1908)
22nd President of the United States (1885-1889)
24th President of the United States (1893-1897)
Political Party: Democratic

A Spirit of Amity and Mutual Concession
和睦互让的精神

Fellow-Citizens:

In the presence of this vast assemblage of my countrymen I am about to supplement and seal by the oath which I shall take the manifestation of the will of a great and free people. In the exercise of their power and right of self-government they have committed to one of their fellow-citizens a supreme and sacred trust, and he here consecrates himself to their service.

This impressive ceremony adds little to the solemn sense of responsibility with which I contemplate the duty I owe to all the people of the land. Nothing can relieve me

同胞们：

在如此众多的同胞面前，我即将代表一个伟大而自由民族的意愿，宣誓就职。人民在行使他们的权力和自治权时，已经将这一崇高而神圣的职责托付给一位公民。在此，他将献身于为人民效力。

这令人难忘的盛典与庄严的责任感十分相称，正是怀着这样的责任感，我期待着为

from anxiety lest by any act of mine their interests may suffer, and nothing is needed to strengthen my resolution to engage every faculty and effort in the promotion of their welfare.

Amid the din of party strife the people's choice was made, but its attendant circumstances have demonstrated anew the strength and safety of a government by the people. In each succeeding year it more clearly appears that our democratic principle needs no apology, and that in its fearless and faithful application is to be found the surest guaranty of good government.

But the best results in the operation of a government wherein every citizen has a share largely depend upon a proper limitation of purely partisan zeal and effort and a correct appreciation of the time when the heat of the partisan should be merged in the patriotism of the citizen.

Today the executive branch of the Government is transferred to new keeping. But this is still the Government of all the people, and it should be none the less an object of their affectionate solicitude. At this hour the animosities of political strife, the bitterness of partisan defeat, and the exultation of partisan triumph should be supplanted by an ungrudging acquiescence in the popular will and a sober, conscientious concern for the general weal. Moreover, if from this hour we cheerfully and honestly abandon all sectional prejudice and distrust, and determine, with manly confidence in one another, to work out harmoniously the achievements of our national destiny, we shall deserve to realize all the benefits which our happy form of government can bestow.

On this auspicious occasion we may well renew the

全体人民担负使命。没有什么能使我免除忧虑，唯恐由于我的不当行动有损于人民的利益，我的决心坚不可摧，我要竭尽所能为民造福。

在党派斗争的喧闹声中，人民作出了选择，但是随之而来的形势已显示出一个民选政府崭新的力量与稳定。年复一年越来越清楚的是，我们的民主原则无可指责，正是毫无畏惧地忠实运用了这一民主原则，令人满意的政府才找到最可靠的保证。

但是，一个由全体公民共同参与的政府，其最出色的治理基本上取决于恰当地限制单纯的党派热情和努力，也取决于当这种党派热情必须同公民的爱国思想结合的时候作出正确的评价。

今天，政府的行政部门已经移交给新的人员。但它依然是全体人民的政府，依然为人民所深切关心。就在此时此刻，政治斗争的敌意，党派斗争失败的痛苦，党派斗争胜利的狂喜，都应该以对公民的意愿慷慨默许所代替，并为公众福利倾注认真而真诚的关注。不仅如此，如果从现在起，我们能满怀诚意地欣然抛弃一切地方主义的偏见和不信任，人与人相互信赖，和睦共事，从而对国家的前途有所建树，那么，我们理应获得这尽善尽美的政治体制所赐予的全部恩惠。

值此吉利的时刻，我们要

Grover Cleveland
格罗佛·克利夫兰 (1837-1908)
22nd, 24th President of the United States (1885-1889, 1893-1897)

pledge of our devotion to the Constitution, which, launched by the founders of the Republic and consecrated by their prayers and patriotic devotion, has for almost a century borne the hopes and the aspirations of a great people through prosperity and peace and through the shock of foreign conflicts and the perils of domestic strife and vicissitudes.

By the Father of his Country our Constitution was commended for adoption as "the result of a spirit of amity and mutual concession." In that same spirit it should be administered, in order to promote the lasting welfare of the country and to secure the full measure of its priceless benefits to us and to those who will succeed to the blessings of our national life. The large variety of diverse and competing interests subject to Federal control, persistently seeking the recognition of their claims, need give us no fear that "the greatest good to the greatest number" will fail to be accomplished if in the halls of national legislation that spirit of amity and mutual concession shall prevail in which the Constitution had its birth. If this involves the surrender or postponement of private interests and the abandonment of local advantages, compensation will be found in the assurance that the common interest is subserved and the general welfare advanced.

In the discharge of my official duty I shall endeavor to be guided by a just and unstrained construction of the Constitution, a careful observance of the distinction between the powers granted to the Federal Government and those reserved to the States or to the people, and by a cautious appreciation of those functions which by the Constitution and laws have been especially assigned to the executive branch of the Government.

重申效忠宪法的誓言。这部宪法是由共和国奠基人所制定的,而人民对宪法的尊崇及其爱国献身的精神使它变得神圣不可侵犯。近一个世纪以来,宪法使伟大的美国人民怀有希望与抱负,使他们经历了繁荣与和平,经受了同国外发生冲突的震惊,还经历了国内斗争与变迁的种种艰险。

我们的国父赞扬这部宪法是"和睦互让的产物"并予以采纳。本着这一精神,宪法的实施应该是为了促进国家的持久安宁,是为了将宪法无限珍贵的利益完整地赐福于我们与我们的后代。受联邦政府管辖的各种各样、形形色色而又互相竞争的利益集团,不断地要求承认他们的权益,但是,我们不必为此而担心,只要国家立法机构充满着和睦互让的精神,而我们的宪法正是这种精神的产物,那么,"为最大多数人谋求最大利益的目标"就一定会实现。如果这涉及放弃或延缓个人利益,并涉及放弃地方优势,那么,由于确保了促进公共利益及一般福利,这种情况将会得到补偿。

我在履行公务时,将努力按照对宪法不加曲解的公正解释行事,密切注意授予联邦政府的权力同留给州政府或人民的权力之间的差别,谨慎地重视由宪法与各项法律专门指定给政府行政部门的职能。

But he who takes the oath today to preserve, protect, and defend the Constitution of the United States only assumes the solemn obligation which every patriotic citizen—on the farm, in the workshop, in the busy marts of trade, and everywhere—should share with him. The Constitution which prescribes his oath, my countrymen, is yours; the Government you have chosen him to administer for a time is yours; the suffrage which executes the will of freemen is yours; the laws and the entire scheme of our civil rule, from the town meeting to the State capitals and the national capital, is yours. Your every voter, as surely as your Chief Magistrate, under the same high sanction, though in a different sphere, exercises a public trust. Nor is this all. Every citizen owes to the country a vigilant watch and close scrutiny of its public servants and a fair and reasonable estimate of their fidelity and usefulness. Thus is the people's will impressed upon the whole framework of our civil polity—municipal, State, and Federal; and this is the price of our liberty and the inspiration of our faith in the Republic.

It is the duty of those serving the people in public place to closely limit public expenditures to the actual needs of the Government economically administered, because this bounds the right of the Government to exact tribute from the earnings of labor or the property of the citizen, and because public extravagance begets extravagance among the people. We should never be ashamed of the simplicity and prudential economies which are best suited to the operation of a republican form of government and most compatible with the mission of the

但是，今天他宣誓要维护和捍卫合众国宪法，这只是承担了一项庄严的责任，这项责任是全体爱国公民——在农场、在工厂、在繁忙的集市以及每一个地方，要与他共同承担的。同胞们，规定他宣誓的宪法是属于你们的；选择他来主持的这届政府的权力是属于你们的；执行自由人民的意志的选举权是属于你们的；从市镇会议到各州首府及国家首都的一切法律和整个治国体制也都是属于你们的。全体选民和总统一样，确实体现了一种公众的信任，尽管其范围各异，但都须获得宪法的批准。不仅如此，每个公民都有义务对国家进行严密监督并仔细考察人民的公仆，对他们的忠诚和效率作出公正而合理的评价。这样，我国的行政机构——在城市、州和联邦——就体现出了全民的意志。这就是我们为自由所付出的代价，也是我们信奉共和政体的启迪。

按照节俭治理政府的实际需要，严格限制公共开支乃是公职人员的责任，因为这把政府对劳动收益或公民财产的征款限制在恰如其分的程度，因为国家的奢侈会在人民中滋长浪费的风气。我们绝不要为简朴和审慎节约的经济而感到羞愧，因为它最适合于共和制政府的治理，最能同美国人民的使命相称。那些

Grover Cleveland

格罗佛·克利夫兰 (1837-1908)
22nd, 24th President of the United States (1885-1889, 1893-1897)

American people. Those who are selected for a limited time to manage public affairs are still of the people, and may do much by their example to encourage, consistently with the dignity of their official functions, that plain way of life which among their fellow-citizens aids integrity and promotes thrift and prosperity.

The genius of our institutions, the needs of our people in their home life, and the attention which is demanded for the settlement and development of the resources of our vast territory dictate the scrupulous avoidance of any departure from that foreign policy commended by the history, the traditions, and the prosperity of our Republic. It is the policy of independence, favored by our position and defended by our known love of justice and by our power. It is the policy of peace suitable to our interests. It is the policy of neutrality, rejecting any share in foreign broils and ambitions upon other continents and repelling their intrusion here. It is the policy of Monroe and of Washington and Jefferson—"Peace, commerce, and honest friendship with all nations; entangling alliance with none."

A due regard for the interests and prosperity of all the people demands that our finances shall be established upon such a sound and sensible basis as shall secure the safety and confidence of business interests and make the wage of labor sure and steady, and that our system of revenue shall be so adjusted as to relieve the people of unnecessary taxation, having a due regard to the interests of capital invested and workingmen employed in American industries, and preventing the accumulation of a surplus in the Treasury to tempt extravagance and waste.

受到挑选、将在有限的时期内管理国事的人仍来自人民，他们会坚持不懈地借担任公职的机会，以其自身的榜样来鼓励简朴的生活方式，这在国民中有助于表现坦诚与正直，并促进节约与繁荣昌盛。

我国制度的本质，我国人民家庭生活的需要，以及对在广袤的领土上定居和开发资源的关切，这些都决定我们要审慎地避免背离由合众国的历史、传统和繁荣所称誉的任何外交政策。这是独立的政策，我们的地位赞同它，我们用对正义的众所周知的热爱和我们的力量捍卫它；这是和平的政策，它与我们的利益相一致；这是中立的政策，它要求我们不参与任何外国的骚乱或觊觎别国领土的活动并击退外国的入侵；这是门罗、华盛顿和杰斐逊所倡导的政策——总之，这就是与所有的国家"保持和平、通商和真诚友谊；不同任何国家缔结联盟"。

为了对全体人民的利益和幸福予以应有的关心，要求我们把财政建立在稳固而明智的基础上，以保障企业的安全与信心，确保工资稳定；这也要求调整我们的税收制度，减轻人民不必要的赋税；应该关心美国工业投资的资本赢利和所雇用的工人，以免国库积累过多而诱发奢侈与浪费。

Care for the property of the nation and for the needs of future settlers requires that the public domain should be protected from purloining schemes and unlawful occupation.

The conscience of the people demands that the Indians within our boundaries shall be fairly and honestly treated as wards of the Government and their education and civilization promoted with a view to their ultimate citizenship, and that polygamy in the Territories, destructive of the family relation and offensive to the moral sense of the civilized world, shall be repressed.

The laws should be rigidly enforced which prohibit the immigration of a servile class to compete with American labor, with no intention of acquiring citizenship, and bringing with them and retaining habits and customs repugnant to our civilization.

The people demand reform in the administration of the Government and the application of business principles to public affairs. As a means to this end, civil-service reform should be in good faith enforced. Our citizens have the right to protection from the incompetency of public employees who hold their places solely as the reward of partisan service, and from the corrupting influence of those who promise and the vicious methods of those who expect such rewards; and those who worthily seek public employment have the right to insist that merit and competency shall be recognized instead of party subserviency or the surrender of honest political belief.

In the administration of a government pledged to do equal and exact justice to all men there should be no pretext for anxiety touching the protection of the freedmen in their rights or their security in the enjoyment of their privileges

出于对国家财产和新开拓者需要的关注，必须保护国有土地，严禁偷盗与非法侵占。

人民凭良知要求我们公平坦诚地对待我国领土上的印第安人，他们将受到政府的监护。我们要提高他们的教育与文化，旨在最终给予他们公民权。印第安人属多婚制，破坏了家庭关系，同时也违背了文明世界的道德观念，因此必须废除。

禁止苦力阶层入境的法律应予以坚决实施，因为他们与美国的劳工进行竞争，尽管他们并不打算取得公民权，却带来而且保留了跟我们的文明不相容的风俗和习惯。

人民要求对政府的行政机关进行改革，把企业原则应用到国事中去。作为达到这一目的的手段，我们要真诚地实施行政机构的改革。我们的公民有权防范不称职的公务人员，他们只是为党派利益效劳而任职；公民有权抑制那些利用公职允诺别人的拙劣影响以及指望获得报酬的卑劣行径；同时，有资格担任公职者则有权坚持对他们的功绩和能力加以承认，而不是承认他们党派方面的阿谀奉承或放弃其真诚的政治信仰。

在一个宣誓以平等与绝对公正对待一切人的行政机构中，人民依据宪法及其修正案享受他们的权利与安全的

Grover Cleveland

格罗佛·克利夫兰 (1837-1908)
22nd, 24th President of the United States (1885-1889,1893-1897)

under the Constitution and its amendments. All discussion as to their fitness for the place accorded to them as American citizens is idle and unprofitable except as it suggests the necessity for their improvement. The fact that they are citizens entitles them to all the rights due to that relation and charges them with all its duties, obligations, and responsibilities.

These topics and the constant and ever-varying wants of an active and enterprising population may well receive the attention and the patriotic endeavor of all who make and execute the Federal law. Our duties are practical and call for industrious application, an intelligent perception of the claims of public office, and, above all, a firm determination, by united action, to secure to all the people of the land the full benefits of the best form of government ever vouchsafed to man. And let us not trust to human effort alone, but humbly acknowledging the power and goodness of Almighty God, who presides over the destiny of nations, and who has at all times been revealed in our country's history, let us invoke His aid and His blessings upon our labors.

特权。我们不应有任何借口对保护该项自由表示担忧。一切涉及他们作为美国公民所获得的地位是否合适的辩论都是空洞而无益的,除非这一辩论是为了改善他们的地位所必需的。作为公民,他们有权享受与公民有关的一切权利,同时他们也要承担全部义务和责任。

以上所说的,以及一个活跃的有进取心的人民的那种持久而又不断变化着的愿望,都要得到联邦法律的制定者与执行者的充分注意,并为其付之爱国行动。我们的职责是实际的,要求毫不松懈地加以应用并明智地理解行政部门的权利,而头等重要的,是要有一个坚毅的决心,依靠同心协力,来保障全国人民从这个有史以来赐予人类的最好的政府中获得全部利益。让我们不仅仅地信任寄托在人的力量上,还要恭敬地承认全能上帝的力量和恩泽。上帝主宰着国家的命运,它时时刻刻都在我国历史中显示。让我们祈求上帝的帮助,保佑我们努力吧。

西奥多·罗斯福：美国第26任总统(1901—1909)。共和党人，1901年出任副总统，同年接任遇刺身亡的麦金莱总统，年仅42岁。对内限制托拉斯势力，缓和劳资关系，对外实行"大棒政策"。1906年因调停日俄关系获诺贝尔和平奖。本篇是唯一不使用第一人称"我"的就职演说。

Theodore Roosevelt
西奥多·罗斯福(1858-1919)
26th President of the United States (1901-1909)
Political Party: Republican (1897-1912)
Progressive Party (1912-1916)

Free Self-government
自由的自治政府

My fellow-citizens,

No people on earth have more cause to be thankful than ours, and this is said reverently, in no spirit of boastfulness in our own strength, but with gratitude to the Giver of Good who has blessed us with the conditions which have enabled us to achieve so large a measure of well-being and of happiness. To us as a people it has been granted to lay the foundations of our national life in a new continent. We are the heirs of the ages, and yet we have had to pay few of the penalties which in old countries are exacted by the dead hand of a bygone civilization. We have not been obliged to fight for our existence against any alien race; and

同胞们：

世界上没有哪一个民族比我们更有理由感到欣慰了，这样说是谦恭的，绝无夸耀我们的力量之意，而是怀着对赐福于我们、使我们能够有条件获得如此巨大的幸福康乐的上帝的感激之情。作为一个民族，我们获得上帝的许可，在新大陆上奠下了国民生活的基础。我们是时代的继承者，然而我们无需像在古老的国家里那样，承受以往文明的遗留影响所强

Theodore Roosevelt
西奥多·罗斯福(1858-1919)
26th President of the United States (1901-1909)

yet our life has called for the vigor and effort without which the manlier and hardier virtues wither away. Under such conditions it would be our own fault if we failed; and the success which we have had in the past, the success which we confidently believe the future will bring, should cause in us no feeling of vainglory, but rather a deep and abiding realization of all which life has offered us; a full acknowledgment of the responsibility which is ours; and a fixed determination to show that under a free government a mighty people can thrive best, alike as regards the things of the body and the things of the soul.

Much has been given us, and much will rightfully be expected from us. We have duties to others and duties to ourselves; and we can shirk neither. We have become a great nation, forced by the fact of its greatness into relations with the other nations of the earth, and we must behave as beseems a people with such responsibilities. Toward all other nations, large and small, our attitude must be one of cordial and sincere friendship. We must show not only in our words, but in our deeds, that we are earnestly desirous of securing their good will by acting toward them in a spirit of just and generous recognition of all their rights. But justice and generosity in a nation, as in an individual, count most when shown not by the weak but by the strong. While ever careful to refrain from wrongdoing others, we must be no less insistent that we are not wronged ourselves. We wish peace, but we wish the peace of justice, the peace of righteousness. We wish it because we think it is right and not because we are afraid. No weak nation that acts manfully and justly should ever have cause to fear us, and no strong power should ever be able to single us out as a

加的惩罚。我们不必为了自己的生存而去同任何异族抗衡。然而,我们的生活要求活力和勤奋,没有这些,雄健刚毅的美德就会消失殆尽。在这种条件下,倘若我们失败了,那便是我们自己的过错;我们在过去获得的成功,我们深信未来将带给我们的成功,不应使我们目空一切,而是要深刻地长久地认识到生活为我们提供的一切,充分认识我们肩负的责任,并矢志表明;在自由政府的领导下,一个强大的民族能够繁荣昌盛,物质生活如此,精神生活必也如此。

我们被赋予的很多,期望于我们的自然也很多。我们对他人负有义务,对自己也负有义务,两者都不能逃避。我们已成为一个伟大的国家,这一事实迫使我们在同世界上其他国家交往时,行为举止必须与负有这种责任的民族相称。对于其他一切国家,无论大国还是小国,我们的态度都必须热诚、真挚、友好。我们必须不仅用语言,而且以行动表明,我们公正、宽宏地承认他们的一切权利,用这种精神对待他们,我们热切希望获得他们的善意。但是,一个国家的公正与宽宏,如同一个人的公正与宽宏一样,不是由弱者而是由强者表现出来时,才为人推崇。在我们极其审慎地避免损害别人时,我们必须同样地坚持自己不受伤害。我

subject for insolent aggression.

Our relations with the other powers of the world are important; but still more important are our relations among ourselves. Such growth in wealth, in population, and in power as this nation has seen during the century and a quarter of its national life is inevitably accompanied by a like growth in the problems which are ever before every nation that rises to greatness. Power invariably means both responsibility and danger. Our forefathers faced certain perils which we have outgrown. We now face other perils, the very existence of which it was impossible that they should foresee. Modern life is both complex and intense, and the tremendous changes wrought by the extraordinary industrial development of the last half century are felt in every fiber of our social and political being. Never before have men tried so vast and formidable an experiment as that of administering the affairs of a continent under the forms of a Democratic republic. The conditions which have told for our marvelous material well-being, which have developed to a very high degree our energy, self-reliance, and individual initiative, have also brought the care and anxiety inseparable from the accumulation of great wealth in industrial centers. Upon the success of our experiment much depends, not only as regards our own welfare, but as regards the welfare of mankind. If we fail, the cause of free self-government throughout the world will rock to its foundations, and therefore our responsibility is heavy, to ourselves, to the world as it is today, and to the generations yet unborn. There is no good reason why we should fear the

们希望和平,但是我们希望的是公正的和平,正义的和平。我们这样希望是因为我们认为这是正确的,而不是因为我们怯懦胆小。行事果敢正义的弱国绝无理由畏惧我们,强国则永远不能挑选我们作为蛮横入侵的对象。

我们同世界上其他强国的关系是重要的,但更为重要的是我们内部之间的关系。随着国家在过去125年中所经历的财富、人口和实力的增长,就像每一个逐步壮大起来的国家所遇到的情况一样,各种问题也都不可避免地相应增加了。实力永远意味着责任和危险。先辈们曾面临某些我们这个时代不复存在的危险。我们现在面临的则是其他危险,这些危险的出现是先人所无法预见的。现代生活既复杂又紧张,我们的社会和政治肌体的每一根纤维都能感觉到,过去半个世纪里,工业的异常发展引起的巨大变化。人们以前从来没有尝试过诸如在民主共和国的形式下管理一个大陆的事务这般庞大而艰巨的实验。创造了奇迹般的物质幸福并将我们的活力、自立能力和个人能动性发展到很高程度的那些条件,也带来了与工业中心巨大的财富积累不可分开的烦恼与焦虑。许多事情取决于我们的实验成功与否,这不仅关系到我们自己的幸福,而且关系到人类的幸福。倘若我们失败了,就会

Theodore Roosevelt
西奥多·罗斯福(1858-1919)
26th President of the United States (1901-1909)

future, but there is every reason why we should face it seriously, neither hiding from ourselves the gravity of the problems before us nor fearing to approach these problems with the unbending, unflinching purpose to solve them aright.

Yet, after all, though the problems are new, though the tasks set before us differ from the tasks set before our fathers who founded and preserved this Republic, the spirit in which these tasks must be undertaken and these problems faced, if our duty is to be well done, remains essentially unchanged. We know that self-government is difficult. We know that no people needs such high traits of character as that people which seeks to govern its affairs aright through the freely expressed will of the freemen who compose it. But we have faith that we shall not prove false to the memories of the men of the mighty past. They did their work, they left us the splendid heritage we now enjoy. We in our turn have an assured confidence that we shall be able to leave this heritage unwasted and enlarged to our children and our children's children. To do so we must show, not merely in great crises, but in the everyday affairs of life, the qualities of practical intelligence, of courage, of hardihood, and endurance, and above all the power of devotion to a lofty ideal, which made great the men who founded this Republic in the days of Washington, which made great the men who preserved this Republic in the days of Abraham Lincoln.

动摇全世界自由的自治政府事业的基础,因此,对于我们自己,对于当今世界,对于尚未出生的后代,我们负有重大责任。我们没有什么理由畏惧未来,但是我们有充分的理由认真地面对未来,既不对自己隐瞒摆在面前的问题的严重性,也不怕以百折不挠的意志面对这些问题,正确予以解决。

然而,要知道,虽然这些是新问题,虽然摆在我们面前的任务不同于摆在创建并维护这个共和国的先辈面前的任务,但是,如果要很好地履行我们的责任,那么,承担这些任务和正视这些问题所必须发扬的精神依然根本没有改变。我们知道,自治是困难的。我们知道,我们力求以组成本民族的自由人自由表达意愿来正确地管理自己的事务,没有哪一个民族需要像我们所需要的这样高尚的特性。但我们相信,我们不会背离先人们在辉煌的过去所创立的事业。他们做了他们的工作,他们为我们留下了我们如今所享受的辉煌的遗产。我们也坚信,我们一定不会浪费这份遗产,而且要进一步充实增加,留给我们的孩子,留给孩子们的后代。为此,我们不仅必须在重大危机中,而且要在日常事务中,都表现出注重实际的智慧、勇敢、刚毅和忍耐,尤其是献身于崇高理想的力量等优秀品质,而这些品质曾使华盛顿时代建立这个共和国的人们名垂青史,而这些品质曾使亚伯拉罕·林肯时代维护这个共和国的人们名垂青史。

伍德罗·威尔逊：美国第28任总统（1913—1921），第一位获博士学位（约翰·霍普金斯大学）和曾任大学校长（普林斯顿大学）的总统。任期内以"新自由"为施政纲领，推行一系列改革，并使美国在第一次世界大战中大获其利。

Woodrow Wilson
伍德罗·威尔逊(1856-1924)
28th President of the United States (1913-1921)
Political Party: Democratic

A Work of Restoration
正本清源的工作

There has been a change of government. It began two years ago, when the House of Representatives became Democratic by a decisive majority. It has now been completed. The Senate about to assemble will also be Democratic. The offices of President and Vice-President have been put into the hands of Democrats. What does the change mean? That is the question that is uppermost in our minds today. That is the question I am going to try to answer, in order, if I may, to interpret the occasion.

It means much more than the mere success of a party.

政府发生了变化。这种变化开始于两年前民主党在众议院取得决定性多数席位的时候，现在已告一段落。即将组成的参议院也将由民主党把持。总统和副总统的职务都已交与民主党执掌。这种变化意味着什么呢？这是如今盘旋于我们脑海中的最主要的问题。这也是今天我要试图回答的问题，如果可以的话，我要阐明其中的缘由。

这种变化不仅仅意味着一

Woodrow Wilson
伍德罗·威尔逊(1856-1924)
28th President of the United States (1913-1921)

The success of a party means little except when the Nation is using that party for a large and definite purpose. No one can mistake the purpose for which the Nation now seeks to use the Democratic Party. It seeks to use it to interpret a change in its own plans and point of view. Some old things with which we had grown familiar, and which had begun to creep into the very habit of our thought and of our lives, have altered their aspect as we have latterly looked critically upon them, with fresh, awakened eyes; have dropped their disguises and shown themselves alien and sinister. Some new things, as we look frankly upon them, willing to comprehend their real character, have come to assume the aspect of things long believed in and familiar with, stuff of our own convictions. We have been refreshed by a new insight into our own life.

We see that in many things that life is very great. It is incomparably great in its material aspects, in its body of wealth, in the diversity and sweep of its energy, in the industries which have been conceived and built up by the genius of individual men and the limitless enterprise of groups of men. It is great, also, very great, in its moral force. Nowhere else in the world have noble men and women exhibited in more striking forms the beauty and the energy of sympathy and helpfulness and counsel in their efforts to rectify wrong, alleviate suffering, and set the weak in the way of strength and hope. We have built up, moreover, a great system of government, which has stood through a long age as in many respects a model for those who seek to set liberty upon foundations that will endure against fortuitous change, against storm and accident. Our

个政党的胜利。一个政党的胜利是不足称道的,除非国家要利用这个政党达到一个重大而明确的目标。谁都不会误解国家现在想利用民主党所要达到的目的。它要利用民主党来阐明国家的规划和立场中的某种变化。我们对某些陈旧的事物虽已逐渐习以为常,而且这些事物已开始不知不觉地进入我们的思想习惯和生活习惯,但是,当我们后来以新的、觉醒的眼光批判地看待这些事物时,它们改变了面貌,卸下了伪装,显得陌生而又邪恶。另一方面,当我们实事求是地看待一些新生事物,并愿意了解它们的实质时,它们便开始呈现出我们久已相信和熟悉的事物特征,即我们自己坚信不移的那些东西。我们以一种新的眼光来洞察自己的生活,从而我们的精神世界也为之一振。

我们从许多事情上看出生活是非常美好的。它在物质方面,在财富主体方面,在能量的种类和范围方面,在根据个人的天赋才干和集体的无限力量所构想、建立的工业方面,都是无比伟大的。它在道德力量方面同样是伟大的,而且是极其伟大的。世界上再没有什么地方有这样高尚的人们能如此出色地表现出同情、互助、协商的美妙境界和巨大能量。他们努力补偏救弊、弭患纾难、扶助弱者,以增加力量和希望。不仅如此,我们还建立起了一个伟大的政治体制,这个政治体制在很长一段时期中经受了考验,在很多方面成为那些试图

life contains every great thing, and contains it in rich abundance.

But the evil has come with the good, and much fine gold has been corroded. With riches has come inexcusable waste. We have squandered a great part of what we might have used, and have not stopped to conserve the exceeding bounty of nature, without which our genius for enterprise would have been worthless and impotent, scorning to be careful, shamefully prodigal as well as admirably efficient. We have been proud of our industrial achievements, but we have not hitherto stopped thoughtfully enough to count the human cost, the cost of lives snuffed out, of energies overtaxed and broken, the fearful physical and spiritual cost to the men and women and children upon whom the dead weight and burden of it all has fallen pitilessly the years through. The groans and agony of it all had not yet reached our ears, the solemn, moving undertone of our life, coming up out of the mines and factories, and out of every home where the struggle had its intimate and familiar seat. With the great Government went many deep secret things which we too long delayed to look into and scrutinize with candid, fearless eyes. The great Government we loved has too often been made use of for private and selfish purposes, and those who used it had forgotten the people.

把自由建立在经得起偶然变故、狂风暴雨和意外事件的基础上的人们的楷模。我们的生活拥有一切伟大事物,丰富而充足。

但是,罪恶与善良俱来,纯金常被腐蚀,不可原谅的浪费与富足并至。我们浪费了一大部分本来可利用的东西,我们至今还没有停止挥霍浪费来保存大自然的超然恩赐。如果没有这些恩赐,我们的创业天赋很可能变得毫无价值而不起作用。我们鄙视谨慎行事,我们效率让人惊叹,却对挥霍浪费不感羞耻。我们一向对我国的工业成就引以为自豪,但我们至今仍不能深谋远虑,没有认真计算一下人类为此付出的代价:包括人们所献出的生命的代价,由于辛劳过度、心力交瘁所付出的精力的代价,以及男人、女人和儿童——工业生产的全部重担成年累月地无情地压在这些人的身上——所付出的骇人听闻的肉体代价和精神代价。这些人的痛楚呻吟尚未传到我们的耳际,而由矿山、工厂,由每一个贫困交迫、痛苦挣扎的家庭传来的这些呻吟则构成了我们生活中的庄严而感人肺腑的和音。伴随伟大政体而来的,还有我们长期以来一直不愿以坦率无畏的眼光去探索、去仔细看的许多讳莫如深的事物。我们所热爱的伟大政体经常被人们用来为个人谋私利,而利用这个政体的那些人则早已把人民大众忘记得一干二净!

Woodrow Wilson
伍德罗·威尔逊(1856-1924)
28th President of the United States (1913-1921)

At last a vision has been vouchsafed us of our life as a whole. We see the bad with the good, the debased and decadent with the sound and vital. With this vision we approach new affairs. Our duty is to cleanse, to reconsider, to restore, to correct the evil without impairing the good, to purify and humanize every process of our common life without weakening or sentimentalizing it. There has been something crude and heartless and unfeeling in our haste to succeed and be great. Our thought has been "Let every man look out for himself, let every generation look out for itself," while we reared giant machinery which made it impossible that any but those who stood at the levers of control should have a chance to look out for themselves. We had not forgotten our morals. We remembered well enough that we had set up a policy which was meant to serve the humblest as well as the most powerful, with an eye single to the standards of justice and fair play, and remembered it with pride. But we were very heedless and in a hurry to be great.

We have come now to the sober second thought. The scales of heedlessness have fallen from our eyes. We have made up our minds to square every process of our national life again with the standards we so proudly set up at the beginning and have always carried at our hearts. Our work is a work of restoration.

We have itemized with some degree of particularity the things that ought to be altered and here are some of the chief items: A tariff which cuts us off from our proper part in the commerce of the world, violates the just principles of taxation, and makes the Government a facile instrument in

我们终于得以看到了生活的全貌。我们看到恶与善、丑与美、颓唐堕落与活力生机并生共存。我们是以这种眼光来处理新生事物的。我们的责任是清除、审查、纠偏、匡正邪恶而不损害善与美，使我们日常生活的每一个过程得以净化、人性化，而不使之衰弱伤感。但我们往往急于求成，有些事情难免做得粗鲁、无情而又冷酷。我们一向认为要"让每一个人自己照管自己，让每一代人自己照管自己"，同时，我们却建立起了庞大的政府机器，使除了那些掌握操纵杆的人之外，任何人都不可能有机会照管自己。我们一向没有忘记我们的道德准则。我们清楚地记得，我们曾经制定过一项政策，说明我们既要为权贵效劳，也要为地位低下者服务，而且我们特别着眼于公正合理的准则，一想到这一点，我们就会感到自豪。但是，我们太不谨慎，太急于求成了。

现在我要谈的是另外一个严肃的想法。我们的眼中已容不得掉以轻心地办事。我们决心要以我们当初自豪地建立起来的，并且始终牢记心中的准则，重新调整国民生活的每一个过程。我们所要做的工作是一项正本清源的工作。

我们已比较详细地列举了应该加以改变的问题，其中最主要的几项是：(一)关税——现行关税把我们排斥于国际贸易的正当角色之外，这违背了公平征税的原则，使政府沦为

the hand of private interests; a banking and currency system based upon the necessity of the Government to sell its bonds fifty years ago and perfectly adapted to concentrating cash and restricting credits; an industrial system which, take it on all its sides, financial as well as administrative, holds capital in leading strings, restricts the liberties and limits the opportunities of labor, and exploits without renewing or conserving the natural resources of the country; a body of agricultural activities never yet given the efficiency of great business undertakings or served as it should be through the instrumentality of science taken directly to the farm, or afforded the facilities of credit best suited to its practical needs; watercourses undeveloped, waste places unreclaimed, forests untended, fast disappearing without plan or prospect of renewal, unregarded waste heaps at every mine. We have studied as perhaps no other nation has the most effective means of production, but we have not studied cost or economy as we should either as organizers of industry, as statesmen, or as individuals.

Nor have we studied and perfected the means by which government may be put at the service of humanity, in safeguarding the health of the Nation, the health of its men and its women and its children, as well as their rights in the struggle for existence. This is no sentimental duty. The firm basis of government is justice, not pity. These are matters of justice. There can be no equality or opportunity, the first essential of justice in the body politic, if men and women and children be not shielded in their lives, their very vitality,

私人利益集团手中的驯服工具;(二)金融货币制度——现行金融货币制度仍以50年前政府出售公债的需要为基础,并完全适合于集中货币和限制贷款;(三)工业体制——无论从哪一方面考虑,无论是在管理方面还是在财务方面,现行工业体制都是以资本为主角,限制自由和限制劳工机会,并一味开发国家自然资源而不予以补充或保护;(四)农业活动——从来没有能使农业发挥其所能发挥的巨大的效能,它没有得到它本该得到的、来自于科学的直接为农场的服务,也未曾获得最切合它实际需要的信贷上的便利。除此之外,还有未经开发的河道,未经开垦的荒地,未予保护的、由于缺乏更新计划和打算而迅速消失的森林,以及各矿区无人过问的废料成堆等问题。世界上也许只有我们曾经研究过最有效的生产手段,但是我们,无论是作为企业组织者、政治家还是个人,都没有研究过生产成本和节约问题。

我们也没有研究和完善政府借以服务于人道,保护国民健康,保护男女老少的健康,以及他们争取生存权利的各种方法。这不是什么多愁善感或多此一举。政府的坚实基础是公正,而不是怜悯。这些都是公正的问题。如果国家不能保护男女老少的生命和健康,使之不受他们所不能改变、控制或

Woodrow Wilson
伍德罗·威尔逊(1856-1924)
28th President of the United States (1913-1921)

from the consequences of great industrial and social processes which they cannot alter, control, or singly cope with. Society must see to it that it does not itself crush or weaken or damage its own constituent parts. The first duty of law is to keep sound the society it serves. Sanitary laws, pure food laws, and laws determining conditions of labor which individuals are powerless to determine for themselves are intimate parts of the very business of justice and legal efficiency.

These are some of the things we ought to do, and not leave the others undone, the old-fashioned, never-to-be-neglected, fundamental safeguarding of property and of individual right. This is the high enterprise of the new day: To lift everything that concerns our life as a Nation to the light that shines from the hearthfire of every man's conscience and vision of the right. It is inconceivable that we should do this as partisans; it is inconceivable we should do it in ignorance of the facts as they are or in blind haste. We shall restore, not destroy. We shall deal with our economic system as it is and as it may be modified, not as it might be if we had a clean sheet of paper to write upon; and step by step we shall make it what it should be, in the spirit of those who question their own wisdom and seek counsel and knowledge, not shallow self-satisfaction or the excitement of excursions whither they cannot tell. Justice, and only justice, shall always be our motto.

独立应付的大工业发展和社会发展后果的影响,就不会有平等和机会,而这正是国家寻求公正的首要前提。社会务必不要自己摧残、削弱或损害其自身的组成部分,法律的首要责任是使其为之服务的社会安然无恙。环境卫生法、食品卫生法,以及个人无力为自己决定的确定劳动条件的法律,这些都是公正与法律效力的重要组成部分。

这些就是我们应该做的事情中的一部分。我们也切不可将其他事情置之不理,诸如永远不可忽视的、十分重要的保护财产和个人权利的老问题。新时代的崇高事业就是:让涉及我们国民生活的一切事情都能点燃每一个人的良知和正义感之光。如果我们党派观念十足,要做到这一点是不可想象的;如果我们对客观事实一无所知,或盲目图快,要做到这一点也是不可想象的。我们需要的是恢复,而不是破坏。我们将按照实际情况和可能办到的方法修改我们的经济体制,而不是把它看成一张白纸,可以在上面随意书写;我们要以那些不自以为是,能征求他人意见,寻求知识的人的精神,一步一步地使经济体制名副其实地完善起来,而不要肤浅自满,忘情于说不出所以然的离题话。公正,只有公正才永远是我们的座右铭。

And yet it will be no cool process of mere science. The Nation has been deeply stirred, stirred by a solemn passion, stirred by the knowledge of wrong, of ideals lost, of government too often debauched and made an instrument of evil. The feelings with which we face this new age of right and opportunity sweep across our heartstrings like some air out of God's own presence, where justice and mercy are reconciled and the judge and the brother are one. We know our task to be no mere task of politics but a task which shall search us through and through, whether we be able to understand our time and the need of our people, whether we be indeed their spokesmen and interpreters, whether we have the pure heart to comprehend and the rectified will to choose our high course of action.

This is not a day of triumph; it is a day of dedication. Here muster, not the forces of party, but the forces of humanity. Men's hearts wait upon us; men's lives hang in the balance; men's hopes call upon us to say what we will do. Who shall live up to the great trust? Who dares fail to try? I summon all honest men, all patriotic, all forward-looking men, to my side. God helping me, I will not fail them, if they will but counsel and sustain me!

但是，这不是单纯的科学研究那样的超然冷漠的过程。国家已经被深深地激动了，被一股庄严的热情所感动，被其对错误的认识、理想的消失、对政府一味腐败而沦为邪恶工具的了解所刺激。我们面对这个权利与机会共存的新时代所产生的感情，犹如上帝亲临时所带来的和风掠过我们的心弦，在上帝面前，公正与怜悯彼此调和，法官和兄弟融为一体。我们知道，我们所承担的任务不仅仅是一项政治任务，而是要彻底考察我们是否能够理解自己所处的时代和人民的需要，我们是否真是人民的代言人和阐述者，我们是否具有纯洁的心胸去理解和正直的意志去选择崇高的行动路线。

今天不是一个胜利的日子，而是一个献身的日子。聚集在这里的不是党派的力量，而是人性的力量。人民的心在期待着我们，人民的生命安危未定，人民的希望要求我们能说明我们所要做的事情。谁将不负重托？谁将不畏失败敢于一试？我号召所有正直的人，所有爱国的人，所有有远见卓识的人，站到我一边来。上帝在庇佑我，只要他们给我建议，支持我，我决不会使他们失望！

Calvin Coolidge
卡尔文·柯立芝 (1872-1933)
30th President of the United States (1923-1929)

卡尔文·柯立芝:美国第 30 任总统(1923—1929)。1920 年当选为副总统,3 年后接替病故的哈定总统入主白宫,次年获连任。执政 6 年间资本主义世界稳定发展,美国经济快速增长,史称"柯立芝繁荣时期"。本文略有删节。

Calvin Coolidge
卡尔文·柯立芝 (1872-1933)
30th President of the United States (1923-1929)
Political Party: Republican

Better International Understandings, Greater Economy, and Lower Taxes
国际上寻求更好了解,国内厉行节约和减税

My Countrymen:

No one can contemplate current conditions without finding much that is satisfying and still more that is encouraging. Our own country is leading the world in the general readjustment to the results of the great conflict. Many of its burdens will bear heavily upon us for years, and the secondary and indirect effects we must expect to experience for some time. But we are beginning to comprehend

同胞们:

任何人在考虑当前形势时,都不能不看到许多令人满意和更为令人鼓舞的情况。我国正在领导全世界进行这场巨大冲突后的全面重建工作。未来数年内,我们将肩负起许多重担,我们也必须承受其次要、间接的影响。不过,

more definitely what course should be pursued, what remedies ought to be applied, what actions should be taken for our deliverance, and are clearly manifesting a determined will faithfully and conscientiously to adopt these methods of relief. Already we have sufficiently rearranged our domestic affairs so that confidence has returned, business has revived, and we appear to be entering an era of prosperity which is gradually reaching into every part of the Nation. Realizing that we cannot live unto ourselves alone, we have contributed of our resources and our counsel to the relief of the suffering and the settlement of the disputes among the European nations. Because of what America is and what America has done, a firmer courage, a higher hope, inspires the heart of all humanity.

These results have not occurred by mere chance. They have been secured by a constant and enlightened effort marked by many sacrifices and extending over many generations. We cannot continue these brilliant successes in the future, unless we continue to learn from the past. It is necessary to keep the former experiences of our country both at home and abroad continually before us, if we are to have any science of government. If we wish to erect new structures, we must have a definite knowledge of the old foundations. We must realize that human nature is about the most constant thing in the universe and that the essentials of human relationship do not change. We must frequently take our bearings from these fixed stars of our political firmament if we expect to hold a true course. If we examine carefully what we have done, we can determine the more accurately what we can do.

If we are to judge by past experience, there is much to be hoped for in international relations from frequent conferences and consultations. We have before us the beneficial results of the Washington conference and the

目前我们正开始更具体地领会我们必须执行的方针、必须使用的补救办法、必须采取的行动,并忠诚而自觉地表明采取这些解救方法的坚定决心。由于我们已在内政上充分地重做安排,从而使我们恢复了信心,振兴了商业,全国各地正逐步进入一个繁荣的纪元。我们认识到我们不能单独地生存下去,所以我们已经为欧洲各国解除困苦与平息争端的工作提供了财力、物力和建议。美国现在和一贯显示的坚定勇气和崇高希望,振奋了全人类的精神。

这些成就不仅仅是靠机遇就能取得的。它们是多少代人作出许多牺牲、不懈地致力于一项进步事业所取得的。如果我们不继续向过去学习,将来我们就不能使这些光辉的成就继续保下去。如果我们讲求治国之道,就必须继续运用我国以往处理内政外交的经验。如果我们想要建立新的结构,就必须对原有基础有个透彻的了解。我们必须认识到:人性是宇宙间永恒不变的,人际关系的本质也是不会改变的。如果我们想把握住正确方向,就必须常常根据政治天空中这些固定的星座来辨认自己的方位。如果我们认真审视过去已做的工作,就能更正确地决定我们今后所能做的工作。

如果我们根据以往的经验来判断,那么从频繁举行的会议和协商中,可以看出国际关系是大有希望的。在我们面前就有华盛顿会议的有益的结果,

Calvin Coolidge

卡尔文·柯立芝 (1872-1933)

30th President of the United States (1923-1929)

various consultations recently held upon European affairs, some of which were in response to our suggestions and in some of which we were active participants. Even the failures cannot but be accounted useful and an immeasurable advance over threatened or actual warfare. I am strongly in favor of continuation of this policy, whenever conditions are such that there is even a promise that practical and favorable results might be secured.

In conformity with the principle that a display of reason rather than a threat of force should be the determining factor in the intercourse among nations, we have long advocated the peaceful settlement of disputes by methods of arbitration and have negotiated many treaties to secure that result. The same considerations should lead to our adherence to the Permanent Court of International Justice. Where great principles are involved, where great movements are under way which promise much for the welfare of humanity by reason of the very fact that many other nations have given such movements their actual support, we ought not to withhold our own sanction because of any small and inessential difference, but only upon the ground of the most important and compelling fundamental reasons. We cannot barter away our independence or our sovereignty, but we ought to engage in no refinements of logic, no sophistries, and no subterfuges, to argue away the undoubted duty of this country by reason of the might of its numbers, the power of its resources, and its position of leadership in the world, actively and comprehensively to signify its approval and to bear its full share of the responsibility of a candid and disinterested attempt at the establishment of a tribunal for the administration of even-handed justice between nation and nation. The weight of our enormous influence must be cast upon the side of a reign not of force but of law and trial, not by battle but by reason.

和最近就欧洲问题举行的各种磋商,其中有些是根据我们的建议举行的,有些是我们积极参与的。即使是失败的磋商,我们也必须把它看作是有益的,同战争威胁或真正的战争相比,这是无可估量的进步。我坚决赞成继续执行这种策略,无论何时即使只达成一项诺言,也会获得实际而有利的结果。

遵照国际交往中应表现理智,而不以武力进行威胁这一原则,我们早就提倡通过仲裁和平地解决争端,并为取得这样的结果而与别国议订了许多条约。根据同样的考虑,我们应该信赖国际永久法庭。在涉及重大原则的地方,掀起了给予人类福利很大希望的伟大运动。鉴于其他许多国家都已实际地支持这些运动,我们绝不能因为任何无关紧要的细小差异而拒绝给予支持,而只能根据最重要的、不得不采取行动的根本理由行事。我们不能拿独立和主权做交易。但是,由于我国人口众多、资源丰富,并在世界上居于领导地位,我们绝不能用咬文嚼字、狡辩、托词等手段去推脱我国无可置疑的责任,而应积极地、全面地表明我们同意并承担起我们对于在国家之间建立一个不偏不倚的公正法庭应负的一份责任,以及为此而进行真诚、无私的努力。我们巨大影响的力量,必须用来支持法律和审讯,而不是支持武力,并且不是通过战争,而是通过理性来进行支持。

We have never any wish to interfere in the political conditions of any other countries. Especially are we determined not to become implicated in the political controversies of the Old World. With a great deal of hesitation, we have responded to appeals for help to maintain order, protect life and property, and establish responsible government in some of the small countries of the Western Hemisphere. Our private citizens have advanced large sums of money to assist in the necessary financing and relief of the Old World. We have not failed, nor shall we fail to respond, whenever necessary to mitigate human suffering and assist in the rehabilitation of distressed nations. These, too, are requirements which must be met by reason of our vast powers and the place we hold in the world. Some of the best thought of mankind has long been seeking for a formula for permanent peace. Undoubtedly the clarification of the principles of international law would be helpful, and the efforts of scholars to prepare such a work for adoption by the various nations should have our sympathy and support. Much may be hoped for from the earnest studies of those who advocate the outlawing of aggressive war. But all these plans and preparations, these treaties and covenants, will not of themselves be adequate. One of the greatest dangers to peace lies in the economic pressure to which people find themselves subjected. One of the most practical things to be done in the world is to seek arrangements under which such pressure may be removed, so that opportunity may be renewed and hope may be revived. There must be some assurance that effort and endeavor will be followed by success and prosperity. In the making and financing of such adjustments there is not only an opportunity, but a real duty, for America to respond with her counsel and her resources. Conditions must be provided under which people can make a living and work out of their difficulties. But there is another element, more

我们从来不想干预任何他国的政治环境，尤其不愿卷入旧世界的政治纠纷。我们踌躇良久才答应西半球的一些小国，帮助它们维持秩序，保护生命和财产，并建立负责的政府。我们的一些公民付出巨额款项以使旧世界获得必需的资金和救济支援。对于减轻人类痛苦和帮助贫困国家的重建工作，无论何时，只要有此需要，我们过去没有不管，今后也绝不会置之不理。由于我们的巨大实力和在世界上所占有的地位，这些工作也是必须完成的。自古以来，人们一直在不断寻求维持永久和平的公式，这是人类的良好愿望之一。毫无疑问，澄清国际法的相关原则对此大有裨益；而学者们也在为构建多国合作的框架做出努力，对于他们的付出，我们十分认同，也很支持。我们从反对侵略性战争合法性的学者那里看到了希望。但是，所以这些的计划、准备，这些条约、协议，他们本身并不能充分地解决问题。动摇和平的最大危险之一是人们所感受到的经济压力。当下最切合实际的一件事情就是去寻求合作，赶走这些压力，如此才能带来新的机遇，孕育新的希望。辛劳和努力定会换来成功和繁荣，这点必须受到保障。在做出调整的同时，我们所面临的不单单是机遇，还有确定的责任，美国要为已付出的人力、财力负责。我们要提供条件，使得人们能够养活自己，脱离贫困。保障和平还有另外一个因素。它比其他因素都重要，缺少了它，永久的和

Calvin Coolidge

卡尔文·柯立芝 (1872-1933)
30th President of the United States (1923-1929)

important than all, without which there cannot be the slightest hope of a permanent peace. That element lies in the heart of humanity. Unless the desire for peace be cherished there, unless this fundamental and only natural source of brotherly love be cultivated to its highest degree, all artificial efforts will be in vain. Peace will come when there is realization that only under a reign of law, based on righteousness and supported by the religious conviction of the brotherhood of man, can there be any hope of a complete and satisfying life. Parchment will fail, the sword will fail, it is only the spiritual nature of man that can be triumphant. It seems altogether probable that we can contribute most to these important objects by maintaining our position of political detachment and independence. We are not identified with any Old World interests. This position should be made more and more clear in our relations with all foreign countries. We are at peace with all of them. Our program is never to oppress, but always to assist. But while we do justice to others, we must require that justice be done to us. With us a treaty of peace means peace, and a treaty of amity means amity. We have made great contributions to the settlement of contentious differences in both Europe and Asia. But there is a very definite point beyond which we cannot go. We can only help those who help themselves. Mindful of these limitations, the one great duty that stands out requires us to use our enormous powers to trim the balance of the world.

While we can look with a great deal of pleasure upon what we have done abroad, we must remember that our continued success in that direction depends upon what we do at home. Since its very outset, it has been found necessary to conduct our Government by means of political parties. That system would not have survived from generation to generation if it had not been fundamentally

平根本无法实现。这个因素就是人性。如果和平的愿望未被珍惜,如果手足之情赖以存在的这个基础未得到坚实地巩固,那么所有人为的努力都会付诸东流。只有在遵守法律的国度,拥有建立在人们宗教般的友爱之情之上的正义感,才能保障所有人的完整、美好的生活。认识到这一点,和平才有可能到来。羊皮纸有一天会腐烂,刀剑有一天会生锈,但人类的精神永恒,会最终取得胜利。综合多方面来看,保持政治上的独立和自主有利于我们实现这些重要目标。我们不为任何旧世界的利益服务。这一点必须在我国的对外交往中得到明确。我们愿与其他国家和平相处。我们从来不去压迫别人,只会提供支援。但是,我们给予别人公平的同时,我们也要求得到同样的回报。对我们而言,和平条约意味着和平,友好条约意味着友好。欧洲和亚洲与美国之间存在着有争议性的差异,但是我们已尽一切努力去化解双方的不同。我们的付出有个临界点,那就是我们只帮助自强进取的国家。虽有种种局限,但仍有一个伟大的使命等待我们完成,那就是用我们强大的力量维护世界的平衡。

在我们十分欣喜地看到我们在国外所进行的工作时,我们必须牢记:国外工作之所以连续获得成功乃有赖于我们在国内的工作。人们从一开始就已经发现必须通过政党来管理政府。如果当初这个制度从根本上说不是稳固的,也没有为

sound and provided the best instrumentalities for the most complete expression of the popular will. It is not necessary to claim that it has always worked perfectly. It is enough to know that nothing better has been devised. No one would deny that there should be full and free expression and an opportunity for independence of action within the party. There is no salvation in a narrow and bigoted partisanship. But if there is to be responsible party government, the party label must be something more than a mere device for securing office. Unless those who are elected under the same party designation are willing to assume sufficient responsibility and exhibit sufficient loyalty and coherence, so that they can cooperate with each other in the support of the broad general principles, of the party platform, the election is merely a mockery, no decision is made at the polls, and there is no representation of the popular will. Common honesty and good faith with the people who support a party at the polls require that party, when it enters office, to assume the control of that portion of the Government to which it has been elected. Any other course is bad faith and a violation of the party pledges.

    When the country has bestowed its confidence upon a party by making it a majority in the Congress, it has a right to expect such unity of action as will make the party majority an effective instrument of government. This Administration has come into power with a very clear and definite mandate from the people. The expression of the popular will in favor of maintaining our constitutional guarantees was overwhelming and decisive. There was a manifestation of such faith in the integrity of the courts that we can consider that issue rejected for some time to come.

最全面地表现公众意愿提供最好的手段,那它就不会一代一代地保留下来。我们没有必要宣称这种制度一直起着完美无瑕的作用。只要知道不能设想出比这更好的制度就够了。没有人会否认在党内应该充分而自由地表达意见,并有独立行动的机会。狭隘、偏执的党派偏见是不可救药的。但是,如果想要有一个负责的党派政府,那么党派标记就不应只是一种取得职位的策略。如果那些根据同一党派指定而当选的人都不愿意承担足够的责任,表现足够的忠诚与一致性,从而说明他们能够互相合作,支持主要的一般原则和党纲,那么选举也仅仅是一种讽刺,投票就决定不了任何事情,也不能代表公众的意愿。一个政党应该与投票支持自己的人民具有同样的正直和诚意,这就要求该党在当选执政时,担负起管理政府的工作。任何其他做法都是不守信用,是对党的誓言的破坏。

当国家使一个政党成为国会中的多数党而给予信任时,国家有权要求这个多数党行动一致,并成为管理政府的有效工具。本届政府是经过人民清楚而明确的授权而执政的。公众为维护我国宪法所规定的各项保证而表现的意愿,是压倒一切的并具有决定意义的。人民已表明相信法院的正直,我们可以认为法

Calvin Coolidge
卡尔文·柯立芝(1872-1933)
30th President of the United States (1923-1929)

Likewise, the policy of public ownership of railroads and certain electric utilities met with unmistakable defeat. The people declared that they wanted their rights to have not a political but a judicial determination, and their independence and freedom continued and supported by having the ownership and control of their property, not in the Government, but in their own hands. As they always do when they have a fair chance, the people demonstrated that they are sound and are determined to have a sound government.

When we turn from what was rejected to inquire what was accepted, the policy that stands out with the greatest clearness is that of economy in public expenditure with reduction and reform of taxation. The principle involved in this effort is that of conservation. The resources of this country are almost beyond computation. No mind can comprehend them. But the cost of our combined governments is likewise almost beyond definition. Not only those who are now making their tax returns, but those who meet the enhanced cost of existence in their monthly bills, know by hard experience what this great burden is and what it does. No matter what others may want, these people want a drastic economy. They are opposed to waste. They know that extravagance lengthens the hours and diminishes the rewards of their labor. I favor the policy of economy, not because I wish to save money, but because I wish to save people. The men and women of this country who toil are the ones who bear the cost of the Government. Every dollar that we carelessly waste means that their life will be so much the more meager. Every dollar that we prudently save means that their life will be so much the more abundant. Economy

院是否正直这个问题已经受到驳斥,今后一段时间内不可再提了。同样地,关于对铁路和某些电力设施实行公有制的政策也遭到明确的失败。人民宣称:他们要求自己的权利得到司法上的、而不是政治上的确认,并要求把财产的所有权和支配权掌握在自己手里,而不是在政府手里,以便保证继续享有独立和自由。就像人民在得到公正的机会时经常做的那样,他们表明他们是有可靠的,而且决意要有一个可靠的政府。

当我们从被人们抵制的问题转向询问被人们接受的问题时,显得最为突出的就是关于压缩公共开支和税制改革的经济政策。这项工作涉及保护资源的原则。我国的资源几乎无法计算,没人能彻底弄清。但是我们联合政府机构的费用同样也是难以确定的。不仅是那些要求退还税款的人,而且那些在每月账单上看到生活费用上涨的人,都从艰难的生活中懂得,这种沉重负担的含义和影响。无论别人想要什么,这些人要求的是严厉的节约措施。他们反对浪费。他们知道铺张浪费使他们延长了劳动时间而减少了报酬。我赞成厉行节约政策,这不是为了省钱,而是要拯救人民。我国辛勤劳动的男男女女是负担政府费用的人。我们随意浪费每一

is idealism in its most practical form. If extravagance were not reflected in taxation, and through taxation both directly and indirectly injuriously affecting the people, it would not be of so much consequence. The wisest and soundest method of solving our tax problem is through economy. Fortunately, of all the great nations this country is best in a position to adopt that simple remedy. We do not any longer need wartime revenues. The collection of any taxes which are not absolutely required, which do not beyond reasonable doubt contribute to the public welfare, is only a species of legalized larceny. Under this republic the rewards of industry belong to those who earn them. The only constitutional tax is the tax which ministers to public necessity. The property of the country belongs to the people of the country. Their title is absolute. They do not support any privileged class; they do not need to maintain great military forces; they ought not to be burdened with a great array of public employees. They are not required to make any contribution to Government expenditures except that which they voluntarily assess upon themselves through the action of their own representatives. Whenever taxes become burdensome a remedy can be applied by the people; but if they do not act for themselves, no one can be very successful in acting for them.

The time is arriving when we can have further tax reduction, when, unless we wish to hamper the people in their right to earn a living, we must have tax reform. The method of raising revenue ought not to impede the transaction

块美元,就意味着将使他们的生活多增加一份贫苦。我们精打细算地省下每一块美元,则意味着将使他们的生活多增加一份改善。节约是一种最实际的理想主义。如果税收束缚不了铺张,而加税却又直接或间接地损害到人民的利益,那么再提税收就不那么重要了。解决我国税收难题的最有效、最成熟的方法是莫过于发展经济。幸运的是,在所有伟大的国家里,我们恰巧碰到了采用这个简单良方的最佳时刻。我们不再需要战时的税收政策。从来没有绝对必征的税收,对公众福祉无益的税收,以上两种只能算是一种合法的窃盗。在共和国里,工业产值的回报属于那些有所付出的人们。唯一符合宪法的税收是为必要民生服务而征收的。国家的财产属于全体人民。他们受之无愧。他们无需为特权阶级服务;他们无需为庞大军事开支买单;他们不应该背负政府人员的开销。除通过议会代表行使主动纳税的原因之外,人民不需要承担任何政府开销。每当课税成为负担时,人民可以去寻找补偿;但是,如果人民不为自己行动的话,那么是没有人能够代表他们的。

我们能够进一步实行减税的时候正在到来,我们必须改革税制,除非我们不想让人民享有谋生的权利。提高税

Calvin Coolidge
卡尔文·柯立芝 (1872-1933)
30th President of the United States (1923-1929)

of business; it ought to encourage it. I am opposed to extremely high rates, because they produce little or no revenue, because they are bad for the country, and, finally, because they are wrong. We cannot finance the country, we cannot improve social conditions, through any system of injustice, even if we attempt to inflict it upon the rich. Those who suffer the most harm will be the poor. This country believes in prosperity. It is absurd to suppose that it is envious of those who are already prosperous. The wise and correct course to follow in taxation and all other economic legislation is not to destroy those who have already secured success but to create conditions under which every one will have a better chance to be successful. The verdict of the country has been given on this question. That verdict stands. We shall do well to heed it.

These questions involve moral issues. We need not concern ourselves much about the rights of property if we will faithfully observe the rights of persons. Under our institutions their rights are supreme. It is not property but the right to hold property, both great and small, which our Constitution guarantees. All owners of property are charged with a service. These rights and duties have been revealed, through the conscience of society, to have a divine sanction. The very stability of our society rests upon production and conservation. For individuals or for governments to waste and squander their resources is to deny these rights and disregard these obligations. The result of economic dissipation to a nation is always moral decay.

收的方法不应妨碍商业交易，而应鼓励商业。我反对把税率定得太高，因为那会减少、甚至没有税收，因为这对国家有害，最后，因为那是错误的做法。我们不能通过侵害别人权利的任何不公正方法来为国家筹措资金，改善社会条件，即使对富人也不可以使用这种方法。因为受害最大的仍将是穷人。我国人民坚信富裕是好事。对已经富裕起来的人感到妒忌，这是很荒唐的。在税制和其他一切经济立法中应遵循明智而正确的方针，不是摧残那些已经获得成功的人，而是创造条件使每一个人都能获得较好的成功机会。我国人民已经对这个问题发表了意见。那种意见依然有效。我们必须认真对待。

这些方面都涉及道德问题。如果我们忠实地尊重个人的权利，我们就不必过分地为财产权担心。在我国的制度下，人民的权利高于一切。我国宪法所保证的不是财产，而是拥有不论多少财产的权利。一切拥有财产的人都被要求承担起义务。这些权利和义务都已通过社会意识表明它们具有神圣的约束力。我们社会的安定在于生产与保护资源。无论个人还是政府，浪费和滥用资源就是否定这些权利、漠视这些义务。对一个国家来说，经济上的挥霍总是导致道德上的堕落。

These policies of better international understandings, greater economy, and lower taxes have contributed largely to peaceful and prosperous industrial relations. Under the helpful influences of restrictive immigration and a protective tariff, employment is plentiful, the rate of pay is high, and wage earners are in a state of contentment seldom before seen. Our transportation systems have been gradually recovering and have been able to meet all the requirements of the service. Agriculture has been very slow in reviving, but the price of cereals at last indicates that the day of its deliverance is at hand.

We are not without our problems, but our most important problem is not to secure new advantages but to maintain those which we already possess. Our system of government made up of three separate and independent departments, our divided sovereignty composed of Nation and State, the matchless wisdom that is enshrined in our Constitution, all these need constant effort and tireless vigilance for their protection and support.

In a republic the first rule for the guidance of the citizen is obedience to law. Under a despotism the law may be imposed upon the subject. He has no voice in its making, no influence in its administration, it does not represent him. Under a free government the citizen makes his own laws, chooses his own administrators, which do represent him. Those who want their rights respected under the Constitution and the law ought to set the example themselves of observing the Constitution and the law. While there may be those of high intelligence who violate the law at times, the barbarian and the defective always violate it. Those who disregard the rules of society are not exhibiting a

在国际上寻求更好的相互了解，在国内厉行节约和减税，这些政策都大大有助于发展和平繁荣的产业关系。在限制移民和保护关税的有利影响下，我们有了充分的就业机会，工资得到了提高，挣得收入的劳动者处于以往少见的满足状态。我们的运输系统已经逐渐恢复，并能满足各方面对运输业务的需要。农业恢复得很慢，但谷物价格终于说明农业问题得以解决的日子即将到来。

我们不是没有问题，但是我们最重要的问题不是争取新的有利条件，而是保持我们已经拥有的有利条件。我们由三个分开而独立的部门所组成的政府体制，我们由国家和州分享的主权，宪法中备受尊重的无与伦比的智慧，所有这些都需要以持续的努力和不懈的警觉来加以保护和支持。

在一个共和国里，指导公民行动的第一准则是遵守法律。在专制政治下，法律可以强加于人民。人民在法律的制定过程中没有发言权，在法律的执行过程中不能产生影响，法律也不代表人民。而在自由政治下，公民制定自己的法律，选择自己的行政人员，这些确实都能代表他们。那些想要根据宪法和法律使自己的权利受到尊重的人，本身应该树立起遵守宪法和法律

Calvin Coolidge

卡尔文·柯立芝(1872-1933)
30th President of the United States (1923-1929)

superior intelligence, are not promoting freedom and independence, are not following the path of civilization, but are displaying the traits of ignorance, of servitude, of savagery, and treading the way that leads back to the jungle.

The essence of a republic is representative government. Our Congress represents the people and the States. In all legislative affairs it is the natural collaborator with the President. In spite of all the criticism which often falls to its lot, I do not hesitate to say that there is no more independent and effective legislative body in the world. It is, and should be, jealous of its prerogative. I welcome its cooperation, and expect to share with it not only the responsibility, but the credit, for our common effort to secure beneficial legislation.

These are some of the principles which America represents. We have not by any means put them fully into practice, but we have strongly signified our belief in them. The encouraging feature of our country is not that it has reached its destination, but that it has overwhelmingly expressed its determination to proceed in the right direction. It is true that we could, with profit, be less sectional and more national in our thought. It would be well if we could replace much that is only a false and ignorant prejudice with a true and enlightened pride of race. But the last election showed that appeals to class and nationality had little effect. We were all found loyal to a common citizenship. The fundamental precept of liberty is toleration. We cannot permit any inquisition either within or without the law or apply any religious test to the holding

的榜样。尽管高知人士有时也会犯法,但经常犯法的却是残暴的人和精神有缺陷的人。那些无视社会纪律的人并没有表现出什么超人的智慧,他们不是在促进自由和独立,不是遵循文明的轨道前进,而是暴露了无知、奴性和野蛮的特征,是踏上了返回丛林时代的道路。

共和政体的实质是代议制政府。我们的国会代表人民和各州。在一切立法事务上,国会是总统的天然合作者。尽管它难免经常受批评,我却要毫不犹豫地说世界上再没有比它更独立、更有效率的立法机关了。它珍惜,而且应该珍惜自己的特权。我欢迎国会的合作,并期望和它一起努力来保证有益的立法,不仅分担责任,而且共享荣誉。

这些是美国所主张的一些原则。我们还没有完全付诸实践,但是我们已经强烈地表明我们对这些原则所抱的信念。我国的特点是令人鼓舞的,这并不是说它已达到了预期的目的,而是说它已非常明确地表示有决心朝着正确的方向前进。我们的确能够在思想上克服地区观念,增强全国观点,而这是很有裨益的。如果我们能以一种正确的、进步的民族自尊心来代替一种完全错误的、无知的偏见,那就好了。但是上次的选举说明,诉诸阶级和民族性收

of office. The mind of America must be forever free.

It is in such contemplations, my fellow countrymen, which are not exhaustive but only representative, that I find ample warrant for satisfaction and encouragement. We should not let the much that is to do obscure the much which has been done. The past and present show faith and hope and courage fully justified. Here stands our country, an example of tranquility at home, a patron of tranquility abroad. Here stands its Government, aware of its might but obedient to its conscience. Here it will continue to stand, seeking peace and prosperity, solicitous for the welfare of the wage earner, promoting enterprise, developing waterways and natural resources, attentive to the intuitive counsel of womanhood, encouraging education, desiring the advancement of religion, supporting the cause of justice and honor among the nations. America seeks no earthly empire built on blood and force. No ambition, no temptation, lures her to thought of foreign dominions. The legions which she sends forth are armed, not with the sword, but with the cross. The higher state to which she seeks the allegiance of all mankind is not of human, but of divine origin. She cherishes no purpose save to merit the favor of Almighty God.

效甚微。人们看到，我们都忠实于共同的公民身份。自由的基本箴言是宽容。我们不能在法律范围内或法律范围外容许任何对异端的镇压，也不能容许在有关担任公职的问题上运用任何宗教的检验标准。美国的思想必须永远是自由的。

同胞们，正是在上述这些并不详尽而只是代表性的思考中，我发现了可以感到满意和鼓舞的充分依据。我们不应该让将做的许多事遮掩住已做的许多事。过去和现在都表明，我们的信念、希望和勇气是有依据的。这里屹立着我们的国家，就国内而言，它是安定的榜样，就国外而言，它是安定的保护者。这里屹立着它的政府，意识到它的力量，服从于它的良心。今后它仍将屹立在这里，追求和平与繁荣，关心挣得收入劳动者的福利，促进企业的发展，开发水路和自然资源，倾听女性的直觉忠告，鼓励教育事业，期望宗教事业的进展，支持国际正义与光荣的事业。美国绝不企图在流血和武力的基础上建立全球性的帝国。任何野心和诱惑都不能吸引它产生统治外国的想法。它所派遣的军团不是用武器和刺刀，而是用十字架武装起来的。她追求全人类的相互忠诚，这个崇高境界具有神圣的、而不是人间的起因。她除了向全能的上帝祈求恩宠外，别无其他的目的。

Herbert Hoover
赫伯特·胡佛(1874-1964)
31st President of the United States (1929-1933)

赫伯特·胡佛：美国第 31 任总统（1929—1933），第一位工程师出身的总统。任期内爆发经济危机，自由放任经济政策失灵，回天乏术，4 年后黯然下台。本文略有删节。

Herbert Hoover
赫伯特·胡佛(1874-1964)
31st President of the United States (1929-1933)
Political Party: Republican

Progress to Higher Standards
向更高的标准前进

This occasion is not alone the administration of the most sacred oath which can be assumed by an American citizen. It is a dedication and consecration under God to the highest office in service of our people. I assume this trust in the humility of knowledge that only through the guidance of Almighty Providence can I hope to discharge its ever-increasing burdens.

It is in keeping with tradition throughout our history that I should express simply and directly the opinions which I hold concerning some of the matters of present importance.

这个场合不仅是一个美国公民举行最神圣宣誓的场合。这是在上帝指引下，为了把自己贡献给我国人民服务的最高职位而举行的仪式。在承担这项职责时，我浅薄的知识告诉我，只要凭借全能上帝的指引，我就有希望履行这种日益繁重的责任。

为了遵循贯穿于我国历史上的一个传统，我必须就当前的一些重要问题简单而直率地发表意见。

Our Progress If we survey the situation of our Nation both at home and abroad, we find many satisfactions; we find some causes for concern. We have emerged from the losses of the Great War and the reconstruction following it with increased virility and strength. From this strength we have contributed to the recovery and progress of the world. What America has done has given renewed hope and courage to all who have faith in government by the people. In the large view, we have reached a higher degree of comfort and security than ever existed before in the history of the world. Through liberation from widespread poverty we have reached a higher degree of individual freedom than ever before. The devotion to and concern for our institutions are deep and sincere. We are steadily building a new race—a new civilization great in its own attainments. The influence and high purposes of our Nation are respected among the peoples of the world. We aspire to distinction in the world, but to a distinction based upon confidence in our sense of justice as well as our accomplishments within our own borders and in our own lives. For wise guidance in this great period of recovery the Nation is deeply indebted to Calvin Coolidge.

But all this majestic advance should not obscure the constant dangers from which self-government must be safeguarded. The strong man must at all times be alert to the attack of insidious disease.

The Relation of Government to Business The election has again confirmed the determination of the American people that regulation of private enterprise and not Government ownership or operation is the course rightly

我们的进展 如果我们审视一下国内外形势,就会看到许多令人满意的事和一些令人担心的事。我们以日益增强的生气和力量,摆脱了世界大战带来的损失,进行了战后的重建工作。我们以这种力量帮助全世界得到了恢复和进步。美国的作为使所有那些相信政府应由人民管理的人产生了新的希望和勇气。广义上而言,我们得到的高度舒适和安定的生活,是世界历史上前所未有的。我们从普遍的贫困中解脱了出来,得到了前所未有的、高度的个人自由。我们对我国的各项制度的忠诚和关切是深刻而真挚的。我们正在坚定不移地建设一种拥有伟大成就的新的民族文化。我国的影响和崇高的目标受到全世界人民的尊重。我们渴望世界性的荣誉,但这种荣誉是以我们的正义感和在自己国土上、在自己生活中取得成就的信心为基础的。我们国家对卡尔文·柯立芝在这个伟大的重建时期所做的明智指导深表感谢。

但是,所有这一切巨大进展都不应掩盖自治政府时时都应提防的各种危险。身体强壮的人也必须随时警惕乘虚而入的疾病的侵袭。

政府与企业之间的关系 这次选举再次证实了美国人民的决心:在政府与企业的关系中应该执行的正确方针是

Herbert Hoover
赫伯特·胡佛(1874-1964)
31st President of the United States (1929-1933)

to be pursued in our relation to business. In recent years we have established a differentiation in the whole method of business regulation between the industries which produce and distribute commodities on the one hand and public utilities on the other. In the former, our laws insist upon effective competition; in the latter, because we substantially confer a monopoly by limiting competition, we must regulate their services and rates. The rigid enforcement of the laws applicable to both groups is the very base of equal opportunity and freedom from domination for all our people, and it is just as essential for the stability and prosperity of business itself as for the protection of the public at large. Such regulation should be extended by the Federal Government within the limitations of the Constitution and only when the individual States are without power to protect their citizens through their own authority. On the other hand, we should be fearless when the authority rests only in the Federal Government.

Cooperation by the Government The larger purpose of our economic thought should be to establish more firmly stability and security of business and employment and thereby remove poverty still further from our borders. Our people have in recent years developed a new-found capacity for cooperation among themselves to effect high purposes in public welfare. It is an advance toward the highest conception of self-government. Self-government does not and should not imply the use of political agencies alone. Progress is born of cooperation in the community—not from governmental restraints. The Government should assist and encourage these movements of collective self-help by itself cooperating with them. Business has by cooperation made

对私人企业进行管理,而不是政府拥有所有权和操纵权。近年来,我们在整个企业管理的方法上,对于从事商业生产与分配的企业和公用事业是区别对待的。对前者,我们的法律坚决要求它们进行有效的竞争;对后者,实质上我们是通过限制竞争而使它们居于垄断地位,但我们必须管理它们的服务工作和收费标准。严格地执行适用于两类不同企业的法律,正是全体人民享有均等机会和不受控制的自由的基础,这对企业本身的稳定和繁荣,以及对保持广大人民的利益,同样是必要的。这种管理应该由联邦政府在宪法许可的范围内加以扩大,但这只有在各州无法以自己的权力保护所辖公民时才能进行,另一方面,我们也不必担心这种权力只由联邦政府来掌握。

政府的合作 我们在经济观念上的更大目标应该是:更坚定地巩固和稳定企业与就业,从而在我国境内进一步消除贫困。近年来,我国人民为了实现公共福利方面的崇高目标,发挥了他们新近发现的相互合作的能力。这是朝着自治政府的最高理想迈进了一大步。自治政府并不是指,也不应该仅仅是指运用政治机构而言。进行来自社会的合作——不是来自政府的管束。政府应该通过与这些

great progress in the advancement of service, in stability, in regularity of employment and in the correction of its own abuses. Such progress, however, can continue only so long as business manifests its respect for law.

There is an equally important field of cooperation by the Federal Government with the multitude of agencies, State, municipal and private, in the systematic development of those processes which directly affect public health, recreation, education, and the home. We have need further to perfect the means by which Government can be adapted to human service.

Education Although education is primarily a responsibility of the States and local communities, and rightly so, yet the Nation as a whole is vitally concerned in its development everywhere to the highest standards and to complete universality. Self-government can succeed only through an instructed electorate. Our objective is not simply to overcome illiteracy. The Nation has marched far beyond that. The more complex the problems of the Nation become, the greater is the need for more and more advanced instruction. Moreover, as our numbers increase and as our life expands with science and invention, we must discover more and more leaders for every walk of life. We cannot hope to succeed in directing this increasingly complex civilization unless we can draw all the talent of leadership from the whole people. One civilization after another has been wrecked upon the attempt to secure sufficient leadership from a single group or class. If we would prevent the growth of class distinctions and would constantly refresh our leadership with the ideals of our people, we must draw constantly from the general mass.

集体自助运动的合作,给它们以帮助和鼓励。企业界通过合作已经在提高服务、加强稳定性、调整就业和纠正本身弊端方面取得了很大的进展。然而,企业界只有在表明它尊重法律的情况下才能继续取得这种进展。

系统地发展能直接影响公众健康、娱乐、教育和家庭的事业,同样也是联邦政府与各州、地方和私人的众多机构进行合作的重要方面。我们需要进一步完善政府的工作方法,使之能适应为人类服务。

教育 正确地说,尽管教育主要是各州政府和地方社会的责任,然而,作为一个整体来说,国家非常关心全国各地教育事业迈向最高标准和全面发展的情况。自治政府只能通过有知识的选民才能得到成功。我们的目标不只是扫除文盲。国家在教育方面的成就远远超过了这一点。国家遇到的问题越复杂,就越需要日趋先进的教育事业。不仅如此,随着我国人口的增加,随着科学发明的进步和生活内容的更为丰富,我们必须为社会各行业发掘更多的领导人才。如果我们不能从全体人民中选拔一切有才能的领导人物,我们就不能在指导我国日益复杂的文化工作中取得成功。以往由于只从某一群体或某一阶层寻找领导

Herbert Hoover

赫伯特·胡佛(1874-1964)
31st President of the United States (1929-1933)

The full opportunity for every boy and girl to rise through the selective processes of education can alone secure to us this leadership.

Public Health In public health the discoveries of science have opened a new era. Many sections of our country and many groups of our citizens suffer from diseases the eradication of which are mere matters of administration and moderate expenditure. Public health service should be as fully organized and as universally incorporated into our governmental system as is public education. The returns are a thousand fold in economic benefits, and infinitely more in reduction of suffering and promotion of human happiness.

World Peace The United States fully accepts the profound truth that our own progress, prosperity, and peace are interlocked with the progress, prosperity, and peace of all humanity. The whole world is at peace. The dangers to a continuation of this peace today are largely the fear and suspicion which still haunt the world. No suspicion or fear can be rightly directed toward our country.

The recent treaty for the renunciation of war as an instrument of national policy sets an advanced standard in our conception of the relations of nations. Its acceptance should pave the way to greater limitation of armament, the offer of which we sincerely extend to the world. But its full realization also implies a greater and greater perfection in the instrumentalities for pacific settlement of controversies

人物,因而使一代又一代的文化受到了损害。如果我们想要防止阶级差别的扩大,并且根据人民的理想不断更新领导人,我们就必须从广大群众中发掘领导人。只要使每个男女学生都有足够的机会通过教育的选择过程而崭露头角,就能为我们找到这种领导人。

公共保健工作 科学的发现开辟了公共保健方面的新纪元。我国有许多地区和许多公民群体遭受疾病的折磨,而消灭这些疾病仅仅需要加强管理和适当的开支。公共保健工作应该和公共教育一样全面地组织起来,并且纳入政府系统。这样做将千百倍地提高经济效益,并且大大地减少疾病和促进人间幸福。

世界和平 美国完全接受这样一条深刻的真理:我们自己的进步、繁荣与和平是同全人类的进步、繁荣与和平联结在一起的。整个世界现在处于和平状态。今天,保持这种和平的危险主要是那依然纠缠着世界的恐惧和猜疑。任何投向我国的猜疑和恐惧都是没有道理的。

最近,有一些国家签订了条约,规定不得以战争作为推行国家政策的工具,这为国与国之间关系的概念树立了一个先进的准则。这个准则如能被接受,则必将为进一步限制军备铺平道路,我们向全世

between nations. In the creation and use of these instrumentalities we should support every sound method of conciliation, arbitration, and judicial settlement. American statesmen were among the first to propose and they have constantly urged upon the world, the establishment of a tribunal for the settlement of controversies of a justiciable character. The Permanent Court of International Justice in its major purpose is thus peculiarly identified with American ideals and with American statesmanship. No more potent instrumentality for this purpose has ever been conceived and no other is practicable of establishment. The reservations placed upon our adherence should not be misinterpreted. The United States seeks by these reservations no special privilege or advantage but only to clarify our relation to advisory opinions and other matters which are subsidiary to the major purpose of the court. The way should, and I believe will, be found by which we may take our proper place in a movement so fundamental to the progress of peace.

Our people have determined that we should make no political engagements such as membership in the League of Nations, which may commit us in advance as a nation to become involved in the settlements of controversies between other countries. They adhere to the belief that the independence of America from such obligations increases its ability and availability for service in all fields of human progress.

I have lately returned from a journey among our sister Republics of the Western Hemisphere. I have received unbounded hospitality and courtesy as their expression of

界诚恳地提议接受这个准则。但是这一准则的全面实现,还意味着和平解决国与国之间的争端的手段将越来越臻于完善。在提出和使用这些手段时,对于调停、仲裁和法律解决的各种正确方法,我们都应给予支持。美国政治家最先提议并一直敦促世界各国:建立一个法庭,以便解决那些应由法庭裁决的争端。国际永久法庭的主要目的特别符合美国的理想和美国的政治见解。人们为达到这一目的而构想的方法再没有比这更有力、更切实可行的了。我们对国际永久法庭的支持是有保留的,这不应引起误解。合众国不是想通过这些保留取得任何特权或利益,而只是为了阐明我们同那些对法庭主要目的而言居于次要地位的咨询性意见及其他问题的关系。我们应该,而且我相信,我们必将设法在推进和平的重要行动中取得适当的地位。

我国人民决定,我们不应承担诸如国际联盟会员国那样的任何政治约束,以免提前作出承诺,被牵扯进解决其他国家的争端之中。我国人民坚信:美国不受这些义务的束缚,就会使自己在为人类进行的各个方面的工作中增强其能力和效力。

我最近刚从西半球的一些兄弟共和国家访问归来。我受到了他们对我国表示友

Herbert Hoover

赫伯特·胡佛(1874-1964)
31st President of the United States (1929-1933)

friendliness to our country. We are held by particular bonds of sympathy and common interest with them. They are each of them building a racial character and a culture which is an impressive contribution to human progress. We wish only for the maintenance of their independence, the growth of their stability, and their prosperity. While we have had wars in the Western Hemisphere, yet on the whole the record is in encouraging contrast with that of other parts of the world. Fortunately the New World is largely free from the inheritances of fear and distrust which have so troubled the Old World. We should keep it so.

It is impossible, my countrymen, to speak of peace without profound emotion. In thousands of homes in America, in millions of homes around the world, there are vacant chairs. It would be a shameful confession of our unworthiness if it should develop that we have abandoned the hope for which all these men died. Surely civilization is old enough, surely mankind is mature enough so that we ought in our own lifetime to find a way to permanent peace. Abroad, to west and east, are nations whose sons mingled their blood with the blood of our sons on the battlefields. Most of these nations have contributed to our race, to our culture, our knowledge, and our progress. From one of them we derive our very language and from many of them much of the genius of our institutions. Their desire for peace is as deep and sincere as our own.

好的热情款待的礼遇。我们和他们是由同情和共同利益的特殊纽带联结起来的。他们各自都建立了自己的民族性格和文化,这对人类进步是一种令人难忘的贡献。我们只希望他们维护自己的独立,增加安定和繁荣。尽管我们在西半球有过战事,但从整体上说,同世界上其他地方相比,这里的情况还是令人鼓舞的。新世界幸而已经在很大程度上摆脱了那些折磨着旧世界的恐惧和猜疑。我们应该保持这种局面。

同胞们,谈到和平就不能不使人寄以深情,在美国成千上万个家庭里,在世界上几百万个家庭里,都有闲置的椅子。如果我们放弃了所有这些人为之而献出生命的希望,那么当我们提到这个卑鄙行为时,就会感到羞耻而忏悔。当然,文明已经够古老的了,人类已经够成熟的了,因而我们应该在我们这一生找到通向持久和平的道路。在国外,无论向西还是向东,那些国家的儿子和我们国家的儿子的血在战场上流在一起。这些国家对我们的民族、我们的文化、我们的知识和我们的进步都做出过贡献。从其中的一个国家,我们得到了我们的语言,从其中的许多国家,我们得到了我们各种制度的精神实质。他们对和平的要求与我们对和平的要求一样深刻而真挚。

Peace can be contributed to by respect for our ability in defense. Peace can be promoted by the limitation of arms and by the creation of the instrumentalities for peaceful settlement of controversies. But it will become a reality only through self-restraint and active effort in friendliness and helpfulness. I covet for this administration a record of having further contributed to advance the cause of peace.

Party Responsibilities   In our form of democracy the expression of the popular will can be effected only through the instrumentality of political parties. We maintain party government not to promote intolerant partisanship but because opportunity must be given for expression of the popular will, and organization provided for the execution of its mandates and for accountability of government to the people. It follows that the government both in the executive and the legislative branches must carry out in good faith the platforms upon which the party was entrusted with power. But the government is that of the whole people; the party is the instrument through which policies are determined and men chosen to bring them into being. The animosities of elections should have no place in our Government, for government must concern itself alone with the common weal.

Special Session of the Congress   Action upon some of the proposals upon which the Republican Party was returned to power, particularly further agricultural relief and limited changes in the tariff, cannot in justice to our farmers, our labor, and our manufacturers be postponed. I shall therefore request a special session of Congress for the consideration of these two questions. I shall deal with each of them upon the assembly of the Congress.

重视我们的防卫能力,就能对和平作出贡献。限制军备和提出和平解决争端的方法,就能推进和平。但是,唯有自我约束地、积极努力地促进友谊与互助,才能使和平成为现实。我渴望本届政府创造一个能进一步推动和平事业的纪录。

政党的职责   在我们的民主形式下,公众的意愿只有通过政党的工具才能表达。我们维护政党政府,不是为了发展褊狭的党派行为,而是由于必须为公众能表达其意愿而提供机会,为执行公众的委托和为政府向人民进行解释提供机构。由此可见,政府的行政部门和立法部门都必须真诚地实现政党所提出并经人民赋予权力的政纲。但是,政府是全体人民的政府;政党是用来决定政策、挑选执行政策的人员的工具。由于选举而引起的怨恨绝不能在我国政府中占有地位,因为政府所关心的必须是人民大众的福利。

召开国会特别会议   对于共和党重新执政时所提的一些建议,特别是进一步支援农业和有限制地变动关税这两项建议,应该迅速采取行动,不能再有拖延,这样才能公正地对待农民、劳工和制造商。我将提请国会召开特别会议,讨论这两个问题。我将在国会开会时就这些问题发表意见。

Herbert Hoover
赫伯特·胡佛(1874-1964)
31st President of the United States (1929-1933)

Other Mandates from the Election It appears to me that the more important further mandates from the recent election were the maintenance of the integrity of the Constitution; the vigorous enforcement of the laws; the continuance of economy in public expenditure; the continued regulation of business to prevent domination in the community; the denial of ownership or operation of business by the Government in competition with its citizens; the avoidance of policies which would involve us in the controversies of foreign nations; the more effective reorganization of the departments of the Federal Government; the expansion of public works; and the promotion of welfare activities affecting education and the home.

These were the more tangible determinations of the election, but beyond them was the confidence and belief of the people that we would not neglect the support of the embedded ideals and aspirations of America. These ideals and aspirations are the touchstones upon which the day-to-day administration and legislative acts of government must be tested. More than this, the Government must, so far as lies within its proper powers, give leadership to the realization of these ideals and to the fruition of these aspirations. No one can adequately reduce these things of the spirit to phrases or to a catalogue of definitions. We do know what the attainments of these ideals should be: the preservation of self-government and its full foundations in local government; the perfection of justice whether in economic or in social fields; the maintenance of ordered liberty; the denial of domination by any group or class; the building up and preservation of equality of opportunity; the stimulation of initiative and individuality; absolute integrity in public affairs; the choice of officials for fitness to office; the direction of economic progress toward prosperity for the further lessening of poverty; the freedom of public opinion; the sustaining of education and of the advancement of

选举中提出的其他委托事项 在我看来,最近这次选举所进一步显示的更重要的委托事项是:维护宪法的完整性;有力地执行法律;继续节约公共开支;继续管理企业防止它对社会的控制;禁止政府拥有或经营的企业同公民进行竞争;避免可能使我们卷入他国争端的政策;整顿联邦政府各部门,使其成为更有效率的机构;扩大公众就业;促进能影响教育与家庭的福利活动。

这些都是选举中人民较明显表明的决心,但更重要的是人民的信心和信念,他们相信我们不会忽视美国人民心坎中的理想和抱负所给予我们的支持。这些理想和抱负都是试金石,政府日常的行政工作和立法工作都得经受它们的考验。而且,政府必须在适当的权力范围内,领导人民实现这些理想,使这些抱负获得结果。任何人都无法用几句话或一套定义来充分地归纳这些事物的精神实质。但我们确实知道,这些理想应该获得的成就是:维护自治政府及其在地方政府的全部基础;在经济和社会范围内完善公正的原则;维护有秩序的自由;制止任何群体或阶层对社会的控制;建立并维护机会均等;鼓励首创精神和个性;提倡公共事务中的绝对正直;选拔称职的官员;指导经济发展,使其走向繁荣,以求进一

knowledge; the growth of religious spirit and the tolerance of all faiths; the strengthening of the home; the advancement of peace.

There is no short road to the realization of these aspirations. Ours is a progressive people, but with a determination that progress must be based upon the foundation of experience. Ill-considered remedies for our faults bring only penalties after them. But if we hold the faith of the men in our mighty past who created these ideals, we shall leave them heightened and strengthened for our children.

Conclusion This is not the time and place for extended discussion. The questions before our country are problems of progress to higher standards; they are not the problems of degeneration. They demand thought and they serve to quicken the conscience and enlist our sense of responsibility for their settlement. And that responsibility rests upon you, my countrymen, as much as upon those of us who have been selected for office.

Ours is a land rich in resources; stimulating in its glorious beauty; filled with millions of happy homes; blessed with comfort and opportunity. In no nation are the institutions of progress more advanced. In no nation are the fruits of accomplishment more secure. In no nation is the government more worthy of respect. No country is more loved by its people. I have an abiding faith in their capacity, integrity and high purpose. I have no fears for the future of our country. It is bright with hope.

步缩小贫困；保护舆论自由；支持教育和科学进展；发展宗教精神，容许各种不同信仰的存在；重视家庭问题；促进和平。

实现这些抱负是没有捷径的。我们的人民是进步的人民，但他们决心要把进步建立在经验的基础之上。用考虑不周的方法来纠正我们的缺点，实行以后只能导致惩罚。然而如果我们继续保持前人在过去辉煌的岁月里提出这些理想时的信念，我们就应该使这些理想发扬光大，然后传给我们的子孙。

结论 此时此地不宜发表长篇大论。我国面临的问题是向更高的标准前进而不是走向衰败。这些问题要求我们深思，唤起我们的良心，激起我们的责任感。同胞们，这个责任同样地落在你们和我们这些被挑选出来任职的人身上。

我们的国土资源丰富；它的壮丽景色令人激赏；全国遍布着几百万个幸福家庭；人民享有安逸的生活和各种机会。任何国家都没有比我们更先进的进步制度。任何国家都不能像我们这样保障各种成就。任何国家都没有像我们这样是一个值得尊重的政府。任何国家都没有像我国这样受到人民的爱戴。我永远相信人民的能力、正直和崇高目标。我毫不担心我国的未来。这充满希望，前途光明。

Herbert Hoover
赫伯特·胡佛(1874-1964)
31st President of the United States (1929-1933)

In the presence of my countrymen, mindful of the solemnity of this occasion, knowing what the task means and the responsibility which it involves, I beg your tolerance, your aid, and your cooperation. I ask the help of Almighty God in this service to my country to which you have called me.

在同胞们面前,我牢记这个庄严的场合,我知道这个任务的意义和它所具有的责任,我恳求能得到你们的宽容、你们的帮助和你们的合作。在你们召唤我来担任的这项为祖国效力的工作中,我祈求全能的上帝赐予帮助。

富兰克林·罗斯福：美国第32任总统(1933—1945)，唯一一位任期超过2届并连任4届的总统。任期内力挽经济危机狂澜，推行著名的"新政"。太平洋战争爆发后，领导美国加入反法西斯战争。本篇是他的第一次就职演说，发表于经济危机肆虐之时，有极强的鼓动性，是就职演说中的名篇。

Franklin D. Roosevelt
富兰克林·罗斯福(1882-1945)
32nd President of the United States(1933-1945)
Political Party: Democratic

The Establishment of a Sound National Economy
建立健全国家经济

I am certain that my fellow Americans expect that on my induction into the Presidency I will address them with a candor and a decision which the present situation of our Nation impels. This is preeminently the time to speak the truth, the whole truth, frankly and boldly. Nor need we shrink from honestly facing conditions in our country today. This great Nation will endure as it has endured, will revive and will prosper. So, first of all, let me assert my firm

我肯定，同胞们都期待我在就任总统时，会像我国目前形势所要求的那样，坦率而果断地向他们讲话。现在正是坦白、勇敢地说出实话，说出全部实话的最好时刻。我们不必畏首畏尾，不敢坦然面对我国今天的情况。这个伟大的国家会一如既往地坚持下

Franklin D. Roosevelt

富兰克林·罗斯福(1882-1945)

32nd President of the United States (1933-1945)

belief that the only thing we have to fear is fear itself—nameless, unreasoning, unjustified terror which paralyzes needed efforts to convert retreat into advance. In every dark hour of our national life a leadership of frankness and vigor has met with that understanding and support of the people themselves which is essential to victory. I am convinced that you will again give that support to leadership in these critical days.

In such a spirit on my part and on yours we face our common difficulties. They concern, thank God, only material things. Values have shrunken to fantastic levels; taxes have risen; our ability to pay has fallen; government of all kinds is faced by serious curtailment of income; the means of exchange are frozen in the currents of trade; the withered leaves of industrial enterprise lie on every side; farmers find no markets for their produce; the savings of many years in thousands of families are gone.

More important, a host of unemployed citizens face the grim problem of existence, and an equally great number toil with little return. Only a foolish optimist can deny the dark realities of the moment.

Yet our distress comes from no failure of substance. We are stricken by no plague of locusts. Compared with the perils which our forefathers conquered because they believed and were not afraid, we have still much to be thankful for. Nature still offers her bounty and human efforts have multiplied it. Plenty is at our doorstep, but a generous use of it languishes in the very sight of the supply.

去,它会复兴和繁荣。因此,让我首先表明我的坚定信念:我们唯一不得不害怕的就是害怕本身——一种莫名其妙的、丧失理智的、毫无根据的恐惧,它会把转退为进所需的种种努力化为泡影。凡在我国生活阴云密布的时刻,坦率而有活力的领导都得到过人民的理解和支持,从而为胜利准备了必不可少的条件。我相信,在这危急时刻,大家会再次给予我们同样的支持。

我和你们都要以这种精神来面对我们共同的困难。感谢上帝,这些困难只是物质方面的。购买力缩水到难以想象的地步;税金增加了,我们的支付能力下降了;各级政府面临着严重的收入短缺;交易方式在贸易过程中遭到了冻结;工业企业枯萎的落叶到处可见;农场主的产品找不到销路;千家万户多年的积蓄付之东流。

更为重要的是,大批失业公民正面临严峻的生存问题,还有大批公民正以艰辛的劳动换取微薄的报酬。只有愚蠢的乐天派会否认当前这些黑暗的现实。

但是,我们的苦恼绝不是因为缺乏物资。我们没有遭到什么蝗虫灾害。我们的先辈曾以信念和无畏一次次转危为安,比起他们经历过的险阻,我们仍大可感到欣慰。大自然仍在给予我们恩惠,人类的努力已使之倍增。富足的

Primarily this is because the rulers of the exchange of mankind's goods have failed, through their own stubbornness and their own incompetence, have admitted their failure, and abdicated. Practices of the unscrupulous money changers stand indicted in the court of public opinion, rejected by the hearts and minds of men.

True they have tried, but their efforts have been cast in the pattern of an outworn tradition. Faced by failure of credit they have proposed only the lending of more money. Stripped of the lure of profit by which to induce our people to follow their false leadership, they have resorted to exhortations, pleading tearfully for restored confidence. They know only the rules of a generation of self-seekers. They have no vision, and when there is no vision the people perish.

The money changers have fled from their high seats in the temple of our civilization. We may now restore that temple to the ancient truths. The measure of the restoration lies in the extent to which we apply social values more noble than mere monetary profit.

Happiness lies not in the mere possession of money; it lies in the joy of achievement, in the thrill of creative effort. The joy and moral stimulation of work no longer must be forgotten in the mad chase of evanescent profits. These dark days will be worth all they cost us if they teach us that our true destiny is not to be ministered unto but to minister to ourselves and to our fellow men.

生活近在咫尺,但就在我们见到这种情景的时候,宽裕的生活却悄然离去。这主要是因为主宰人类物资交换的统治者们失败了,他们固执己见而又无能为力,因而已经承认失败,并撒手不管了,贪得无厌的货币兑换商的种种行径,将受到舆论法庭的起诉,将受到人类心灵和理智的唾弃。

不错,他们做出过努力,但他们的努力一直囿于陈旧的传统方式。面对信用的失败,他们提议的只有更多的贷款。当利润失去了吸引力,不能再用来诱使人们服从他们的错误领导时,他们就转而依靠规劝,眼泪汪汪地请求人们重建信心。他们只知道追求私利的那一代人的原则。他们缺乏远见,而没有远见,人民就要遭殃。

货币兑换商已从我们文明庙堂的高位上溜之大吉了。我们现在可以按古老的真理来恢复庙堂了。至于能恢复到什么程度,这要看我们如何运用社会价值,使它比纯粹的金钱利润更可贵。

幸福并不在于单纯地占有金钱;幸福还在于取得成就后的喜悦,在于创造性努力时的激情。务必不能再忘记劳动带来的喜悦和激励,而去疯狂地追逐那转瞬即逝的利润。如果这些暗淡的时日能使我们认识到,我们真正的天命不是被别人侍奉,而是为自己和同胞们服务,那么,我们付出的所有代价就是值得的。

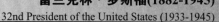

Franklin D. Roosevelt
富兰克林·罗斯福(1882-1945)
32nd President of the United States (1933-1945)

Recognition of the falsity of material wealth as the standard of success goes hand in hand with the abandonment of the false belief that public office and high political position are to be valued only by the standards of pride of place and personal profit; and there must be an end to a conduct in banking and in business which too often has given to a sacred trust the likeness of callous and selfish wrongdoing. Small wonder that confidence languishes, for it thrives only on honesty, on honor, on the sacredness of obligations, on faithful protection, on unselfish performance; without them it cannot live.

Restoration calls, however, not for changes in ethics alone. This Nation asks for action, and action now.

Our greatest primary task is to put people to work. This is no unsolvable problem if we face it wisely and courageously. It can be accomplished in part by direct recruiting by the Government itself, treating the task as we would treat the emergency of a war, but at the same time, through this employment, accomplishing greatly needed projects to stimulate and reorganize the use of our natural resources.

Hand in hand with this we must frankly recognize the overbalance of population in our industrial centers and, by engaging on a national scale in a redistribution, endeavor to provide a better use of the land for those best fitted for the land. The task can be helped by definite efforts to raise the values of agricultural products and with this the power to purchase the output of our cities. It can be helped by preventing realistically the tragedy of the growing loss through foreclosure of our small homes and our farms. It can be helped by insistence that the Federal, State, and

认识到把物质财富当作成功的标准是错误的,我们就会抛弃以地位尊严和个人收益为唯一标准来衡量公职和高级政治地位的错误信念;我们必须制止银行界和企业界的一种行为,它常常使神圣的信任混同于无情和自私的不正当行为。信心的减弱并不足为奇。因为增强信心只有靠诚实、荣誉感、神圣的责任感,忠实地加以维护和无私地履行职责;而没有这些,就不可能有信心。

但是,复兴不仅仅要求改变伦理观念。这个国家要求行动起来,现在就行动起来。

我们压倒一切的首要任务是安排人们工作。如果明智地、勇敢地面对这个问题,这就不是什么解决不了的问题。我们可以像处理战时紧急情况那样,通过政府本身的直接招雇来解决部分问题,并通过这种招雇,同时完成迫切需要的工程,促进和调整自然资源的使用。

与此同时,我们要坦白地承认,我们的工业中心已人口过剩。因此要通过全国性的重新分配,努力为最善于使用土地的人提供更好的使用条件。为了促进这项工作,可以通过具体的努力来提高农产品的价值,并以此提高对城市产品的购买力;可以通过从实际出发,防止出现小房产主和农场主因丧失赎回权而不断

local governments act forthwith on the demand that their cost be drastically reduced. It can be helped by the unifying of relief activities which today are often scattered, uneconomical, and unequal. It can be helped by national planning for and supervision of all forms of transportation and of communications and other utilities which have a definitely public character. There are many ways in which it can be helped, but it can never be helped merely by talking about it. We must act and act quickly.

Finally, in our progress toward a resumption of work we require two safeguards against a return of the evils of the old order; there must be a strict supervision of all banking and credits and investments; there must be an end to speculation with other people's money, and there must be provision for an adequate but sound currency.

There are the lines of attack. I shall presently urge upon a new Congress in special session detailed measures for their fulfillment, and I shall seek the immediate assistance of the several States.

Through this program of action we address ourselves to putting our own national house in order and making income balance outgo. Our international trade relations, though vastly important, are in point of time and necessity secondary to the establishment of a sound national economy. I favor as a practical policy the putting of first things first. I shall spare no effort to restore world trade by international economic readjustment, but the emergency at home cannot wait on that accomplishment.

The basic thought that guides these specific means of

蒙受损失的悲剧；可以通过坚持联邦政府、州政府和地方政府立即按要求大幅度削减经费；可以通过统筹安排救济工作，改变目前那种常常是分散的、浪费的和不公平的局面；可以通过由国家统一规划和监督各种形式的运输、交通以及明确具有公共性质的其他设施。总之，可以通过许多方法来促进这项工作，但光说不做永远无济于事。我们必须采取行动，迅速地采取行动。

最后，在继续工作的进程中，我们需要两项保护措施防止重新出现旧秩序的种种弊端；必须严格监督所有的银行、信贷和投资；必须制止利用他人的钱财进行投机；必须要有充足而健全的货币供应。

我们有几条进攻路线。我会立即敦促新一届国会召开特别会议，对实施这些路线的详细措施进行审议，我还将寻求有关各州立即援助。

通过这个行动纲领，我们要致力于整顿国库和平衡收支。我们的国际贸易关系虽然很重要，但从时间和需要而言，要服从于建立健全的国家经济。我赞成讲究实际，最重要的事情最先做。我将不遗余力地通过国际经济调整来恢复世界贸易，但是，不能等到这项工作完成后再来处理国内的紧急情况。

国家复兴的这些具体方

Franklin D. Roosevelt
富兰克林·罗斯福(1882-1945)
32nd President of the United States (1933-1945)

national recovery is not narrowly nationalistic. It is the insistence, as a first consideration, upon the interdependence of the various elements in all parts of the United States—a recognition of the old and permanently important manifestation of the American spirit of the pioneer. It is the way to recovery. It is the immediate way. It is the strongest assurance that the recovery will endure.

In the field of world policy I would dedicate this Nation to the policy of the good neighbor—the neighbor who resolutely respects himself and, because he does so, respects the rights of others—the neighbor who respects his obligations and respects the sanctity of his agreements in and with a world of neighbors.

If I read the temper of our people correctly, we now realize as we have never realized before our interdependence on each other; that we cannot merely take but we must give as well; that if we are to go forward, we must move as a trained and loyal army willing to sacrifice for the good of a common discipline, because without such discipline no progress is made, no leadership becomes effective. We are, I know, ready and willing to submit our lives and property to such discipline, because it makes possible a leadership which aims at a larger good. This I propose to offer, pledging that the larger purposes will bind upon us all as a sacred obligation with a unity of duty hitherto evoked only in time of armed strife.

With this pledge taken, I assume unhesitatingly the leadership of this great army of our people dedicated to a disciplined attack upon our common problems.

法，其基本指导思想不是狭隘的民族主义。它首先考虑的是坚持合众国各个部分、各种因素的相互依靠——即认识到这是美国拓荒精神的传统和永远重要的体现。这是通向复兴的道路。这是直接的道路。这是持久复兴最坚强的保证。

在外交政策方面，我认为美国应当献身于睦邻政策——做一个决心尊重自己，因而也尊重其他国家的权利的邻国——做一个遵守自己的义务，遵守与世界各国的神圣协议的邻国。

如果我对我国人民的情绪理解得正确，那就是：我们现在比以往任何时候更加认识到我们必须相互依靠；我们不能只求有所得，还要有所给；我们要前进就必须像一支受过训练的忠诚的军队那样行动，并甘愿为共同的纪律有所牺牲，因为没有这种纪律，我们就不可能前进，就不可能形成有效的领导。我知道，我们准备并且愿意为这种纪律献出生命和财产，因为它使一个以更远大的利益为目标的领导成为可能。这就是我想要提供的领导。我保证，这些远大目标将如同一种神圣的义务对我们大家都产生约束，产生只有在战争时期才有过的共同责任感。

作了这项保证，我毫不犹豫地开始领导这支由我国人民组成的大军，纪律严明地向我们共同的问题发起进攻。

Action in this image and to this end is feasible under the form of government which we have inherited from our ancestors. Our Constitution is so simple and practical that it is possible always to meet extraordinary needs by changes in emphasis and arrangement without loss of essential form. That is why our constitutional system has proved itself the most superbly enduring political mechanism the modern world has produced. It has met every stress of vast expansion of territory, of foreign wars, of bitter internal strife, of world relations.

It is to be hoped that the normal balance of executive and legislative authority may be wholly adequate to meet the unprecedented task before us. But it may be that an unprecedented demand and need for undelayed action may call for temporary departure from that normal balance of public procedure.

I am prepared under my constitutional duty to recommend the measures that a stricken nation in the midst of a stricken world may require. These measures, or such other measures as the Congress may build out of its experience and wisdom, I shall seek, within my constitutional authority, to bring to speedy adoption.

But in the event that the Congress shall fail to take one of these two courses, and in the event that the national emergency is still critical, I shall not evade the clear course of duty that will then confront me. I shall ask the Congress for the one remaining instrument to meet the crisis—broad Executive power to wage a war against the emergency, as great as the power that would be given to me if we were in fact invaded by a foreign foe.

我们继承了先辈创立的政体，因此，用这样的行动并达到这样的目的是可行的。我们的宪法简明而实用，总是可以在不失去基本形式的情况下，通过着重点和排列的变化来迎合特殊的需要。正因为如此，我们的宪制才不愧为现代世界所产生的最经得起考验的政治机制。它经受住了大规模的领土扩张、对外战争、痛苦的内战和国际关系等种种压力。

我希望，行政权和立法权之间的正常平衡完全能应付我们面临的空前任务。但是，史无前例的要求和迅速行动的需要，也可能使我们暂时背离公共程序上的这种正常平衡。

根据宪法赋予我的职责，我准备建议一些措施，而一个受灾世界中的受灾国家也许需要这些措施。对于这些措施，以及国会根据本身的经验和智慧可能制订的其他类似措施，我将在宪法赋予我的权限内，设法迅速地予以通过。

但是，如果国会拒不采纳这两条路线中的一条，如果国家紧急情况依然如故，我将不回避我所面临的明确的尽责方向。我将要求国会准许我使用唯一剩下的手段来应付危机——向非常情况开战的广泛的行政权，就像我们真的遭到外敌入侵时赋予我那样的广泛权力。

Franklin D. Roosevelt
富兰克林·罗斯福(1882-1945)
32nd President of the United States (1933-1945)

For the trust reposed in me I will return the courage and the devotion that befit the time. I can do no less.

We face the arduous days that lie before us in the warm courage of the national unity; with the clear consciousness of seeking old and precious moral values; with the clean satisfaction that comes from the stern performance of duty by old and young alike. We aim at the assurance of a rounded and permanent national life.

We do not distrust the future of essential democracy. The people of the United States have not failed. In their need they have registered a mandate that they want direct, vigorous action. They have asked for discipline and direction under leadership. They have made me the present instrument of their wishes. In the spirit of the gift I take it.

In this dedication of a Nation we humbly ask the blessing of God. May He protect each and every one of us. May He guide me in the days to come.

对大家给予我的信任,我一定报以时代所要求的勇气和献身精神,我会竭尽全力。

让我们正视面前的严峻岁月,怀着举国一致给我们带来的热情和勇气,怀着寻求传统的、珍贵的道德观念的明确意识,怀着老老少少都能通过恪尽职守而得到的问心无愧的满足。我们的目标是要保证国民生活的圆满和长治久安。

我们并不怀疑基本民主制度的未来。合众国人民并没有失败。他们在困难中表达了自己的委托,即要求采取直接而有力的行动。他们要求有领导的纪律和方向。他们现在选择了我作为实现他们愿望的工具。我接受这份厚赠。

在此举国奉献之际,我们谦卑地请求上帝赐福。愿上帝保佑我们大家和每一个人,愿上帝在未来的日子里指引我。

第二次就职演讲：1936 年罗斯福在竞选中以压倒性优势战胜堪萨斯州州长阿尔弗雷德·兰顿（共和党改良主义者）。在 1937 年 1 月 20 日的第二次就职演说中，罗斯福弹奏出自信和实用主义的调子，描绘了一个正在忙于探寻解决办法并正在积极解决问题的政府形象；但是他承认，大萧条继续造成惨重的损失。当罗斯福政府努力使议会同意设立新的行政机构为老人提供社会保险，为失业者提供工作，维持农产品价格时，大萧条仍在摧残人们的生命。

Franklin D. Roosevelt
富兰克林·罗斯福(1882-1945)
32nd President of the United States(1933-1945)
Political Party: Democratic

We Will Carry on
持久进步之路

When four years ago we met to inaugurate a President, the Republic, single-minded in anxiety, stood in spirit here. We dedicated ourselves to the fulfillment of a vision—to speed the time when there would be for all the people that security and peace essential to the pursuit of happiness. We of the Republic pledged ourselves to drive from the temple of our ancient faith those who had profaned it; to end by action, tireless and unafraid, the stagnation and despair of that day. We did those first things first.

4 年前，当我们聚在一起举行总统就职典礼，合众国忧心如焚，群情激奋。我们致力于实现一个理想——让全体人民追求幸福所必不可少的安全与和平环境早日到来。我们合众国人民立下誓言：要把玷污我们传统信仰的人赶出庙堂；要坚韧不拔地、无所畏惧地用行动来结束当时的萧条和失望。我们首先解决了这些当务之急。

● 108

Franklin D. Roosevelt

富兰克林·罗斯福(1882-1945)
32nd President of the United States (1933-1945)

Our covenant with ourselves did not stop there. Instinctively we recognized a deeper need—the need to find through government the instrument of our united purpose to solve for the individual the ever-rising problems of a complex civilization. Repeated attempts at their solution without the aid of government had left us baffled and bewildered. For, without that aid, we had been unable to create those moral controls over the services of science which are necessary to make science a useful servant instead of a ruthless master of mankind. To do this we knew that we must find practical controls over blind economic forces and blindly selfish men.

We of the Republic sensed the truth that democratic government has innate capacity to protect its people against disasters once considered inevitable, to solve problems once considered unsolvable. We would not admit that we could not find a way to master economic epidemics just as, after centuries of fatalistic suffering, we had found a way to master epidemics of disease. We refused to leave the problems of our common welfare to be solved by the winds of chance and the hurricanes of disaster.

In this we Americans were discovering no wholly new truth; we were writing a new chapter in our book of self-government.

This year marks the one hundred and fiftieth anniversary of the Constitutional Convention which made us a nation. At that Convention our forefathers found the way out of the chaos which followed the Revolutionary War; they created a strong government with powers of united

我们的誓约没有就此止步。我们本能地认识到更深一层的需要——需要通过政府找到实现共同目标的手段，为每个人去解决复杂文明社会所日益产生的问题。试图不要政府的帮助来解决这些问题，已使我们屡屡碰壁和一筹莫展。因为，没有这种帮助，我们就无法从道德上来控制科学的使用；有了这种必要的控制，才能把科学变成人类的有用的仆人，而不是无情的主人。为了做到这一点，我们知道必须找到切实可行的办法，控制那些盲目的经济力量和利令智昏的人。

我们合众国人民认识到一条真理：民主政府生来就有能力保护人民，使他们免遭一度认为是不可避免的灾难，解决一度认为是不可解决的问题。我们听天由命地忍受了几个世纪之后，找到了控制瘟疫的办法，所以，我们不承认找不到控制经济瘟疫的办法。我们拒绝把我们的共同福利问题交给机会的阵风和灾难的飓风去摆布。

在这方面，我们美国人不是在发明全新的真理。而是在为我们的自治史册写下新的篇章。

今年是制宪会议召开150周年，那次会议使我们成为一个国家。在那次会议上，我们的前辈为摆脱革命战争后的混乱局面找到了出路；他

action sufficient then and now to solve problems utterly beyond individual or local solution. A century and a half ago they established the Federal Government in order to promote the general welfare and secure the blessings of liberty to the American people.

Today we invoke those same powers of government to achieve the same objectives.

Four years of new experience have not belied our historic instinct. They hold out the clear hope that government within communities, government within the separate States, and government of the United States can do the things the times require, without yielding its democracy. Our tasks in the last four years did not force democracy to take a holiday.

Nearly all of us recognize that as intricacies of human relationships increase, so power to govern them also must increase—power to stop evil; power to do good. The essential democracy of our Nation and the safety of our people depend not upon the absence of power, but upon lodging it with those whom the people can change or continue at stated intervals through an honest and free system of elections. The Constitution of 1787 did not make our democracy impotent.

In fact, in these last four years, we have made the exercise of all power more democratic; for we have begun to bring private autocratic powers into their proper subordination to the public's government. The legend that they were invincible—above and beyond the processes of a democracy—has been shattered. They have been challenged and beaten.

们创立了步调一致、坚强有力的政府，使我们足以在当时和现在都能解决个人或地方根本无法解决的问题，他们在一个半世纪以前建立起联邦政府，目的就是要增进美国人民的普遍福利，确保美国人民的自由幸福。

今天，我们要同样运用政府的力量来达到同样的目标。

4年来的新经验并没有使我们的历史直觉落空。这4年清楚地展现了一条希望之路，即地方政府、州政府和合众国政府都能按时代的要求行事而无需放弃民主。我们过去4年的任务并没有迫使民主去休假。

我们几乎所有的人都认识到，由于人类关系日趋复杂，支配这种关系的权力也必须加强——包括抑恶的权力和扬善的权力，我国的基本民主和人民安全的依据不是不要权力，而是通过诚实和自由的选举制度，把权力交给可以由人民定期更换或连任的人。1787年的宪法并没有使我们的民主软弱无力。

事实上，在过去4年中，我们使一切权力的行使都变得更加民主；因为我们已经开始使私人专断的种种权力恰当地服从于大众的政府。所谓它们不可战胜——凌驾于民主程序之上又超脱于民主程序之外——这个神话已经被粉碎，它们遭到了挑战，并且已经被击败。

Franklin D. Roosevelt

富兰克林·罗斯福(1882-1945)

32nd President of the United States (1933-1945)

Our progress out of the depression is obvious. But that is not all that you and I mean by the new order of things. Our pledge was not merely to do a patchwork job with secondhand materials. By using the new materials of social justice we have undertaken to erect on the old foundations a more enduring structure for the better use of future generations.

In that purpose we have been helped by achievements of mind and spirit. Old truths have been relearned; untruths have been unlearned. We have always known that heedless self-interest was bad morals; we know now that it is bad economics. Out of the collapse of a prosperity whose builders boasted their practicality has come the conviction that in the long run economic morality pays. We are beginning to wipe out the line that divides the practical from the ideal; and in so doing we are fashioning an instrument of unimagined power for the establishment of a morally better world.

This new understanding undermines the old admiration of worldly success as such. We are beginning to abandon our tolerance of the abuse of power by those who betray for profit the elementary decencies of life.

In this process evil things formerly accepted will not be so easily condoned. Hard-headedness will not so easily excuse hardheartedness. We are moving toward an era of good feeling. But we realize that there can be no era of good feeling save among men of good will.

我们摆脱萧条所取得的进步是显而易见的。但是,那还不是你们和我所说的事物新秩序的全部,我们的誓言并非仅仅用旧材料做些修补工作。我们已经在用社会公正这种新材料,开始从原有基础上建立更持久的结构,以便未来几代人更好地利用。

在这方面,我们已经得益于思想和精神上所取得的成就。古老的真理得到了重温;假话虚话遭到了抛弃。我们一直知道,无动于衷的自私自利是不道德的,我们现在还知道,它是不利于经济的。经济繁荣的建筑师们曾自诩符合实际,但随着繁荣的破灭,人们都已经深信,从长远来看经济道德会带来效益。我们正在开始消除实际与理想之间的界线;通过这种做法,我们正在为建立道德更高尚的世界,制作一件力大无比的工具。

这种新的认识,打破了以追名逐利为荣的传统观念。我们开始不再容忍某些人滥用权力,这些人为了利润而背弃了起码的生活准则。

在这个过程中,以前得到认可的歪风邪气不会那么轻易地得到宽恕,冷静的头脑不会那么轻易地原谅冷酷的心肠。我们正在走向一个好心肠时代,但是,我们认识到,除非在有善良愿望的人之间外,是不可能存在好心肠时代的。

For these reasons I am justified in believing that the greatest change we have witnessed has been the change in the moral climate of America.

Among men of good will, science and democracy together offer an ever-richer life and ever-larger satisfaction to the individual. With this change in our moral climate and our rediscovered ability to improve our economic order, we have set our feet upon the road of enduring progress.

Shall we pause now and turn our back upon the road that lies ahead? Shall we call this the promised land? Or, shall we continue on our way? For "Each age is a dream that is dying, or one that is coming to birth."

Many voices are heard as we face a great decision. Comfort says, "Tarry a while." Opportunism says, "This is a good spot." Timidity asks, "How difficult is the road ahead?"

True, we have come far from the days of stagnation and despair. Vitality has been preserved. Courage and confidence have been restored. Mental and moral horizons have been extended.

But our present gains were won under the pressure of more than ordinary circumstances. Advance became imperative under the goad of fear and suffering. The times were on the side of progress.

To hold to progress today, however, is more difficult. Dulled conscience, irresponsibility, and ruthless self-interest already reappear. Such symptoms of prosperity may become portents of disaster! Prosperity already tests the

出于这些原因,我理所当然地认为,我们所目睹的最重大变化就是美国道德风尚的变化。

在有善良愿望的人之间,科学与民主一道为个人提供了日益富足的生活和日益增大的满足感。随着道德风尚的这种变化和我们重新发现了改进经济秩序的能力,我们已经踏上了持久进步之路。

我们现在就停下来,从前进的道路上向后转吗?我们要把现在的美国称为希望之乡吗?或者,我们要继续走自己的路吗?因为谚语云:"每一个时代都是一场梦,不是在消逝,就是在诞生。"

我们在面临重大抉择时听到了许多声音。贪图安逸者说:"歇一会吧。"机会主义者说:"这是个好地方。"胆小怕事者问:"前面的路有多难走啊?"

不错,我们已经把萧条和沮丧的日子远远甩到了后面。我们维持了活力。我们恢复了勇气和信心。我们扩大了思想和道德领域的疆界。

但是,我们目前的成绩是在超常形势的压力下取得的。在恐惧和痛苦的刺激下,前进是迫不得已的。当时的形势是有利于进步的。

然而,今天要坚持进步就比较困难了。麻木不仁、不负责任、冷酷无情的自私自利已经重新抬头。这类繁荣的症

Franklin D. Roosevelt
富兰克林·罗斯福(1882-1945)
32nd President of the United States (1933-1945)

persistence of our progressive purpose.

Let us ask again: Have we reached the goal of our vision of that fourth day of March 1933? Have we found our happy valley?

I see a great nation, upon a great continent, blessed with a great wealth of natural resources. Its hundred and thirty million people are at peace among themselves; they are making their country a good neighbor among the nations. I see a United States which can demonstrate that, under democratic methods of government, national wealth can be translated into a spreading volume of human comforts hitherto unknown, and the lowest standard of living can be raised far above the level of mere subsistence.

But here is the challenge to our democracy: In this nation I see tens of millions of its citizens—a substantial part of its whole population—who at this very moment are denied the greater part of what the very lowest standards of today call the necessities of life.

I see millions of families trying to live on incomes so meager that the pall of family disaster hangs over them day by day.

I see millions whose daily lives in city and on farm continue under conditions labeled indecent by a so-called polite society half a century ago.

I see millions denied education, recreation, and the opportunity to better their lot and the lot of their children.

I see millions lacking the means to buy the products of farm and factory and by their poverty denying work and productiveness to many other millions.

状可能成为灾难的征兆！繁荣已经在考验我们进步的决心能否持久。

让我们再问一问：我们已经达到1933年3月4日那天憧憬的目标了吗？我们已经找到快乐之谷了吗？

我看到一个伟大的国家，地处辽阔的大陆，天赐富饶的自然资源。它的一亿三千万人民和睦相处；他们正在使自己的国家成为各国的好邻居，我看到一个合众国，它能够作出示范，即采用民主管理的方法，可以把国家财富转变成日益广泛的、闻所未闻的人类生活情趣，可以把最低生活标准提高到远远超过仅仅糊口的水平。

但是，我们的民主正面临种种挑战：在这个国家，我看到几千万公民——占人口总数相当大一部分——此时此刻得不到按目前最低标准所规定的大部分生活必需品。

我看到几百万个家庭以微薄收入勉强度日，日复一日处于家庭灾难的威胁之下。

我看到几百万城乡居民，他们的日常生活仍处于半个世纪以前被所谓上流社会称作的不体面状况。

我看到几百万人得不到教育和娱乐，得不到改善自己及其子女命运的机会。

我看到几百万人无力购买工农业产品，而他们的贫困又使其他数百万人无法投入工作和生产。

I see one-third of a nation ill-housed, ill-clad, ill-nourished.

It is not in despair that I paint you that picture. I paint it for you in hope—because the Nation, seeing and understanding the injustice in it, proposes to paint it out. We are determined to make every American citizen the subject of his country's interest and concern; and we will never regard any faithful law-abiding group within our borders as superfluous. The test of our progress is not whether we add more to the abundance of those who have much; it is whether we provide enough for those who have too little.

If I know aught of the spirit and purpose of our Nation, we will not listen to Comfort, Opportunism, and Timidity. We will carry on.

Overwhelmingly, we of the Republic are men and women of good will; men and women who have more than warm hearts of dedication; men and women who have cool heads and willing hands of practical purpose as well. They will insist that every agency of popular government use effective instruments to carry out their will.

Government is competent when all who compose it work as trustees for the whole people. It can make constant progress when it keeps abreast of all the facts. It can obtain justified support and legitimate criticism when the people receive true information of all that government does.

我看到全国三分之一的人住不好，穿不好，吃不好。

我不是怀着失望向你们描绘这幅图景的。我是怀着希望来描绘的——因为，当全国都看到并认识到这是不公正现象，就会建议把它消除掉。我们决心使每个美国公民都成为国家注意和关心的对象；我们决不会把境内任何忠诚守法的群体看作是多余的。检验我们进步的标准，不是看我们是否为富裕者锦上添花，而是看我们是否使贫困者丰衣足食。

如果我对我国的精神和目标有所了解，那么，我们一定不会去理睬贪图安逸者、机会主义者和胆小怕事者，我们一定会继续前进。

我们合众国绝大多数人都是善良的人，不论男人还是女人；他们不仅都有热诚的奉献之心，而且还有为达到实际目的所需要的冷静的头脑和勤劳的双手。他们会坚持认为，人民政府的各个机构都要运用有效的手段来执行人民的意志。

政府的各个成员都作为全体人民的委托人那样去工作，这个政府就是称职的政府。政府随时了解所有情况，它就能不断前进。人民了解到政府所作所为的真实情况，政府就能得到应有的支持和合理的批评。

Franklin D. Roosevelt
富兰克林·罗斯福(1882-1945)
32nd President of the United States (1933-1945)

If I know aught of the will of our people, they will demand that these conditions of effective government shall be created and maintained. They will demand a nation uncorrupted by cancers of injustice and, therefore, strong among the nations in its example of the will to peace.

Today we reconsecrate our country to long-cherished ideals in a suddenly changed civilization. In every land there are always at work forces that drive men apart and forces that draw men together. In our personal ambitions we are individualists. But in our seeking for economic and political progress as a nation, we all go up, or else we all go down, as one people.

To maintain a democracy of effort requires a vast amount of patience in dealing with differing methods, a vast amount of humility. But out of the confusion of many voices rises an understanding of dominant public need. Then political leadership can voice common ideals, and aid in their realization.

In taking again the oath of office as President of the United States, I assume the solemn obligation of leading the American people forward along the road over which they have chosen to advance.

While this duty rests upon me I shall do my utmost to speak their purpose and to do their will, seeking Divine guidance to help us each and every one to give light to them that sit in darkness and to guide our feet into the way of peace.

如果我对我国人民的意志有所了解,那么,他们会要求务必创造并维持使政府有效的上述条件。他们会要求我国不被不公正的致命弊病所腐蚀,从而在决心实现和平方面为各国树立起坚强的榜样。

今天,我们在突然发生变化的文明世界上、再一次把我们的国家奉献给珍视已久的理想。世界各地历来存在使人们分离或聚合的力量。从个人抱负而言,我们是个人主义者。但是,当我们作为一个国家去谋求经济和政治进步时,我们就是一个整体,要么共同兴旺起来,要么一起衰落下去。

要维持民主的力量,需要以极大的耐心来应付各种不同方法,还要有虚怀若谷的气度,但是,在众说纷纭之中,可以了解到公众需要的主流。于是,政治领导人就能够发表共同的理想并帮助实现这些理想。

值此再度宣誓就任合众国总统之际,我担当起领导美国人民沿着他们选定的前进道路前行的神圣职责。

在担任这个职务期间,我要尽最大努力按照人民的意愿说话,按照人民的意志办事,我要祈求上帝的指引,来帮助我们大家把光亮送给黑暗中的人,并引导大家踏上和平之路。

哈里·杜鲁门：美国第 33 任总统（1945—1953），1945 年出任副总统，罗斯福逝世后接任总统，4 年后连任。任期内推行"公平施政"，是"冷战"的始作俑者，这在本篇演说中均有反映。本文略有删节。

Harry S. Truman
哈里·杜鲁门(1884-1972)
33rd President of the United States (1945-1953)
Political Party: Democratic

The Initiative Is Ours.
主动权在我们手中

Mr. Vice President, Mr. Chief Justice, and fellow citizens,

I accept with humility the honor which the American people have conferred upon me. I accept it with a deep resolve to do all that I can for the welfare of this Nation and for the peace of the world.

In performing the duties of my office, I need the help and prayers of every one of you. I ask for your encouragement and your support. The tasks we face are difficult, and we can accomplish them only if we work together.

副总统先生，大法官先生，同胞们：

我怀着谦恭的心情接受美国人民授予我的荣誉。我以坚定的决心接受这一荣誉，为我国人民的幸福和世界和平，我将尽我所能。

在履行公职时，我需要诸位的帮助和祈祷。我请求你们给予鼓励和支持。我们面临的任务是艰巨的，因此，我们只有共同努力才能完成这些任务。

Harry S. Truman
哈里·杜鲁门(1884-1972)
33rd President of the United States (1945-1953)

Each period of our national history has had its special challenges. Those that confront us now are as momentous as any in the past. Today marks the beginning not only of a new administration, but of a period that will be eventful, perhaps decisive, for us and for the world.

It may be our lot to experience, and in large measure to bring about, a major turning point in the long history of the human race. The first half of this century has been marked by unprecedented and brutal attacks on the rights of man, and by the two most frightful wars in history. The supreme need of our time is for men to learn to live together in peace and harmony.

The peoples of the earth face the future with grave uncertainty, composed almost equally of great hopes and great fears. In this time of doubt, they look to the United States as never before for good will, strength, and wise leadership.

It is fitting, therefore, that we take this occasion to proclaim to the world the essential principles of the faith by which we live, and to declare our aims to all peoples.

The American people stand firm in the faith which has inspired this Nation from the beginning. We believe that all men have a right to equal justice under law and equal opportunity to share in the common good. We believe that all men have the right to freedom of thought and expression. We believe that all men are created equal because they are created in the image of God.

我国历史上的各个时期都面临过特殊的挑战。我们现在面临的挑战和过去面临的任何挑战一样严重,今天不仅标志着一届新政府的起点,而且标志着一个新时期的开始。对我们来说,对整个世界来说,这个时期将是个多事之秋,也许还将是决定性的岁月。

也许命运注定我们要去体验,或者在更大程度上是去促成人类漫长历史中的一个重大转折。本世纪上半叶的特点是,人权遭到史无前例的粗暴践踏,并经历了历史上最可怕的两场战争。我们这个时代最迫切的需要是学会和睦相处。

世界各国人民都怀着忐忑不安的心情面对着未来,他们既充满希望又满腹忧虑。在这疑虑的时刻,他们比以往任何时候更期待合众国的善意、力量以及明智的领导。

因此,我们审时度势,利用这一时机向全世界宣布指导我们生活的信念的基本原则,向所有的民族宣布我们的目标。

美国人民坚持立国以来就激励着这一国家的信念。我们认为,在法律面前人人平等,分享公共利益的机会均等,这是每个人的权利。我们认为,思想自由和言论自由是每个人的权利。我们认为人人生而平等,因为他们都是上帝按照自己的形象创造出来的。

From this faith we will not be moved.

The American people desire, and are determined to work for, a world in which all nations and all peoples are free to govern themselves as they see fit, and to achieve a decent and satisfying life. Above all else, our people desire, and are determined to work for, peace on earth—a just and lasting peace—based on genuine agreement freely arrived at by equals.

Since the end of hostilities, the United States has invested its substance and its energy in a great constructive effort to restore peace, stability, and freedom to the world.

We have sought no territory and we have imposed our will on none. We have asked for no privileges we would not extend to others.

We have constantly and vigorously supported the United Nations and related agencies as a means of applying democratic principles to international relations. We have consistently advocated and relied upon peaceful settlement of disputes among nations.

We have made every effort to secure agreement on effective international control of our most powerful weapon, and we have worked steadily for the limitation and control of all armaments.

We have encouraged, by precept and example, the expansion of world trade on a sound and fair basis.

Almost a year ago, in company with 16 free nations of

秉持这种信念,我们就不会动摇。

美国人民渴望世界上所有的国家和所有的民族都自由地根据自己认为合适的方法来管理自己,自由地过着体面而满意的生活,并决心为建立这样的世界而努力。最重要的是美国人民渴望在地球上实现和平,决心为此而作出努力。这是一种公正持久的和平,一种以平等而无约束地达成真诚一致为基础的和平。

战争结束以来,合众国为了让世界上恢复和平、稳定和自由,已经投入了物力和精力到大量的建设性工作中。

我们并没有谋求别国的一寸领土,也没有把我们的意志强加于任何人。我们并没有要求任何特权,也不会向任何人提供这样的特权。

我们经常向联合国及其有关机构提供有力的支持,因为这些机构是将民主原则运用于国际关系的工具。我们一贯提倡国家之间和平解决争端,并依赖这种解决方法。

为了保证达成在国际上有效地控制我们最有威力的武器的协议,我们已作出了一切努力。为了限制和控制军备,我们已坚持不懈地进行了工作。

我们用法律和实例鼓励在公平合理的基础上扩大世界贸易。

将近一年前,我们和欧洲

Harry S. Truman
哈里·杜鲁门(1884-1972)
33rd President of the United States (1945-1953)

Europe, we launched the greatest cooperative economic program in history. The purpose of that unprecedented effort is to invigorate and strengthen democracy in Europe, so that the free people of that continent can resume their rightful place in the forefront of civilization and can contribute once more to the security and welfare of the world.

Our efforts have brought new hope to all mankind. We have beaten back despair and defeatism. We have saved a number of countries from losing their liberty. Hundreds of millions of people all over the world now agree with us, that we need not have war—that we can have peace.

The initiative is ours.

We are moving on with other nations to build an even stronger structure of international order and justice. We shall have as our partners countries which, no longer solely concerned with the problem of national survival, are now working to improve the standards of living of all their people. We are ready to undertake new projects to strengthen the free world.

In the coming years, our program for peace and freedom will emphasize four major courses of action.

First, we will continue to give unfaltering support to the United Nations and related agencies, and we will continue to search for ways to strengthen their authority and increase their effectiveness. We believe that the United Nations will be strengthened by the new nations which are being formed in lands now advancing toward self-government under democratic principles.

的16个自由国家一起,发起了历史上规模最大的经济合作计划。这项前所未有的工作的宗旨是为了加强和巩固欧洲的民主,使这一大陆上的自由人民恢复他们在文明世界前沿的合法地位,并能再次为全世界的安全和幸福作出贡献。

我们的努力为全人类带来了新希望。我们已经战胜了绝望和失败主义。我们拯救了许多国家,使他们没有丧失自由。全世界数亿人民现在都同意我们的观点:我们不需要战争,我们能够享有和平。

主动权在我们手中。

我们正和其他国家一起,为国际秩序和公正建立一个更加坚强的结构。我们将把那些不再仅仅关心民族生存问题、目前正在为提高全体人民生活水平而努力的国家作为自己的伙伴。为了巩固自由世界,我们准备实施新的计划。

在今后几年内,我们的和平自由纲领将着重于四项主要的行动方针。

第一,我们将继续坚定不移地支持联合国及其有关机构,继续寻求各种方法来加强这些机构的权威和增加这些机构的效率。今天,不少新的国家正在成立,正在民主原则的指引下向自治方向迈进,我们相信,联合国将因这些新国家而得到加强。

Second, we will continue our programs for world economic recovery.

This means, first of all, that we must keep our full weight behind the European recovery program. We are confident of the success of this major venture in world recovery. We believe that our partners in this effort will achieve the status of self-supporting nations once again.

In addition, we must carry out our plans for reducing the barriers to world trade and increasing its volume. Economic recovery and peace itself depend on increased world trade.

Third, we will strengthen freedom-loving nations against the dangers of aggression.

We are now working out with a number of countries a joint agreement designed to strengthen the security of the North Atlantic area. Such an agreement would take the form of a collective defense arrangement within the terms of the United Nations Charter.

We have already established such a defense pact for the Western Hemisphere by the Treaty of Rio de Janeiro.

The primary purpose of these agreements is to provide unmistakable proof of the joint determination of the free countries to resist armed attack from any quarter. Each country participating in these arrangements must contribute all it can to the common defense.

If we can make it sufficiently clear, in advance, that any armed attack affecting our national security would be met with overwhelming force, the armed attack might never occur.

I hope soon to send to the Senate a treaty respecting the North Atlantic security plan.

第二，我们将继续执行我们制定的世界经济复兴计划。

这意味着我们必须首先全力支持欧洲复兴计划。对于世界复兴中这一重大事业的成功，我们充满了信心。我们相信，通过这项工作，我们的伙伴将再一次取得自给国家的地位。

此外，我们还必须执行为减少世界贸易壁垒、增加世界贸易额而制定的计划。经济复兴与和平本身都取决于世界贸易的增加。

第三，我们要加强热爱自由的国家的力量，以抵御侵略的威胁。

我们正和许多国家一起，为增加北大西洋地区的安全起草一项共同协议。这种协议将根据联合国宪章的规定，采取集体防御协定的形式。

我们已经根据《里约热内卢公约》为西半球建立了这样一个防御同盟。

这些协议的主要目的是明确表示自由国家抵抗来自任何地方的武装进攻的共同决心。参加这些协议的每个国家必须为共同防御贡献出全部力量。

如果我们能预先充分地表明，任何影响到我们国家安全的武装进攻必将遭到强大的抵抗，那么武装进攻也许就永远不会发生。

我希望关于北大西洋安全计划的条约不久将呈送参议院。

Harry S. Truman
哈里·杜鲁门(1884-1972)
33rd President of the United States (1945-1953)

In addition, we will provide military advice and equipment to free nations which will cooperate with us in the maintenance of peace and security.

Fourth, we must embark on a bold new program for making the benefits of our scientific advances and industrial progress available for the improvement and growth of underdeveloped areas.

More than half the people of the world are living in conditions approaching misery. Their food is inadequate. They are victims of disease. Their economic life is primitive and stagnant. Their poverty is a handicap and a threat both to them and to more prosperous areas.

For the first time in history, humanity possesses the knowledge and the skill to relieve the suffering of these people.

The United States is pre-eminent among nations in the development of industrial and scientific techniques. The material resources which we can afford to use for the assistance of other peoples are limited. But our imponderable resources in technical knowledge are constantly growing and are inexhaustible.

I believe that we should make available to peace-loving peoples the benefits of our store of technical knowledge in order to help them realize their aspirations for a better life. And, in cooperation with other nations, we should foster capital investment in areas needing development.

Our aim should be to help the free peoples of the world, through their own efforts, to produce more food, more clothing, more materials for housing, and more mechanical power to lighten their burdens.

此外,我们还将向在维护和平与安全时与我们进行合作的自由国家,提供军事顾问和军事装备。

第四,我们必须着手拟定一项大胆的新计划,使不发达地区的进步与发展能受益于我们科学和工业的进步。

全世界半数以上的人口正濒临悲惨的境地,他们食不果腹、疾病加身。他们的经济生活原始落后,滞缓不振。无论对于他们自己还是对于比较繁荣的地区来说,他们的贫困既是一种阻碍又是一种威胁。

人类有史以来第一次掌握了能够解除这些人苦难的知识和技术。

合众国在工业和科学技术发展方面居各国之首。尽管我们用来援助其他国家人民的物质资源是有限的,但我们在技术知识方面的资源却是无法估量的,是不断增长和用之不竭的。

我认为,为了帮助热爱和平的民族实现美好生活的愿望,我们应该使他们受惠于我们丰富的技术知识。同时,我们还应该和其他国家合作,加强对急待开发的地区进行投资。

我们的目标应该是帮助世界上各个自由民族通过他们自己的努力,生产更多的食物,更多的衣物,更多的建筑材料,以及更多的机器来减轻他们的负担。

We invite other countries to pool their technological resources in this undertaking. Their contributions will be warmly welcomed. This should be a cooperative enterprise in which all nations work together through the United Nations and its specialized agencies wherever practicable. It must be a worldwide effort for the achievement of peace, plenty, and freedom.

With the cooperation of business, private capital, agriculture, and labor in this country, this program can greatly increase the industrial activity in other nations and can raise substantially their standards of living.

Such new economic developments must be devised and controlled to benefit the peoples of the areas in which they are established. Guarantees to the investor must be balanced by guarantees in the interest of the people whose resources and whose labor go into these developments.

The old imperialism—exploitation for foreign profit—has no place in our plans. What we envisage is a program of development based on the concepts of democratic fair-dealing.

All countries, including our own, will greatly benefit from a constructive program for the better use of the world's human and natural resources. Experience shows that our commerce with other countries expands as they progress industrially and economically.

Greater production is the key to prosperity and peace. And the key to greater production is a wider and more vigorous application of modern scientific and technical knowledge.

我们邀请其他国家汇集他们的技术力量来进行这项工作。我们热烈欢迎他们作出贡献。这应该是一种合作事业，所有国家通过联合国及其专门机构在任何可行的方面为此共同工作。这必须是在世界范围内为实现和平、繁荣和自由而作出的努力。

在我国企业、私人资本、农业和劳工等方面的协作下，这一计划能够极大促进其他国家的工业活动，从实质上提高他们的生活水平。

这种新的经济发展必须加以规划和控制，从而使被开发地区的人民有所得益。在保证投资者利益的同时，必须兼顾人民的利益，因为在这些经济发展中倾注着人民的才智和劳动。

在我们的计划中，剥削他国利润的老牌帝国主义没有立足之地。我们拟定的是一个以民主的公平交易的概念为基础的发展规划。

所有国家，包括我国在内，将极大地受益于为更合理地使用世界上的人力资源和自然资源而制定的一项建设性计划。经验证明，我们同其他国家的贸易将随着这些国家在工业和经济上的发展而扩大。

提高生产是繁荣与和平的关键，而提高生产的关键是更广泛、更积极地运用现代科学技术知识。

Harry S. Truman
哈里·杜鲁门(1884-1972)
33rd President of the United States (1945-1953)

Only by helping the least fortunate of its members to help themselves can the human family achieve the decent, satisfying life that is the right of all people.

Democracy alone can supply the vitalizing force to stir the peoples of the world into triumphant action, not only against their human oppressors, but also against their ancient enemies—hunger, misery, and despair.

On the basis of these four major courses of action we hope to help create the conditions that will lead eventually to personal freedom and happiness for all mankind.

If we are to be successful in carrying out these policies, it is clear that we must have continued prosperity in this country and we must keep ourselves strong.

Slowly but surely we are weaving a world fabric of international security and growing prosperity.

We are aided by all who wish to live in freedom from fear—even by those who live today in fear under their own governments.

We are aided by all who want relief from the lies of propaganda—who desire truth and sincerity.

We are aided by all who desire self-government and a voice in deciding their own affairs.

We are aided by all who long for economic security—for the security and abundance that men in free societies can enjoy.

We are aided by all who desire freedom of speech,

人类大家庭只有通过帮助最不幸的成员自助,才能享受体面的、令人满意的生活,而所有人都有权过上这样的生活。

只有民主政治才能产生生机勃勃的力量,以激励世界人民进行斗争,不仅为了反抗人类的压迫者,而且为了反抗人类古老的敌人——饥饿、贫困、失望。

根据这四项主要的行动方针,我们希望有助于创造各种条件,最终实现个人自由和全人类的幸福。

我们要成功地执行这些政策,那么很明显,我们必须继续保持我国的繁荣,我们必须保持自身的强大。

我们正在缓慢而又踏实地编织一张国际安全和日益繁荣的世界网络。

我们得到了所有希望摆脱恐惧生活的人们的帮助,甚至还得到了那些今天在自己政府统治之下仍生活在恐惧中的人们的帮助。

我们得到了所有希望摆脱宣传谎言、渴望真理和诚实的人们的帮助。

我们得到了渴望自治、渴望在决定自己事务中能表达意见的人们的帮助。

我们得到了所有渴望经济保障的人们的帮助,他们渴望自由社会的人们能够享受的保障和富裕。

我们得到了所有渴望言

freedom of religion, and freedom to live their own lives for useful ends.

Our allies are the millions who hunger and thirst after righteousness.

In due time, as our stability becomes manifest, as more and more nations come to know the benefits of democracy and to participate in growing abundance, I believe that those countries which now oppose us will abandon their delusions and join with the free nations of the world in a just settlement of international differences.

Events have brought our American democracy to new influence and new responsibilities. They will test our courage, our devotion to duty, and our concept of liberty.

But I say to all men, what we have achieved in liberty, we will surpass in greater liberty.

Steadfast in our faith in the Almighty, we will advance toward a world where man's freedom is secure.

To that end we will devote our strength, our resources, and our firmness of resolve. With God's help, the future of mankind will be assured in a world of justice, harmony, and peace.

论自由、宗教自由和为达到有益目标而自由选择生活方式的人们的帮助。

千百万如饥似渴地追求公正的人们都是我们的盟友。

随着我们的国家显示出稳定，随着越来越多的国家了解到民主政治的益处，共同来享受日益富裕的生活，我相信，现在反对我们的那些国家到适当的时候会放弃他们的妄想，并和世界上的自由国家一起，公正地解决国家之间的分歧。

一些重大事件已经赋予我们美国的民主政治以新的力量和新的义务。这些事件将检验我们的勇气，检验我们对自己职责的忠诚以及我们的自由观念。

但我要禀告所有的人，我们已经实现了自由的目标，我们还将迈向更高的自由目标。

我们坚定地信仰全能的上帝，我们将迈向一个保障人类自由的世界。

为了达到这个目标，我们将奉献出我们的力量、才智和坚定的决心。在上帝的帮助下，人类的未来必将是一个公正、融洽、和平的世界。

Dwight D. Eisenhower
德怀特·艾森豪威尔(1890-1969)
34th President of the United States (1953-1961)

德怀特·艾森豪威尔：美国第34任总统（1953—1961），第二次世界大战期间盟军最高统帅，自称"自由保守主义者"，任期内继续推行"冷战"政策。

Dwight D. Eisenhower
德怀特·艾森豪威尔(1890-1969)
34th President of the United States (1953-1961)
Political Party: Republican

Building a Peace with Justice
以正义建立和平

Mr. Chairman, Mr. Vice President, Mr. Chief Justice, Mr. Speaker, members of my family and friends, my countrymen, and the friends of my country, wherever they may be,

We meet again, as upon a like moment four years ago, and again you have witnessed my solemn oath of service to you.

I, too, am a witness, today testifying in your name to the principles and purposes to which we, as a people, are pledged.

Before all else, we seek, upon our common labor as a

主席先生，副总统先生，大法官先生，主持先生，我的家人和朋友，我的同胞们，美利坚合众国的朋友们：

我们又像4年前的此刻一样汇聚一堂，你们又目睹了我庄严地宣誓为大家服务。

今天，我也是一个见证人，我以你们的名义证明，我们作为一个民族对原则和目标所作的誓约。

首先，依靠全国的共同努

nation, the blessings of Almighty God. And the hopes in our hearts fashion the deepest prayers of our whole people.

May we pursue the right—without self-righteousness.

May we know unity—without conformity.

May we grow in strength—without pride in self.

May we, in our dealings with all peoples of the earth, ever speak truth and serve justice.

And so shall America—in the sight of all men of good will—prove true to the honorable purposes that bind and rule us as a people in all this time of trial through which we pass.

We live in a land of plenty, but rarely has this earth known such peril as today.

In our nation work and wealth abound. Our population grows. Commerce crowds our rivers and rails, our skies, harbors, and highways. Our soil is fertile, our agriculture productive. The air rings with the song of our industry—rolling mills and blast furnaces, dynamos, dams, and assembly lines—the chorus of America the bountiful.

This is our home—yet this is not the whole of our world. For our world is where our full destiny lies—with men, of all people, and all nations, who are or would be free. And for them—and so for us—this is no time of ease or of rest.

力，我们寻求全能上帝的赐福。我们心中的希望形成了我们整个民族衷心的祈祷。

愿我们追随正义而不自封公正。

愿我们懂得团结而不分派别。

愿我们强大起来而不自傲。

愿我们在和全世界各民族交往时，永远坦诚相待，尊崇正义。

这样，美国一定会在所有善良的人的面前，证明自己对崇高目标的忠诚。作为一个民族，我们经历了这个考验的时代的全部过程，这些目标制约着和支配着我们。

我们生活在一片富饶的土地上，但它很少经历过像今天这样的危险。

我国有大量的工作机会和财富。我国的人口不断增加。在江河、铁路、天空、港口和公路上，商业贸易川流不息。我国土地肥沃，农产丰盛。天空中回响着工业的乐曲，轧钢机、高炉、发电机、水坝和装配线为富足的美利坚而同声歌唱。

这就是我们的家园，但这不是我们的世界的全部。因为我们的世界是我们的全部命运所在——包括自由的或将获得自由的所有的民族和所有的国家。对他们来说，以及对我们来说，现在不是可以贪图安逸和休闲的时候。

Dwight D. Eisenhower
德怀特·艾森豪威尔(1890-1969)
34th President of the United States (1953-1961)

In too much of the earth there is want, discord, danger. New forces and new nations stir and strive across the earth, with power to bring, by their fate, great good or great evil to the free world's future. From the deserts of North Africa to the islands of the South Pacific one third of all mankind has entered upon an historic struggle for a new freedom; freedom from grinding poverty. Across all continents, nearly a billion people seek, sometimes almost in desperation, for the skills and knowledge and assistance by which they may satisfy from their own resources, the material wants common to all mankind.

No nation, however old or great, escapes this tempest of change and turmoil. Some, impoverished by the recent World War, seek to restore their means of livelihood. In the heart of Europe, Germany still stands tragically divided. So is the whole continent divided. And so, too, is all the world.

The divisive force is International Communism and the power that it controls.

The designs of that power, dark in purpose, are clear in practice. It strives to seal forever the fate of those it has enslaved. It strives to break the ties that unite the free. And it strives to capture—to exploit for its own greater power—all forces of change in the world, especially the needs of the hungry and the hopes of the oppressed.

在世界上，贫困、争执和危险的地方太多了。新的势力和新的国家在全世界奋发向上，努力抗争，它们以自己的力量和命运，为自由世界的未来带来最大的幸福或最大的灾难。从北非沙漠到南太平洋岛屿，人类的三分之一开始了为摆脱难熬的贫困、争取新的自由而进行的历史性斗争。遍及各大洲的近10亿人口在寻求，有时几乎是不惜一切地寻求技术、知识和援助。有了这些，他们就能够运用自己的资源来满足全人类共同的物质需要。

任何国家，无论多么古老或多么伟大，都无法躲避这场变革和动荡的风暴。有些国家在最近的一场世界大战中陷入贫困，它们力图恢复自己维持生存的手段。在欧洲的心脏地区，德国仍悲惨地分裂成两半。整个欧洲大陆也分裂成两半。整个世界也是如此。

造成这种分裂的势力就是国际共产主义及其控制的势力。

尽管这股势力的目的秘而不宣，但其做法却是世人皆知。它试图永远决定受其奴役的人民的命运。它试图破坏使自由人民团结起来的纽带。而且它还试图占有全世界所有能引起变革的力量，特别是利用饥饿者的需要和被压迫者的希望，以便扩大自己的势力。

Yet the world of International Communism has itself been shaken by a fierce and mighty force: the readiness of men who love freedom to pledge their lives to that love. Through the night of their bondage, the unconquerable will of heroes has struck with the swift, sharp thrust of lightning. Budapest is no longer merely the name of a city; henceforth it is a new and shining symbol of man's yearning to be free.

Thus across all the globe there harshly blow the winds of change. And, we—though fortunate be our lot—know that we can never turn our backs to them.

We look upon this shaken earth, and we declare our firm and fixed purpose—the building of a peace with justice in a world where moral law prevails.

The building of such a peace is a bold and solemn purpose. To proclaim it is easy. To serve it will be hard. And to attain it, we must be aware of its full meaning—and ready to pay its full price.

We know clearly what we seek, and why.

We seek peace, knowing that peace is the climate of freedom. And now, as in no other age, we seek it because we have been warned, by the power of modern weapons, that peace may be the only climate possible for human life itself.

Yet this peace we seek cannot be born of fear alone: it must be rooted in the lives of nations. There must be justice,

然而，国际共产主义世界本身已被一股猛烈的力量所动摇：这股力量就是热爱自由的人们准备为自己所热爱的自由献出生命。在他们被束缚的黑夜里，英雄们不可征服的意志像迅疾尖利的闪电劈开黑暗。布达佩斯已不再仅仅是一座城市的名称；从此之后，它成了人类渴望自由的闪闪发光的新标志。

因此，强劲的变革之风已吹遍全球，虽然我们很幸运，但我们知道，决不能置之不理。

我们注视着这一震撼的世界，并宣告我们坚定不移的目标：在奉行道德法则的世界上以正义来建立和平。

建立这样的和平是大胆而神圣的目标。宣布这一目标易如反掌，但达到这一目标却困难重重。为了实现这一目标，我们必须充分认识它的意义，并随时准备为此付出全部代价。

我们非常明白我们寻求的是什么，以及为什么要寻求。

我们寻求和平，是因为我们知道和平是自由的条件，与其他时代不同的是，我们今天寻求和平，是因为我们已经收到现代武器威力的警告：和平可能已成为人类生活本身唯一可以依赖的条件。

但是，我们所寻求的和平不能只是因恐惧而产生，和平

Dwight D. Eisenhower
德怀特·艾森豪威尔(1890-1969)
34th President of the United States (1953-1961)

sensed and shared by all peoples, for, without justice the world can know only a tense and unstable truce. There must be law, steadily invoked and respected by all nations, for without law, the world promises only such meager justice as the pity of the strong upon the weak. But the law of which we speak, comprehending the values of freedom, affirms the equality of all nations, great and small.

Splendid as can be the blessings of such a peace, high will be its cost: in toil patiently sustained, in help honorably given, in sacrifice calmly borne.

We are called to meet the price of this peace.

To counter the threat of those who seek to rule by force, we must pay the costs of our own needed military strength, and help to build the security of others.

We must use our skills and knowledge and, at times, our substance, to help others rise from misery, however far the scene of suffering may be from our shores. For wherever in the world a people knows desperate want, there must appear at least the spark of hope, the hope of progress—or there will surely rise at last the flames of conflict.

We recognize and accept our own deep involvement in the destiny of men everywhere. We are accordingly pledged

必须根植于各国人民的生活之中。必须有一种正义,它能力一切民族所感受和分享,因为,如果没有正义,世界上就只有一种紧张而不稳定的休战。必须有一种法律,它能被一切国家坚定地奉行和尊重,因为,如果没有法律,世界上就只有强者怜悯弱者那样的无力的正义。但我们所说的法律,应包括自由的全部价值,并确认国家不论大小,一律平等。

这样的和平所产生的幸福是辉煌的,其代价是高昂的,需要耐心地忍受艰辛,正直地给予援助,安然地承受牺牲。

我们被召唤来为这种和平付出代价。

为了制止那些企图用武力实行统治的人所造成的威胁,我们必须为我们所需要的军备力量付出代价,并帮助其他民族建立他们的安全保障。

我们必须运用我们的技术和知识,有时甚至运用我们的物资,去帮助其他民族摆脱痛苦,不论这些痛苦的所在地离我们的海岸有多远。因为在世界的任何地方,一个民族只要知道自己迫切需要什么,那里就必然会出现希望的火花,出现进步的希望,换句话说,最后必定会燃起抗争的火焰。

我们认识到,并承认我们自己已深深地同世界各地人

to honor, and to strive to fortify, the authority of the United Nations. For in that body rests the best hope of our age for the assertion of that law by which all nations may live in dignity.

And, beyond this general resolve, we are called to act a responsible role in the world's great concerns or conflicts—whether they touch upon the affairs of a vast region, the fate of an island in the Pacific, or the use of a canal in the Middle East. Only in respecting the hopes and cultures of others will we practice the equality of all nations. Only as we show willingness and wisdom in giving counsel—in receiving counsel—and in sharing burdens, will we wisely perform the work of peace.

For one truth must rule all we think and all we do. No people can live to itself alone. The unity of all who dwell in freedom is their only sure defense. The economic need of all nations—in mutual dependence—makes isolation an impossibility; not even America's prosperity could long survive if other nations did not also prosper. No nation can longer be a fortress, lone and strong and safe. And any people, seeking such shelter for themselves, can now build only their own prison.

Our pledge to these principles is constant, because we believe in their rightness.

We do not fear this world of change. America is no stranger to much of its spirit. Everywhere we see the seeds

民的命运联在一起。所以,我们发誓要尊重并努力加强联合国的权威。因为在这个机构中,寄托着我们这个时代最美好的希望——维护所有国家尊严的法律。

除了这个总的决心之外,我们还受命在世界重大事件或冲突中负起责任,无论这些事件涉及的是某个广大地区的事务,还是太平洋上某个岛屿的命运,或是中东某条运河的使用。只有尊重其他国家的希望和文化,我们才能做到各国之间的平等。只有在提出忠告,接受忠告,分担重任时表现出我们的意愿和智慧,我们才能明智地履行和平的任务。

我们的一切思想和一切行为都必须服从一条真理:任何民族都无法独自生存。所有自由国家团结起来,才是它们唯一可靠的防御。相互依存的经济需求使任何国家不能闭关自守;如果其他国家不繁荣起来,甚至美国的繁荣也不会持久。任何一个国家都不可能长久地成为一个单独的、强大的、安全的堡垒。任何一个为自己寻求这种保护的国家,现在只能为自己建立牢狱。

我们遵奉这些原则的誓言是坚定不移的,因为我们相信这些原则是正确的。

我们并不害怕这个变革的世界。美国对其中的许多

Dwight D. Eisenhower
德怀特·艾森豪威尔(1890-1969)
34th President of the United States (1953-1961)

of the same growth that America itself has known. The American experiment has, for generations, fired the passion and the courage of millions elsewhere seeking freedom, equality, and opportunity. And the American story of material progress has helped excite the longing of all needy peoples for some satisfaction of their human wants. These hopes that we have helped to inspire, we can help to fulfill.

In this confidence, we speak plainly to all peoples.

We cherish our friendship with all nations that are or would be free. We respect, no less, their independence. And when, in time of want or peril, they ask our help, they may honorably receive it; for we no more seek to buy their sovereignty than we would sell our own. Sovereignty is never bartered among freemen.

We honor the aspirations of those nations which, now captive, long for freedom. We seek neither their military alliance nor any artificial imitation of our society. And they can know the warmth of the welcome that awaits them when, as must be, they join again the ranks of freedom.

We honor, no less in this divided world than in a less tormented time, the people of Russia. We do not dread, rather do we welcome, their progress in education and industry. We wish them success in their demands for more intellectual freedom, greater security before their own laws, fuller enjoyment of the rewards of their own toil. For as

精神并不陌生。我们到处看到我们熟知的,使美国本身成长的同样种子。几代人以来,美国的实验已激起了世界各地成千上万人寻求自由、平等和机会的热情和勇气。美国物质发展的故事有助于激起贫困人们的愿望,使他们要求获得某种程度的满足。对于我们已帮助激起的希望,我们也能够帮助他们实现。

怀着这种信心,我们对所有的民族坦诚相告。

我们珍视我们同所有自由的或即将获得自由的国家所结成的友谊。我们同样尊重他们的独立。当他们面临贫困和危难而向我们求助时,他们能够体面地得到帮助。因为我们既不会出卖自己的主权,也不打算购买他们的主权。在自由人士中间,主权是绝不能当做交易的。

我们尊重那些今天仍受人控制、渴望自由的国家的愿望。我们既不打算同它们建立军事同盟,也不要求它们人为地模仿我们的社会。当他们重新加入自由的行列时——这是必定无疑的——他们就会知道,等待着他们的是热情欢迎。

在这个分裂的世界里,如同在一个比较安定的时代里一样,我们都同样尊敬俄国人民。我们并不害怕他们在教育和工业方面取得的进步,相反,我们确实欢迎他们能获得

such things come to pass, the more certain will be the coming of that day when our peoples may freely meet in friendship.

So we voice our hope and our belief that we can help to heal this divided world. Thus may the nations cease to live in trembling before the menace of force. Thus may the weight of fear and the weight of arms be taken from the burdened shoulders of mankind.

This, nothing less, is the labor to which we are called and our strength dedicated.

And so the prayer of our people carries far beyond our own frontiers, to the wide world of our duty and our destiny.

May the light of freedom, coming to all darkened lands, flame brightly—until at last the darkness is no more.

May the turbulence of our age yield to a true time of peace, when men and nations shall share a life that honors the dignity of each, the brotherhood of all.

这种进步。我们祝愿他们在更多地追求知识、自由方面，在他们自己的法律面前要求更多的安全方面，在更充分地享受他们自己的辛劳所得方面，都能取得成功。因为这些成果一经实现，那么我们两个民族友好地自由地进行交往的日子，就能够更确定无疑地到来。

因此，我们表露了我们可以协助愈合这一分裂的世界的希望和信心。这样，各国就不再会心惊胆战地生活在武力的威胁之中。这样，人类从肩负的重担中，就能卸下恐惧和武器的重担。

这就是我们被召唤来从事的、我们将为之奉献出力量的艰辛工作，而且一点也不能少。

所以，我国人民的祈祷远远超出了我们的国界，传向我们的责任和我们的命运所系的广阔世界。

愿自由之火燃烧发光，到达一切黑暗的地方，直至黑暗最终消失。

愿我们这个动乱的年代让位于一个真正的和平时代，到那时，所有的人和所有国家都将分享那受到尊重和四海一家的生活。

John F. Kennedy
约翰·肯尼迪(1917-1963)
35th President of the United States (1961-1963)

约翰·肯尼迪：美国第35任总统(1961—1963)，经选举产生的最年轻的总统(43岁)。任期内推出"新边疆"施政纲领，但执政仅千日便遇刺身亡。本篇文采飞扬，堪称精品。

John F. Kennedy
约翰·肯尼迪(1917-1963)
35th President of the United States (1961-1963)
Political Party: Democratic

This Much We Pledge—and More
我们的许诺

Vice President Johnson, Mr. Speaker, Mr. Chief Justice, President Eisenhower, Vice President Nixon, President Truman, reverend clergy, fellow citizens,

　　We observe today not a victory of party, but a celebration of freedom—symbolizing an end, as well as a beginning—signifying renewal, as well as change. For I have sworn before you and Almighty God the same solemn oath our forebears prescribed nearly a century and three quarters ago.

副总统约翰逊先生，主持先生，大法官先生，艾森豪威尔总统，尼克松副总统，杜鲁门总统，尊敬的教士和全国同胞们：

　　今天我们庆祝的不是政党的胜利，而是自由的胜利。这象征着一个结束，也象征着一个开端；意味着延续也意味着变革。因为我已在你们和全能的上帝面前，宣读了我们的先辈在170多年前拟定的庄严誓言。

The world is very different now. For man holds in his mortal hands the power to abolish all forms of human poverty and all forms of human life. And yet the same revolutionary beliefs for which our forebears fought are still at issue around the globe—the belief that the rights of man come not from the generosity of the state, but from the hand of God.

We dare not forget today that we are the heirs of that first revolution. Let the word go forth from this time and place, to friend and foe alike, that the torch has been passed to a new generation of Americans—born in this century, tempered by war, disciplined by a hard and bitter peace, proud of our ancient heritage—and unwilling to witness or permit the slow undoing of those human rights to which this Nation has always been committed, and to which we are committed today at home and around the world.

Let every nation know, whether it wishes us well or ill, that we shall pay any price, bear any burden, meet any hardship, support any friend, oppose any foe, in order to assure the survival and the success of liberty.

This much we pledge—and more.

To those old allies whose cultural and spiritual origins we share, we pledge the loyalty of faithful friends. United, there is little we cannot do in a host of cooperative ventures. Divided, there is little we can do—for we dare not meet a powerful challenge at odds and split asunder.

现在的世界已大不相同了,因为人类的巨手掌握着既能消灭人间的各种贫困,又能毁灭人间的各种生活的力量。但我们的先辈为之奋斗的那些革命信念,在世界各地仍然有着争论。这个信念就是:人的权利并非来自国家的慷慨,而是来自上帝恩赐。

今天,我们不敢忘记我们是第一次革命的继承者。让我们的朋友和敌人同样听见我此时此地的讲话:火炬已经传给新一代美国人。这一代人在本世纪诞生,在战争中受过锻炼,在艰难困苦的和平时期受过训练,他们为我国悠久的传统感到自豪——他们不愿目睹或听任我国一向保证的、今天仍在国内外作出保证的人权渐趋毁灭。

让每个国家都知道——不论它希望我们繁荣还是希望我们衰落——为确保自由的存在和自由的胜利,我们将付出任何代价,承受任何负担,应付任何艰难,支持任何朋友,反抗任何敌人。

这些就是我们的保证——而且还有更多的保证。

对那些和我们有着共同文化和精神渊源的老盟友、我们保证待以忠实朋友那样的忠诚。我们如果团结一致,就能在许多合作事业中无往不胜;我们如果分歧对立,就会一事无成——因为我们不敢在争吵不休、四分五裂时迎接强大的挑战。

John F. Kennedy
约翰·肯尼迪(1917-1963)
35th President of the United States (1961-1963)

To those new States whom we welcome to the ranks of the free, we pledge our word that one form of colonial control shall not have passed away merely to be replaced by a far more iron tyranny. We shall not always expect to find them supporting our view. But we shall always hope to find them strongly supporting their own freedom—and to remember that, in the past, those who foolishly sought power by riding the back of the tiger ended up inside.

To those peoples in the huts and villages across the globe struggling to break the bonds of mass misery, we pledge our best efforts to help them help themselves, for whatever period is required—not because the Communists may be doing it, not because we seek their votes, but because it is right. If a free society cannot help the many who are poor, it cannot save the few who are rich.

To our sister republics south of our border, we offer a special pledge—to convert our good words into good deeds—in a new alliance for progress—to assist free men and free governments in casting off the chains of poverty. But this peaceful revolution of hope cannot become the prey of hostile powers. Let all our neighbors know that we shall join with them to oppose aggression or subversion anywhere in the Americas. And let every other power know that this Hemisphere intends to remain the master of its own house.

To that world assembly of sovereign states, the United Nations, our last best hope in an age where the instruments

对那些我们欢迎其加入自由行列中来的新国家,我们恪守我们的誓言:决不让一种更为残酷的暴政来取代一种消失的殖民统治。我们并不总是指望他们会支持我们的观点。但我们始终希望看到他们坚强地维护自己的自由——而且要记住,在历史上,凡愚蠢地狐假虎威者,终将葬身虎口。

对世界各地身居茅舍和乡村、为摆脱普遍贫困而斗争的人们,我们保证尽最大努力帮助他们自立,不管需要花多长时间——之所以这样做,并不是因为共产党可能正在这样做,也不是因为我们需要他们的选票,而是因为这样做是正确的。自由社会如果不能帮助众多的穷人,也就无法挽救少数富人。

对我国南面的姐妹共和国,我们提出一项特殊的保证——在争取进步的新同盟中,把我们善意的话变为善意的行动,帮助自由的人们和自由的政府摆脱贫困的枷锁。但是,这种充满希望的和平革命绝不可以成为敌对国家的牺牲品。我们要让所有邻国都知道,我们将和他们在一起,反对在美洲任何地区进行侵略和颠覆活动。让所有其他国家都知道,本半球的人仍然想做自己家园的主人。

联合国是主权国家的世界性议事场所,是我们在战争

of war have far outpaced the instruments of peace, we renew our pledge of support—to prevent it from becoming merely a forum for invective—to strengthen its shield of the new and the weak—and to enlarge the area in which its writ may run.

Finally, to those nations who would make themselves our adversary, we offer not a pledge but a request: that both sides begin anew the quest for peace, before the dark powers of destruction unleashed by science engulf all humanity in planned or accidental self-destruction.

We dare not tempt them with weakness. For only when our arms are sufficient beyond doubt can we be certain beyond doubt that they will never be employed.

But neither can two great and powerful groups of nations take comfort from our present course—both sides overburdened by the cost of modern weapons, both rightly alarmed by the steady spread of the deadly atom, yet both racing to alter that uncertain balance of terror that stays the hand of mankind's final war.

So let us begin anew—remembering on both sides that civility is not a sign of weakness, and sincerity is always subject to proof. Let us never negotiate out of fear. But let us never fear to negotiate.

Let both sides explore what problems unite us instead of belaboring those problems which divide us.

Let both sides, for the first time, formulate serious and

John F. Kennedy
约翰·肯尼迪(1917-1963)
35th President of the United States (1961-1963)

precise proposals for the inspection and control of arms—and bring the absolute power to destroy other nations under the absolute control of all nations.

Let both sides seek to invoke the wonders of science instead of its terrors. Together let us explore the stars, conquer the deserts, eradicate disease, tap the ocean depths, and encourage the arts and commerce.

Let both sides unite to heed in all corners of the earth the command of Isaiah—to "undo the heavy burdens ... and to let the oppressed go free."

And if a beachhead of cooperation may push back the jungle of suspicion, let both sides join in creating a new endeavor, not a new balance of power, but a new world of law, where the strong are just and the weak secure and the peace preserved.

All this will not be finished in the first 100 days. Nor will it be finished in the first 1,000 days, nor in the life of this Administration, nor even perhaps in our lifetime on this planet. But let us begin.

In your hands, my fellow citizens, more than in mine, will rest the final success or failure of our course. Since this country was founded, each generation of Americans has been summoned to give testimony to its national loyalty. The graves of young Americans who answered the call to service surround the globe.

和军备控制制订认真而又明确的提案,把毁灭他国的绝对力量置于所有国家的绝对控制之下。

让双方寻求利用科学的奇迹,而不是利用科学造成的恐怖。让我们一起探索星球,征服沙漠,根除疾患,开发深海,并鼓励艺术和商业的发展。

让双方团结起来,在全世界各个角落倾听以赛亚的训令——"解下轭上的索,使被欺压的得自由。"(注:《圣经·旧约全书·以塞亚书》第58章6节。)

如果合作的滩头阵地能逼退猜忌的丛林,那么就让双方共同作一次新的努力;不是建立一种新的权力平衡,而是创造一个新的法治世界,在这个世界中,强者公正,弱者安全、和平将得到维护。

所有这一切不可能在今后一百天内完成,也不可能在今后一千天或者在本届政府任期内完成,甚至也许不可能在我们居住在这个星球上的有生之年内完成。但是,让我们开始吧。

公民们,我们方针的最终成败与其说掌握在我手中,不如说掌握在你们手中。自从合众国建立以来,每一代美国人都曾受到召唤去证明他们对国家的忠诚。响应召唤而献身的美国青年的坟墓遍及全球。

Now the trumpet summons us again—not as a call to bear arms, though arms we need; not as a call to battle, though embattled we are—but a call to bear the burden of a long twilight struggle, year in and year out, "rejoicing in hope, patient in tribulation"—a struggle against the common enemies of man: tyranny, poverty, disease, and war itself.

Can we forge against these enemies a grand and global alliance, North and South, East and West, that can assure a more fruitful life for all mankind? Will you join in that historic effort?

In the long history of the world, only a few generations have been granted the role of defending freedom in its hour of maximum danger. I do not shank from this responsibility—I welcome it. I do not believe that any of us would exchange places with any other people or any other generation. The energy, the faith, the devotion which we bring to this endeavor will light our country and all who serve it—and the glow from that fire can truly light the world.

And so, my fellow Americans: ask not what your country can do for you—ask what you can do for your country.

My fellow citizens of the world: ask not what America will do for you, but what together we can do for the freedom of man.

Finally, whether you are citizens of America or citizens of the world, ask of us the same high standards of strength and sacrifice which we ask of you. With a good conscience our only sure reward, with history the final judge

现在,号角已再次吹响——不是召唤我们拿起武器,虽然我们需要武器;不是召唤我们去作战,虽然我们严阵以待。它召唤我们为迎接黎明而肩负起漫长斗争的重任,年复一年,从希望中得到欢乐,在磨难中保持耐性,对付人类共同的敌人——专制、贫困、疾病和战争本身。

为反对这些敌人,确保人类更为丰裕的生活,我们能够组成一个包括东西南北各方的全球大联盟吗?你们愿意参加这一历史性的努力吗?

在漫长的世界历史中,只有少数几代人在自由处于最危急的时刻被赋予保卫自由的责任。我不会推卸这一责任,我欢迎这一责任。我不相信我们中间有人想同其他人或其他时代的人交换位置。我们为这一努力所奉献的精力、信念和忠诚,将照亮我们的国家和所有为国效劳的人,而这火焰发出的光芒定能照亮全世界。

因此,美国同胞们,不要问国家能为你们做些什么,而要问你们能为国家做些什么。

全世界的公民们,不要问美国将为你们做些什么,而要问我们共同能为人类的自由做些什么。

最后,不论你们是美国公民还是其他国家的公民,你们应要求我们献出我们同样要求于你们的实力和牺牲的高

John F. Kennedy
约翰·肯尼迪(1917-1963)
35th President of the United States (1961-1963)

of our deeds, let us go forth to lead the land we love, asking His blessing and His help, but knowing that here on earth God's work must truly be our own.

标准。问心无愧是我们唯一可靠的奖赏,历史是我们行动的最终裁判,让我们走向前去,引导我们所热爱的国家。我们祈求上帝的福佑和帮助,但我们知道,确切地说,上帝在尘世的工作必定是我们自己的工作。

林顿·约翰逊:美国第36任总统(1963—1969)。1961年当选副总统,1963年肯尼迪遇刺,任总统,两年后获连任。任期内提出"伟大社会"的执政纲领,后因扩大侵越战争而失去民心。由于反战运动高涨,他就在防弹玻璃罩内宣誓就职并发表了这篇演说。

Lyndon Johnson
林顿·约翰逊(1908-1973)
36th President of the United States (1963-1969)
Political Party: Democratic

The American Covenant: Justice, Liberty, and Union
美国公约:公正、自由、团结

My fellow countrymen, on this occasion, the oath I have taken before you and before God is not mine alone, but ours together. We are one nation and one people. Our fate as a nation and our future as a people rest not upon one citizen, but upon all citizens.

This is the majesty and the meaning of this moment.

For every generation, there is a destiny. For some,

同胞们,此时此刻,我在你们和上帝面前宣誓,这个誓言不只是我个人的,而是我们大家的。我们同住在一个国家,同属一个民族。我们国家的命运和我们民族的未来并不是靠一个公民,而是要靠所有的公民。

这就是这一时刻的庄严及其意义所在。

每一代人都有自己的命

Lyndon Johnson
林顿·约翰逊(1908—1973)
36th President of the United States (1963-1969)

history decides. For this generation, the choice must be our own.

Even now, a rocket moves toward Mars. It reminds us that the world will not be the same for our children, or even for ourselves in a short span of years. The next man to stand here will look out on a scene different from our own, because ours is a time of change—rapid and fantastic change bearing the secrets of nature, multiplying the nations, placing in uncertain hands new weapons for mastery and destruction, shaking old values, and uprooting old ways.

Our destiny in the midst of change will rest on the unchanged character of our people, and on their faith.

They came here—the exile and the stranger, brave but frightened—to find a place where a man could be his own man. They made a covenant with this land. Conceived in justice, written in liberty, bound in union, it was meant one day to inspire the hopes of all mankind; and it binds us still. If we keep its terms, we shall flourish.

First, justice was the promise that all who made the journey would share in the fruits of the land.

In a land of great wealth, families must not live in

运。就某些时代的人而言,历史决定了他们的命运。至于我们这一代人,我们必须选择自己的命运。

此时此刻,一枚火箭正向着火星飞去。这提醒我们,对我们的子孙来说,甚至对我们自己来说,在短短几年内,世界将不会再像现在一样。下一任总统站在这里时,他将展望一个和我们现在不同的景象。因为我们的时代是一个变革的时代。迅速而又急剧的变革,揭示了自然的奥秘,使国家成倍地增加,让靠不住的人掌握了能征服和毁灭人类的新式武器,动摇了旧的价值观念、改变了旧的生活方式。

在这场变革中,我们的命运将取决于我国人民始终不变的性格,取决于我们的信念。

我们的祖辈,那些背井离乡的异乡人,那些勇敢而受惊的异乡人,为寻找一块个人可以自主的地方而来到这里。他们在这块土地上订立了公约。这一公约以公正表达,用自由写成,受团结约束,指望总有一天会激励全人类的理想,这一公约至今仍约束着我们。我们如果遵循公约的规定,就将繁荣昌盛。

公约的第一条是公正,就是允许所有迁徙到这里的人共享土地的硕果。

在一块富饶的土地上,家

hopeless poverty. In a land rich in harvest, children just must not go hungry. In a land of healing miracles, neighbors must not suffer and die unattended. In a great land of learning and scholars, young people must be taught to read and write.

For the more than 30 years that I have served this Nation, I have believed that this injustice to our people, this waste of our resources, was our real enemy. For 30 years or more, with the resources I have had, I have vigilantly fought against it. I have learned, and I know, that it will not surrender easily.

But change has given us new weapons. Before this generation of Americans is finished, this enemy will not only retreat—it will be conquered.

Justice requires us to remember that when any citizen denies his fellow, saying, "His color is not mine," or "His beliefs are strange and different," in that moment he betrays America, though his forebears created this Nation.

Liberty was the second article of our covenant. It was self-government. It was our Bill of Rights. But it was more. America would be a place where each man could be proud to be himself: stretching his talents, rejoicing in his work, important in the life of his neighbors and his nation.

This has become more difficult in a world where change and growth seem to tower beyond the control and

家户户不能生活在毫无希望的贫困中。在一块收获丰盛的土地上，孩子们不能遭受饥馑之苦。在一块充满救死扶伤奇迹的土地上，我们的邻居不能无人照料，遭受病痛的折磨而离开人世。在一块知识普及、学者众多的伟大土地上，年轻人必须受到教育，学会读写。

在我为这个国家服务的30多年中，我一直认为，不公正地对待我们的人民，浪费我们的资源，乃是我们真正的敌人。30多年来，我竭尽所能，时刻提防这一敌人并与之作斗争。我认识到，也深深懂得，这个敌人不会轻易屈服。

但是，变革为我们提供了新的武器。在这一代美国人的有生之年，这个敌人不仅会退却，而且还会被征服。

公正就是要求我们记住，倘若任何一个公民不承认自己的同胞，宣称"某某人的肤色和我的肤色不同"，或者"某某人的信仰奇怪异样"，这个公民便背叛了美国，尽管他的先辈创立了这个国家。

公约的第二条是自由，就是自治。这就是我们的权利法案，但不仅如此。美国将成为一个人人都能感到自豪的地方，每个人都可以施展才能，愉快地工作，在邻里和国家的生活中发挥重要的作用。

但是，在变革和发展似乎已超出人们控制，甚至超出人

Lyndon Johnson
林顿·约翰逊(1908-1973)
36th President of the United States (1963-1969)

even the judgment of men. We must work to provide the knowledge and the surroundings which can enlarge the possibilities of every citizen.

The American covenant called on us to help show the way for the liberation of man. And that is today our goal. Thus, if as a nation there is much outside our control, as a people no stranger is outside our hope.

Change has brought new meaning to that old mission. We can never again stand aside, prideful in isolation. Terrific dangers and troubles that we once called "foreign" now constantly live among us. If American lives must end, and American treasure be spilled, in countries we barely know, that is the price that change has demanded of conviction and of our enduring covenant.

Think of our world as it looks from the rocket that is heading toward Mars. It is like a child's globe, hanging in space, the continents stuck to its side like colored maps. We are all fellow passengers on a dot of earth. And each of us, in the span of time, has really only a moment among our companions.

How incredible it is that in this fragile existence, we should hate and destroy one another. There are possibilities enough for all who will abandon mastery over others to pursue mastery over nature. There is world enough for all to seek their happiness in their own way.

们判断力的世界里,实现自由已经变得更为困难。因此,我们必须努力提供各种知识和环境,为每个公民增加机遇。

美国公约要求我们为帮助全人类的解放指明道路。这就是我们今天的奋斗目标。因此,作为一个国家,我们无法控制许多事情;但作为一个民族,我们对所有的人充满希望。

变革给这一古老的使命增添了新义。我们再也不能袖手旁观,以孤立为荣了。那些曾被我们称之为"外国的"可怕的危险和动乱,现在却时时在我们的生活中发生。如果美国人必须在不甚了解的国家中献出生命并消耗钱财,那也是变革向我们的信念以及向我们不朽的公约索取的代价。

我们不妨想象一下坐在飞向火星的火箭上看地球时的情景。地球就像小孩玩的地球仪,悬在太空中,陆地就像贴在球体表面的彩色地图。我们都是这个小小地球上的旅客。在时间的长河中,我们每个人实际上只在自己的同伴中度过短暂的一瞬。

人的生存是如此脆弱,可我们竟然彼此仇恨,相互残杀,这是多么难以令人置信。凡意愿放弃统治他人的人,有足够的机会来实现对自然的统治。天地广阔,足以让每个人以自己的方式寻求幸福。

Our Nation's course is abundantly clear. We aspire to nothing that belongs to others. We seek no dominion over our fellow man, but man's dominion over tyranny and misery.

But more is required. Men want to be a part of a common enterprise—a cause greater than themselves. Each of us must find a way to advance the purpose of the Nation, thus finding new purpose for ourselves. Without this, we shall become a nation of strangers.

The third article was union. To those who were small and few against the wilderness, the success of liberty demanded the strength of union. Two centuries of change have made this true again.

No longer need capitalist and worker, farmer and clerk, city and countryside, struggle to divide our bounty. By working shoulder to shoulder, together we can increase the bounty of all. We have discovered that every child who learns, every man who finds work, every sick body that is made whole—like a candle added to an altar—brightens the hope of all the faithful.

So let us reject any among us who seek to reopen old wounds and to rekindle old hatreds. They stand in the way of a seeking nation.

Let us now join reason to faith and action to experience, to transform our unity of interest into a unity of purpose. For the hour and the day and the time are here to achieve progress without strife, to achieve change without hatred—not without difference of opinion, but without the

我国的方针是明确的。我们并不奢求获得别人的东西。我们并不寻求统治别人，而只希望人类能战胜专制和苦难。

但是我们需要做更多的事情。人们希望成为共同事业的参与者——这是比他们本身更为伟大的事业。我们每个人都必须想方设法为实现我国的目标作出贡献，因而也为自己找到新的目标。如果缺少这些，我国就会变成一个由陌生人组成的国家。

公约的第三条是团结。对那些当年同荒野作斗争的势单力薄的移民来讲，实现自由需要团结的力量。两个世纪的变革再次证实了这点。

资本家和工人，农场主和雇员，城市和农村再也不必为分配利益而争斗，我们只要肩并肩共同努力，就能够增加所有人的利益。我们已经看到，每一个学习的儿童，每一个在职的成人，每一个康复的病人，都像圣坛上的蜡烛，照亮了全体信徒的希望。

因此，让我们唾弃我们中间任何企图重提旧伤、重燃旧恨的人。因为对这个不停地追求的国家来说，他们是道路上的障碍。

现在，让我们把理性和信念融成一体，将行动和经验融成一体，把利益的一致转变成目标的一致。因为无需冲突便能取得进步，不结仇恨便能

Lyndon Johnson
林顿·约翰逊(1908-1973)
36th President of the United States (1963-1969)

deep and abiding divisions which scar the union for generations.

Under this covenant of justice, liberty, and union we have become a nation—prosperous, great, and mighty. And we have kept our freedom. But we have no promise from God that our greatness will endure. We have been allowed by Him to seek greatness with the sweat of our hands and the strength of our spirit.

I do not believe that the Great Society is the ordered, changeless, and sterile battalion of the ants. It is the excitement of becoming—always becoming, trying, probing, falling, resting, and trying again—but always trying and always gaining.

In each generation, with toil and tears, we have had to earn our heritage again.

If we fail now, we shall have forgotten in abundance what we learned in hardship: that democracy rests on faith, that freedom asks more than it gives, and that the judgment of God is harshest on those who are most favored.

If we succeed, it will not be because of what we have, but it will be because of what we are; not because of what we own, but, rather because of what we believe.

For we are a nation of believers. Underneath the clamor of building and the rush of our day's pursuits, we are believers in justice and liberty and union, and in our

实现变革的时刻已经来临——这不是说没有不同的观点，而是不会再有给几代人的团结留下伤痕的根深蒂固的分歧。

在这个以公正、自由、团结为宗旨的公约指导下，我们已经成为一个繁荣、伟大和强盛的国家。我们还维护了我们的自由。但是，上帝没有保证我们的伟大国家经久不衰。上帝准许我们用自己的双手、用汗水、用精神力量来争取我们的伟大。

我认为，"伟大社会"不是一个等级森严、毫无变化、枯燥乏味的蚁群社会。"伟大社会"因转化而充满激情——不停地变革、尝试、探索、失败、休整、再尝试——但总是在尝试，总是有所收获。

我们每一代人都必须用汗水和泪水重新获得我们的传统。

倘若我们现在失败了，这是因为我们在富裕中忘记了在艰难岁月中懂得的那些道理：民主依赖于信仰，自由的要求大于它的赠予，上帝最严厉地评判最受恩宠的人们。

倘若我们成功了，这并不是因为我们具备了什么条件，而是由于我们本身的原因；并不是因为我们拥有什么东西，而是由于我们的信仰所致。

因为我们是一个有信仰的民族。我们闹嚷嚷地创业，急匆匆地追逐生活目标，但在

own Union. We believe that every man must someday be free. And we believe in ourselves.

Our enemies have always made the same mistake. In my lifetime—in depression and in war—they have awaited our defeat. Each time, from the secret places of the American heart, came forth the faith they could not see or that they could not even imagine. It brought us victory. And it will again.

For this is what America is all about. It is the uncrossed desert and the unclimbed ridge. It is the star that is not reached and the harvest sleeping in the unplowed ground. Is our world gone? We say "Farewell." Is a new world coming? We welcome it—and we will bend it to the hopes of man.

To these trusted public servants and to my family and those close friends of mine who have followed me down a long, winding road, and to all the people of this Union and the world, I will repeat today what I said on that sorrowful day in November 1963: "I will lead and I will do the best I can."

But you must look within your own hearts to the old promises and to the old dream. They will lead you best of all.

For myself, I ask only, in the words of an ancient leader: "Give me now wisdom and knowledge, that I may go out and come in before this people: for who can judge this thy people, that is so great?"

这些表象背后,我们是公正、自由和团结的信仰者,是自己联邦的信徒。我们相信,总有一天,人人都会获得自由。而且,我们相信自己有力量。

我们的敌人总是犯相同的错误。在我这一生中——在萧条年代和战争岁月——他们期待着我们的失败。但每一次,在美国人民的心灵深处,都会产生出他们无法理解,甚至无法想象的信念。这种信念曾给我们带来胜利,它将再次给我们带来胜利。

因为这就是美国。这是一块未曾跨越的沙漠,是一座尚未攀登的山脉。这是一颗人迹还没有到过的星球,是沉睡在未开垦土地中的硕果。我们的世界已经过去了吗?我们对它说声"再见"。新的世界来临了吗?我们欢迎它——并将使它服从人类的愿望。

对那些肩负重任的公仆,对我的家人,对跟我走过漫长而又曲折的道路的朋友们,对联邦全体人民和全世界人民,我今天重述我在1963年11月那悲痛的一天说过的话:"我将领导大家,并将竭尽所能。"

但是,你们必须在内心铭记旧时的承诺和梦想。这才是你们最好的向导。

至于我自己,借用一位古代领袖的话,我只"求你赐我智慧聪明,我好在人民面前出入;不然,谁能判断这众多的民众呢?"

Richard Nixon
理查德·尼克松(1913-1994)
37th President of the United States (1969-1974)

理查德·尼克松:美国第37任总统(1969—1974)。任期内提出尼克松主义,推行均势外交。1972年访华,开创中美关系新阶段。1974年因水门事件下台。

Richard Nixon
理查德·尼克松(1913-1994)
37th President of the United States (1969-1974)
Political Party: Republican

Greatness Comes in Simple Trappings
伟大孕育于质朴无华

Senator Dirksen, Mr. Chief Justice, Mr. Vice President, President Johnson, Vice President Humphrey, my fellow Americans—and my fellow citizens of the world community:

I ask you to share with me today the majesty of this moment. In the orderly transfer of power, we celebrate the unity that keeps us free.

Each moment in history is a fleeting time, precious and unique. But some stand out as moments of beginning, in which courses are set that shape decades or centuries.

德克森议员,大法官先生,副总统先生,约翰逊总统,汉弗莱副总统,美国同胞,世界大家庭的公民们:

今天,我请你们和我一起度过这庄严的时刻。值此井然有序地进行权力移交之际,我们盛赞使我们能享受自由的举国团结。

历史的每一个时刻转瞬即逝,它既珍贵又独特。可是,其中某些显然是揭开序幕的时刻,此时,一代先河得以开创,它决定了未来数十年或几个世纪的航向。

This can be such a moment.

Forces now are converging that make possible, for the first time, the hope that many of man's deepest aspirations can at last be realized. The spiraling pace of change allows us to contemplate, within our own lifetime, advances that once would have taken centuries.

In throwing wide the horizons of space, we have discovered new horizons on earth.

For the first time, because the people of the world want peace, and the leaders of the world are afraid of war, the times are on the side of peace.

Eight years from now America will celebrate its 200th anniversary as a nation. Within the lifetime of most people now living, mankind will celebrate that great new year which comes only once in a thousand years—the beginning of the third millennium.

What kind of nation we will be, what kind of world we will live in, whether we shape the future in the image of our hopes, is ours to determine by our actions and our choices.

The greatest honor history can bestow is the title of peacemaker. This honor now beckons America—the chance to help lead the world at last out of the valley of turmoil, and onto that high ground of peace that man has dreamed of since the dawn of civilization.

If we succeed, generations to come will say of us now living that we mastered our moment, that we helped make the world safe for mankind.

现在可能就是这样一个时刻。

现在，各方力量正在汇聚起来，使我们第一次可以望人类的许多夙愿最终能够实现。不断加快的变革速度，使我们能在我们这一代期望过去花了几百年才出现的种种进步。

由于开辟了太空的天地，我们在地球上也发现了新的天地。

由于世界人民希望和平，而世界各国领袖害怕战争，因此，目前形势第一次变得有利于和平。

从现在起，再过8年，美国将庆祝建国200周年。在现在大多数人的有生之年，人类将庆祝千载难逢的、辉煌无比的新年——第三个百年盛世的开端。

我们的国家将变成怎样的国家，我们将生活在怎样的世界上，我们要不要按照我们的希望铸造未来，这些都将由我们根据自己的行动和选择来决定。

历史所能赐予我们的最大荣誉，莫过于和平缔造者这一称号。这一荣誉现在正在召唤美国——这是领导世界最终脱离动乱的幽谷，走向自文明开端以来人类一直梦寐以求的和平高地的一个机会。

我们若获成功，下几代人在谈及现在在世的我们时会说，正是我们掌握了时机，正是我们协力相助，使普天之下国泰民安。

Richard Nixon
理查德·尼克松(1913-1994)
37th President of the United States (1969-1974)

This is our summons to greatness.

I believe the American people are ready to answer this call.

The second third of this century has been a time of proud achievement. We have made enormous strides in science and industry and agriculture. We have shared our wealth more broadly than ever. We have learned at last to manage a modern economy to assure its continued growth.

We have given freedom new reach, and we have begun to make its promise real for black as well as for white.

We see the hope of tomorrow in the youth of today. I know America's youth. I believe in them. We can be proud that they are better educated, more committed, more passionately driven by conscience than any generation in our history.

No people has ever been so close to the achievement of a just and abundant society, or so possessed of the will to achieve it. Because our strengths are so great, we can afford to appraise our weaknesses with candor and to approach them with hope.

Standing in this same place a third of a century ago, Franklin Delano Roosevelt addressed a Nation ravaged by depression and gripped in fear. He could say in surveying the Nation's troubles: "They concern, thank God, only material things."

这是要我们创立宏伟大业的召唤。

我相信,美国人民准备响应这一召唤。

20世纪30年代到60年代是取得辉煌成就的时期。我们在科学和工农业方面都取得了长足的进步。我们比以往任何时候都更广泛地分享了我们的财富。我们终于学会了怎样管理现代经济,确保经济的持续增长。

我们已将自由扩大到新的领域。我们已开始不仅为白人,而且也为黑人,把自由的许诺变成现实。

我们把明天的希望寄予今天的青年人。我理解美国的青年。我信任他们。我们可以引以为荣的是,同我国历史上任何一代青年人相比,今天的青年更有教养,更富有献身精神,更强烈地受良心的支配。

没有一个民族如此接近于建成一个公正而富裕的社会,没有一个民族如此具有建成这个社会的意志。我们的力量如此强大,因此我们能坦率地估量自己的弱点,并能满怀希望地看待这些弱点。

30多年以前,富兰克林·德拉诺·罗斯福也是站在这个地方,向一个受到经济萧条打击并处于恐惧之中的国家发表了演说。他在审视当时的国难时尚能说:"谢天谢地!这些困难只是物质方面的。"

Our crisis today is the reverse.

We have found ourselves rich in goods, but ragged in spirit; reaching with magnificent precision for the moon, but falling into raucous discord on earth.

We are caught in war, wanting peace. We are torn by division, wanting unity. We see around us empty lives, wanting fulfillment. We see tasks that need doing, waiting for hands to do them.

To a crisis of the spirit, we need an answer of the spirit.

To find that answer, we need only look within ourselves.

When we listen to "the better angels of our nature", we find that they celebrate the simple things, the basic things—such as goodness, decency, love, kindness.

Greatness comes in simple trappings.

The simple things are the ones most needed today if we are to surmount what divides us, and cement what unites us.

To lower our voices would be a simple thing.

In these difficult years, America has suffered from a fever of words; from inflated rhetoric that promises more than it can deliver; from angry rhetoric that fans discontents into hatreds; from bombastic rhetoric that postures instead of persuading.

We cannot learn from one another until we stop shouting at one another—until we speak quietly enough so

我们今天的危机恰恰相反。

我们发觉,我们的物质虽然丰富,但精神却很匮乏;我们以无比的精确性奔向月球,但在地球上却陷入吵嚷不和之中。

我们被战争所纠缠,因而希望和平。我们四分五裂,因而希望团结。我们见到周围的人们精神空虚,因而需要充实。我们看到有许多任务需要完成,等待着人们去做。

对于精神危机,我们需要用精神来回答。

为了找到答案,我们只要审视自身。

当我们在聆听"我们本性中的善良天使"时,我们发现她们歌颂的是一些简单的东西、一些基本的东西——如善良、体面、博爱和仁慈。

伟大孕育于质朴无华。

假如我们要克服那些使我们分裂的东西,巩固那些把我们团结起来的东西,那么今天最需要的就是做一些简单的事情。

压低嗓门就是一件简单的事情。

在这些艰难的年代里,美国备受狂言高调之苦:难以践诺的信口开河;煽动不满与仇恨的过激言词;装腔作势而不是相规以善的夸夸其谈,等等。

如果我们不停止相互叫嚷——如果我们不心平气和

Richard Nixon
理查德·尼克松(1913-1994)
37th President of the United States (1969-1974)

that our words can be heard as well as our voices.

For its part, government will listen. We will strive to listen in new ways—to the voices of quiet anguish, the voices that speak without words, the voices of the heart—to the injured voices, the anxious voices, the voices that have despaired of being heard.

Those who have been left out, we will try to bring in.

Those left behind, we will help to catch up.

For all of our people, we will set as our goal the decent order that makes progress possible and our lives secure.

As we reach toward our hopes, our task is to build on what has gone before—not turning away from the old, but turning toward the new.

In this past third of a century, government has passed more laws, spent more money, initiated more programs, than in all our previous history.

In pursuing our goals of full employment, better housing, excellence in education; in rebuilding our cities and improving our rural areas; in protecting our environment and enhancing the quality of life—in all these and more, we will and must press urgently forward.

We shall plan now for the day when our wealth can be transferred from the destruction of war abroad to the urgent needs of our people at home.

地讲话,从而使我们说话的声音和内容都能让人听得清楚,我们便不能相互学习。

对政府来说,我们将倾听一切。我们将通过各种新渠道尽力倾听——默默受苦的声音、无言倾诉的声音、发自肺腑的声音——倾听备受伤害的声音、忧虑焦急的声音、感到无望的声音。

我们要设法带领那些被遗弃的人加入我们的行列。

我们要帮助那些落伍的人迎头赶上。

对全体人民来说,我们要把使进步得以实现,使我们的生活得到保障的良好秩序定为我们的目标。

在我们向着我们的希望奋进之际,我们的任务是要在以往的基础上有所建树——不是抛开过去,而是朝向未来。

在过去的30多年里,政府通过的法律、花费的金钱和着手的项目,超过了我国以往历史上的总和。

在实现充分就业、改善住房条件、施行优良教育的目标方面;在重建城市、改进农业地区条件方面;在保护环境和提高生活质量方面——在所有这些以及其他方面,我们务必加紧步伐,奋勇向前。

我们现在就要有所规划,以便到时候能把用于国外毁灭性战争的钱财用于国内人民的急迫需要方面。

The American dream does not come to those who fall asleep.

But we are approaching the limits of what government alone can do.

Our greatest need now is to reach beyond government, and to enlist the legions of the concerned and the committed.

What has to be done, has to be done by government and people together or it will not be done at all. The lesson of past agony is that without the people we can do nothing; with the people we can do everything.

To match the magnitude of our tasks, we need the energies of our people—enlisted not only in grand enterprises, but more importantly in those small, splendid efforts that make headlines in the neighborhood newspaper instead of the national journal.

With these, we can build a great cathedral of the spirit—each of us raising it one stone at a time, as he reaches out to his neighbor, helping, caring, doing.

I do not offer a life of uninspiring ease. I do not call for a life of grim sacrifice. I ask you to join in a high adventure—one as rich as humanity itself, and as exciting as the times we live in.

The essence of freedom is that each of us shares in the shaping of his own destiny.

Until he has been part of a cause larger than himself, no man is truly whole.

美国人的理想绝不会由那些麻木不仁的人来实现。

不过，政府单枪匹马地进行工作，已经到达了种种极限。

现在，我们最大的需要是超越政府的范围，争取大批关心者和献身者的支持。

凡必须办的事，就要由政府和人民共同来办，否则根本无法完成。过去切肤之痛的教训是，没有人民的参加，我们一事无成；而有了人民的参加，我们无所不能。

为了完成我们的宏图大业，我们需要人民的力量——不仅赖以开展宏大的计划，而且更重要的是赖以进行小型而出色的工作，尽管这些工作将在地区报刊而不是在全国性报刊上成为头条新闻。

有了这些，我们就可以建造起宏伟的精神大厦——当我们每个人把手递给邻居，帮助他、关心他、为他做事，我们就为这座大厦添了砖加了瓦。

我无意提出一种平庸安逸的生活。我也无意要求你们过一种恼人而作出牺牲的生活。我请求你们参加一项崇高的冒险事业——它同人类本身一样丰富多彩，同我们所生活的时代一样激动人心。

自由的要旨是，我们大家共同来决定自己的命运。

任何一个人只有在他成为高于自己的事业的一部分时，才真正是完美无缺的。

Richard Nixon
理查德·尼克松(1913-1994)
37th President of the United States (1969-1974)

The way to fulfillment is in the use of our talents; we achieve nobility in the spirit that inspires that use.

As we measure what can be done, we shall promise only what we know we can produce, but as we chart our goals we shall be lifted by our dreams.

No man can be fully free while his neighbor is not. To go forward at all is to go forward together.

This means black and white together, as one nation, not two. The laws have caught up with our conscience. What remains is to give life to what is in the law: to ensure at last that as all are born equal in dignity before God, all are born equal in dignity before man.

As we learn to go forward together at home, let us also seek to go forward together with all mankind.

Let us take as our goal: where peace is unknown, make it welcome; where peace is fragile, make it strong; where peace is temporary, make it permanent.

After a period of confrontation, we are entering an era of negotiation.

Let all nations know that during this administration our lines of communication will be open.

We seek an open world—open to ideas, open to the

通往完善的道路在于运用我们的才能;我们本着这种能激励我们运用自己才能的精神来达到崇高的境地。

当我们衡量可以完成哪些工作时,我们只能保证我们知道自己能够完成的那一切。可是我们在确定目标时,我们的理想将使我们升华。

任何人在他的邻居尚未取得自由时,都不可能充分地享有自由。真要前进,那就是共同前进。

这意味着白人黑人要一起前进,他们是一个民族,而不是两个民族。各种法律的制订已经能反映出我们的良知。尚待完成的是让法律条文发挥作用,并最终确保每个人在他人面前有天生平等的尊严,就像每个人在上帝面前有天生平等的尊严一样。

正如我们懂得在国内我们是共同前进的,让我们也谋求与全人类共同前进。

让我们把下述作为我们的目标:凡是和平不为人们所知的地方,使和平在那里受到人们的欢迎;凡是和平很脆弱的地方,使它变得牢固起来;凡是和平只是短暂的地方,使和平得以持久下去。

经过一段对抗时期,我们正进入一个谈判时代。

让所有国家都知道,在本届政府任期内,交流通道是敞开的。

我们谋求一个开放的世

exchange of goods and people—a world in which no people, great or small, will live in angry isolation.

We cannot expect to make everyone our friend, but we can try to make no one our enemy.

Those who would be our adversaries, we invite to a peaceful competition—not in conquering territory or extending dominion, but in enriching the life of man.

As we explore the reaches of space, let us go to the new world together—not as new worlds to be conquered, but as a new adventure to be shared.

With those who are willing to join, let us cooperate to reduce the burden of arms, to strengthen the structure of peace, to lift up the poor and the hungry.

But to all those who would be tempted by weakness, let us leave no doubt that we will be as strong as we need to be for as long as we need to be.

Over the past twenty years, since I first came to this Capital as a freshman Congressman, I have visited most of the nations of the world.

I have come to know the leaders of the world, and the great forces, the hatreds, the fears that divide the world.

I know that peace does not come through wishing for it—that there is no substitute for days and even years of patient and prolonged diplomacy.

界——对各种思想开放，对物资和人员的交流开放，在这个世界中，任何民族，不论大小，都不会生活在怏怏不乐的孤立之中。

我们不能指望每个人都成为我们的朋友，可是我们能设法使不与人我为敌。

我们邀请那些很可能是我们对手的人进行一场和平竞赛——不是要征服领土或扩张版图，而是要丰富人类的生活。

在探索宇宙空间的时候，让我们一起走向新的世界——不是走向被征服的新世界，而是共同进行一次新的探险。

让我们同那些愿意加入这一行列的人共同合作，减少军备负担，加固和平结构，提高贫穷挨饿的人们的生活水平。

但是，对所有那些见软就欺的人来说，让我们不容置疑地表明，我们需要多么强大就会多强大，需要强大多久，就会强大多久。

自从我作为新当选的国会议员首次来到国会大厦之后的20多年里，我已经出访过世界上大多数国家。

我结识了世界各国的领导人，了解到使世界陷于四分五裂的各种强大势力，各种深仇大恨，各种恐惧心理。

我知道，和平不会单凭愿望就能到来——这需要日复一日，甚至年复一年地进行耐心而持久的外交努力，除此别无他法。

Richard Nixon
理查德·尼克松(1913-1994)
37th President of the United States (1969-1974)

I also know the people of the world.

I have seen the hunger of a homeless child, the pain of a man wounded in battle, the grief of a mother who has lost her son. I know these have no ideology, no race.

I know America. I know the heart of America is good.

I speak from my own heart, and the heart of my country, the deep concern we have for those who suffer, and those who sorrow.

I have taken an oath today in the presence of God and my countrymen to uphold and defend the Constitution of the United States. To that oath I now add this sacred commitment: I shall consecrate my office, my energies, and all the wisdom I can summon, to the cause of peace among nations.

Let this message be heard by strong and weak alike:

The peace we seek to win is not victory over any other people, but the peace that comes "with healing in its wings"; with compassion for those who have suffered; with understanding for those who have opposed us; with the opportunity for all the peoples of this earth to choose their own destiny.

Only a few short weeks ago, we shared the glory of man's first sight of the world as God sees it, as a single sphere reflecting light in the darkness.

As the Apollo astronauts flew over the moon's gray surface on Christmas Eve, they spoke to us of the beauty of earth—and in that voice so clear across the lunar distance,

我也了解世界各国人民。

我见过无家可归的儿童在忍饥挨饿,战争中挂彩负伤的男人在痛苦呻吟,失去孩子的母亲在无限悲伤。我知道,这些并没有意识形态和种族之分。

我了解美国。我了解美国的心是善良的。

我从心底里,从我国人民的心底里,向那些蒙受不幸和痛苦的人们表达我们的深切关怀。

今天,我在上帝和我国同胞面前宣誓,拥护和捍卫合众国宪法。除了这一誓言,我现在还要补充一项神圣的义务:我将把自己的职责、精力以及我所能使唤的一切智慧,一并奉献给各国之间的和平事业。

让强者和弱者都能听到这一信息:

我们企求赢得的和平不是战胜任何一个民族,而是"和平天使"带来的为治愈创伤的和平;是对遭受苦难者予以同情的和平;是对那些反对过我们的人予以谅解的和平;是地球上各族人民都有选择自己命运的机会的和平。

就在几星期以前,人类如同上帝凝望这个世界一样,第一次端视了这个世界,一个在冥冥黑暗中辉映发光的独特的星球。我们分享了这一荣光。

阿波罗号上的宇航员在圣诞节前夕飞越月球灰色的表面时,向我们说起地球的美丽——从穿过月距而传来的

we heard them invoke God's blessing on its goodness.

In that moment, their view from the moon moved poet Archibald MacLeish to write:

"**To** see the earth as it truly is, small and blue and beautiful in that eternal silence where it floats, is to see ourselves as riders on the earth together, brothers on that bright loveliness in the eternal cold—brothers who know now they are truly brothers."

In that moment of surpassing technological triumph, men turned their thoughts toward home and humanity—seeing in that far perspective that man's destiny on earth is not divisible; telling us that however far we reach into the cosmos, our destiny lies not in the stars but on Earth itself, in our own hands, in our own hearts.

We have endured a long night of the American spirit. But as our eyes catch the dimness of the first rays of dawn, let us not curse the remaining dark. Let us gather the light.

Our destiny offers, not the cup of despair, but the chalice of opportunity. So let us seize it, not in fear, but in gladness—and, "riders on the earth together," let us go forward, firm in our faith, steadfast in our purpose, cautious of the dangers; but sustained by our confidence in the will of God and the promise of man.

如此清晰的声音中,我们听到他们在祈祷上帝赐福人间。

在那一时刻,他们从月球上发出的意愿,激励着诗人阿奇博尔德·麦克利什写下了这样的篇章:

"在永恒的宁静中,那渺小、斑斓、美丽的地球在浮动。要真正地观望地球,就得把我们自己都看作是地球的乘客,看作是一群兄弟,他们共处于漫漫的、寒冷的宇宙中,仰赖着光明的挚爱——这群兄弟懂得,而今他们是真正的兄弟。"

在那个比技术胜利更有意义的时刻,人们把思绪转向了家乡和人类——他们从那个遥远的视角中发现,地球上人类的命运是不能开的;他们告诉我们,不管我们在宇宙中走得多远,我们的命运不是在别的星球上,而是在地球上,在我们自己手中,在我们的心头。

我们已经度过了一个反映美国精神的漫漫长夜。可是,当我们瞥见黎明前的第一缕曙光,切莫诅咒那尚未消散的黑暗。让我们迎接光明吧。

我们的命运所赐予的不是绝望的苦酒,而是机会的美餐。因此,让我们不是充满恐惧,而是满怀喜悦地去抓住这个机会吧——"地球的乘客们",让我们以坚定的信念,朝着稳定的目标,在提防着危险中前进吧!我们对上帝的意志和人类的希望充满了信心,这将使我们持之以恒。

Jimmy Carter
吉米·卡特(1924-)
39th President of the United States (1977-1981)

吉米·卡特:美国第39任总统(1977—1981),民主党人。作为美国独立后跨入第三个百年的第一位总统,他在外交上较有建树,首创"人权"外交。他曾多次访华,2002年获诺贝尔和平奖。

Jimmy Carter
吉米·卡特(1924-)
39th President of the United States (1977-1981)
Political Party: Democratic

Unchanging Principles
不变的原则

For myself and for our Nation, I want to thank my predecessor for all he has done to heal our land.

In this outward and physical ceremony we attest once again to the inner and spiritual strength of our Nation. As my high school teacher, Miss Julia Coleman, used to say: "We must adjust to changing times and still hold to unchanging principles."

Here before me is the Bible used in the inauguration of

我谨代表我个人和我们的国家,向前任总统为治愈我们国家所做的一切努力表示感谢。

值此公开的和有形的庆典之际,我们再次证明了我们国家内在的和无形的精神力量。正如我的高中教师朱莉娅·科尔曼女士经常说的:"我们必须适应变化的时代,同时必须坚持恒定不变的原则。"

我的面前是一本1789年

our first President, in 1789, and I have just taken the oath of office on the Bible my mother gave me a few years ago, opened to a timeless admonition from the ancient prophet Micah:

"He hath showed thee, O man, what is good; and what doth the Lord require of thee, but to do justly, and to love mercy, and to walk humbly with thy God." (Micah 6: 8)

This inauguration ceremony marks a new beginning, a new dedication within our Government, and a new spirit among us all. A President may sense and proclaim that new spirit, but only a people can provide it.

Two centuries ago our Nation's birth was a milestone in the long quest for freedom, but the bold and brilliant dream which excited the founders of this Nation still awaits its consummation. I have no new dream to set forth today, but rather urge a fresh faith in the old dream.

Ours was the first society openly to define itself in terms of both spirituality and of human liberty. It is that unique self-definition which has given us an exceptional appeal, but it also imposes on us a special obligation, to take on those moral duties which, when assumed, seem invariably to be in our own best interests.

You have given me a great responsibility—to stay close to you, to be worthy of you, and to exemplify what you are. Let us create together a new national spirit of unity and trust. Your strength can compensate for my weakness, and

我国首任总统就职时使用过的《圣经》，我刚才宣誓就职时用的是几年前母亲给我的那本《圣经》，这本《圣经》打开的地方写着古代先知弥迦所留下的一则永恒的训诫：

"世人啊，耶和华已指示你何为善。他向你所要的是什么呢？只要你行公义、好怜悯、存谦卑的心。与你的神同行。"

今天的就职典礼标志着一个新开端，标志着政府的新奉献，标志着全体人民的新精神。总统可以感悟并宣扬这种新精神，但唯有人民才能赋予这种精神。

两个世纪以前，我们国家的诞生是长期寻求自由的一个里程碑。但是，激励了建国先贤们的这个勇敢而光辉的理想，依然有待于完成。今天我无意提出新的理想，而是要在原有的理想中提出一种新的信念。

我们的社会是第一个依据精神价值和人类自由来公开阐明自己的社会。正是这种独特的自我定义使我们具有特殊的号召力——但同时也赋予我们特殊的义务——道德义务，这种义务一旦承担起来，似乎总是符合我们的最大利益。

你们已给予我一项重大责任——同你们紧密站在一起，不负众望，作出表率。让我们共同创造一种新的、团结

Jimmy Carter

吉米·卡特(1924-)

39th President of the United States (1977-1981)

your wisdom can help to minimize my mistakes.

Let us learn together and laugh together and work together and pray together, confident that in the end we will triumph together in the right.

The American dream endures. We must once again have full faith in our country—and in one another. I believe America can be better. We can be even stronger than before.

Let our recent mistakes bring a resurgent commitment to the basic principles of our Nation, for we know that if we despise our own government we have no future. We recall in special times when we have stood briefly, but magnificently, united. In those times no prize was beyond our grasp.

But we cannot dwell upon remembered glory. We cannot afford to drift. We reject the prospect of failure or mediocrity or an inferior quality of life for any person.

Our Government must at the same time be both competent and compassionate.

We have already found a high degree of personal liberty, and we are now struggling to enhance equality of opportunity. Our commitment to human rights must be absolute, our laws fair, our natural beauty preserved; the powerful must not persecute the weak, and human dignity must be enhanced.

We have learned that "more" is not necessarily

和信任的国家精神。你们的力量能弥补我的弱点,你们的智慧能帮助我尽量少犯错误。

让我们一起学习,一起欢笑,一起工作,一起祈祷,坚信站在正义这边的我们终将共同获胜。

美国的理想持久不衰。我们必须再次对我们的国家和对我们彼此充满信心。我相信美国能变得更美好。我们能比过去任何时候更强大。

让我们检讨最近犯的错误,以便对我国的基本原则重新承担起义务,因为我们知道,如果轻视自己的政府,我们就没有任何前途。我们记得,我们在一些特殊的时期有过短暂而意义深远的团结;在那个时候,我们取得了无数珍贵的成就。

但是,我们不能沉溺于昔日的荣耀。我们不能随波逐流,我们不要那种失败的、碌碌无为的,或者使任何人过着一种低质量生活的远景。

我们的政府既要称职,又要富于同情心。

我们已经达到了高度的个人自由,我们现在正在为促进机会均等而斗争。我们为维护人权所作的承诺必须是绝对的,我们的法律必须是公正的,我们天身的美德必须保持;强者绝不可以欺凌弱者,人的尊严必须提高。

我们懂得,"更多"未必

"better", that even our great Nation has its recognized limits, and that we can neither answer all questions nor solve all problems. We cannot afford to do everything, nor can we afford to lack boldness as we meet the future. So, together, in a spirit of individual sacrifice for the common good, we must simply do our best.

Our Nation can be strong abroad only if it is strong at home. And we know that the best way to enhance freedom in other lands is to demonstrate here that our democratic system is worthy of emulation.

To be true to ourselves, we must be true to others. We will not behave in foreign places so as to violate our rules and standards here at home, for we know that the trust which our Nation earns is essential to our strength.

The world itself is now dominated by a new spirit. Peoples more numerous and more politically aware are craving and now demanding their place in the sun—not just for the benefit of their own physical condition, but for basic human rights.

The passion for freedom is on the rise. Tapping this new spirit, there can be no nobler nor more ambitious task for America to undertake on this day of a new beginning than to help shape a just and peaceful world that is truly humane.

We are a strong nation, and we will maintain strength so sufficient that it need not be proven in combat—a quiet strength based not merely on the size of an arsenal, but on

就是"更好"。即便我们伟大的国家也有公认的局限性,我们既回答不了也解决不了所有的问题。我们不能包揽一切,但我们在面对未来时不能缺乏勇气。因此,让我们一起怀着为了共同利益而作出个人牺牲的精神,务必尽力而为之。

我们的国家只有自强,才能对外称强。我们还懂得,要增进其他国家的自由,最好的方式,就是在这里证实我们的民主制度是值得仿效的。

要对自己真诚,我们必须对别人真诚。我们不会到别国领土上去违反我们国内奉行的规范与准则,因为,我们懂得,我们国家所赢得的信任,对加强我国的力量是不可或缺的。

现在,世界本身正受着一种新的精神支配。那些人数较多、在政治上日益觉醒的民族,正渴望并要求在阳光下拥有一席之地——不只是为了他们自身的物质条件,而且也是为了获得基本的人权。

人们对自由的渴望正在高涨,为了发扬这种新精神,美国在这个新开始的日子里所要从事的崇高而雄心勃勃的使命,莫过于帮助塑造一个公正、和平、真正合乎人道主义的世界。

我们的国家是一个强大的国家,我们要保持无比坚强的力量。这种力量无需在战

Jimmy Carter
吉米·卡特(1924-   )
39th President of the United States (1977-1981)

the nobility of ideas.

We will be ever vigilant and never vulnerable, and we will fight our wars against poverty, ignorance, and injustice—for those are the enemies against which our forces can be honorably marshaled.

We are a purely idealistic Nation, but let no one confuse our idealism with weakness.

Because we are free we can never be indifferent to the fate of freedom elsewhere. Our moral sense dictates a clearcut preference for these societies which share with us an abiding respect for individual human rights. We do not seek to intimidate, but it is clear that a world which others can dominate with impunity would be inhospitable to decency and a threat to the well-being of all people.

The world is still engaged in a massive armaments race designed to ensure continuing equivalent strength among potential adversaries. We pledge perseverance and wisdom in our efforts to limit the world's armaments to those necessary for each nation's own domestic safety. And we will move this year a step toward ultimate goal—the elimination of all nuclear weapons from this Earth. We urge all other people to join us, for success can mean life instead of death.

争中加以证实——一种不仅仅是建立在武器库规模的基础之上,也是建立在崇高思想的基础之上的无声的力量。

我们要时刻保持警惕,毫不松懈,我们要向贫困、无知和非正义开战,因为这些都是我们的敌人,我们可以光荣地聚集我们的力量来战斗。

我们的国家是一个怀有无限自豪的理想主义国家,但是我们不允许别人把我们的理想主义误认为是软弱。

因为我们是自由的,所以我们绝不能对其他地方的自由命运漠不关心。我们的道德观使我们明显地偏爱那些同我们一样一贯尊重个人人权的社会。我们并不试图恫吓他人,可是,一个由他人可以肆无忌惮地加以支配的世界,不仅有悖情理,而且也是对全人类幸福的一种威胁,这是显而易见的。

这个世界依然有人从事大规模的军备竞赛,目的是确保与潜在的对手继续维持均势。我们保证以毅力与智慧,努力使世界的军备局限于各个国家确保其安全所需的范围。此外,今年,我们还将向我们的最终目标——在地球上销毁一切核武器——迈出一步。我们迫切要求各国人民加入我们的行列,因为此举的成功意味着生存而不是死亡。

Within us, the people of the United States, there is evident a serious and purposeful rekindling of confidence. And I join in the hope that when my time as your President has ended, people might say this about our Nation:

—**that** we had remembered the words of Micah and renewed our search for humility, mercy, and justice;

—**that** we had torn down the barriers that separated those of different race and region and religion, and where there had been mistrust, built unity, with a respect for diversity;

—**that** we had found productive work for those able to perform it;

—**that** we had strengthened the American family, which is the basis of our society;

—**that** we had ensured respect for the law, and equal treatment under the law, for the weak and the powerful, for the rich and the poor;

—**and** that we had enabled our people to be proud of their own Government once again.

I would hope that the nations of the world might say that we had built a lasting peace, built not on weapons of war but on international policies which reflect our own most precious values.

These are not just my goals, and they will not be my accomplishments, but the affirmation of our Nation's continuing moral strength and our belief in an undiminished, ever-expanding American dream.

在我们合众国人民之中，显然存在一种认真而坚定地恢复信心的倾向。我同大家一样希望，在我担任总统届满时，人们会这样论及我们的国家：

我们记得弥迦的话，我们重新寻求谦卑、怜悯和公义；

我们已经隔开了不同种族、不同地区和不同信仰的障碍拆除，我们以尊重多样化的方式使缺乏信任的地方建立起团结；

我们已经为能够从事工作的人们找到了工作；

我们已经巩固了美国的家庭，这是我们的社会基础；

我们已经确保尊重法律，无论弱者还是强者，富人还是穷人，在法律面前一律平等；

我们已使人民重新对自己的政府感到骄傲。

我希望世界各国都会这样说：我们不是依靠武器而是依靠反映我们最珍视的价值观的国际政策，建立起持久的和平。

这些不仅仅是我个人的目标，它们也将不是我个人的成就，而是对我国持续不断的道德力量的一种肯定，也是对我们从未减弱的、不断发展的美国理想的一种肯定。

Ronald Reagan
罗纳德·里根(1911-2004)
40th President of the United States (1981-1989)

罗纳德·里根:美国第40任总统(1981—1989),美国历史上最长寿(享年93岁)、就任时最年迈(差16天70岁)的总统。他当过演员,善于辞令,上台后实行减税以振兴经济,增加军费以"重振国威"。本篇严厉抨击了民主党奉行的"大政府"信条。

Ronald Reagan
罗纳德·里根(1911-2004)
40th President of the United States (1981-1989)
Political Party: Republican

We the People
我们是美国人

Senator Hatfield, Mr. Chief Justice, Mr. President, Vice President Bush, Vice President Mondale, Senator Baker, Speaker O'Neill, Reverend Moomaw, and my fellow citizens:

To a few of us here today, this is a solemn and most momentous occasion; and yet, in the history of our Nation, it is a commonplace occurrence. The orderly transfer of authority as called for in the Constitution routinely takes place as it has for almost two centuries and few of us stop to think how unique we really are. In the eyes of many in the

海特菲尔德议员、法官先生、总统先生、副总统布什、蒙代尔先生、议员贝克先生、发言人奥尼尔先生、尊敬的摩麦先生,以及广大支持我的美国同胞们:

对今天在场的少数几个人来说,这是一个庄严而极为隆重的时刻。可是,在我国历史上,这是件很普通的事情。《宪法》所规定的井然有序的权力移交已照例进行了将近两个世纪;我们当中很少有人

world, this every-4-year ceremony we accept as normal is nothing less than a miracle.

Mr. President, I want our fellow citizens to know how much you did to carry on this tradition. By your gracious cooperation in the transition process, you have shown a watching world that we are a united people pledged to maintaining a political system which guarantees individual liberty to a greater degree than any other, and I thank you and your people for all your help in maintaining the continuity which is the bulwark of our Republic.

The business of our nation goes forward. These United States are confronted with an economic affliction of great proportions. We suffer from the longest and one of the worst sustained inflations in our national history. It distorts our economic decisions, penalizes thrift, and crushes the struggling young and the fixed-income elderly alike. It threatens to shatter the lives of millions of our people.

Idle industries have cast workers into unemployment, causing human misery and personal indignity. Those who do work are denied a fair return for their labor by a tax system which penalizes successful achievement and keeps us from maintaining full productivity.

But great as our tax burden is, it has not kept pace with public spending. For decades, we have piled deficit upon deficit, mortgaging our future and our children's future for the temporary convenience of the present. To continue this long trend is to guarantee tremendous social,

会去想,我们究竟有什么独特之处。但在世界上许多人看来,我们视为平常的四年一度的典礼,简直是一个奇迹。

总统先生,我想让公民们知道,您为坚持这一传统作了多大努力。您在移交过程中的谦和合作,向正在注视我们的世界表明:我们是一个团结的民族,正致力于维护一种比任何其他制度更能确保个人自由的政治制度,我感谢您和您的部下为维持作为我们共和政体支柱的连续性所给予的全部协助。

我们国家的事业在继续前进。合众国正面临巨大的经济困难。我们遭遇到我国历史上历时最长、最严重之一的通货膨胀。它扰乱着我们的经济决策,打击着节俭的风气,压迫着正在挣扎谋生的青年人和收入固定的中年人,威胁着要摧毁我国千百万人民的生计。

停滞的工业使工人失业、蒙受痛苦并失去了个人尊严。即使那些有工作的人,也因税收制度的缘故而得不到公正的劳动报酬,因为这种税收制度使我们无法在事业上取得成就,使我们无法保持充分的生产力。

尽管我们的纳税负担相当沉重,但还是跟不上公共开支的增长。数十年来,我们的赤字额屡屡上升,我们为图目前一时之便,把自己和子孙的

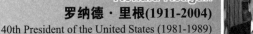

Ronald Reagan
罗纳德·里根(1911-2004)
40th President of the United States (1981-1989)

cultural, political, and economic upheavals.

You and I, as individuals, can, by borrowing, live beyond our means, but for only a limited period of time. Why, then, should we think that collectively, as a nation, we are not bound by that same limitation?

We must act today in order to preserve tomorrow. And let there be no misunderstanding—we are going to begin to act, beginning today.

The economic ills we suffer have come upon us over several decades. They will not go away in days, weeks, or months, but they will go away. They will go away because we, as Americans, have the capacity now, as we have had in the past, to do whatever needs to be done to preserve this last and greatest bastion of freedom.

In this present crisis, government is not the solution to our problem. Government is the problem.

From time to time, we have been tempted to believe that society has become too complex to be managed by self-rule, that government by an elite group is superior to government for, by, and of the people. But if no one among us is capable of governing himself, then who among us has the capacity to govern someone else? All of us together, in and out of government, must bear the burden. The solutions we seek must be equitable, with no one group singled out to pay a higher price.

前途抵押出去了。这一趋势如果长此以往，必然引起社会、文化、政治和经济等方面的大动荡。

作为个人，你们和我可以靠借贷过一种入不敷出的生活，然而只能维持一段有限的时期。我们怎么可以认为，作为一个国家整体，我们就不应受到同样的约束呢？

为了保住明天，我们今天就必须行动起来。大家都要明白无误地懂得——我们从今天起就要采取行动。

我们深受其害的经济弊病，几十年来一直袭击着我们。这些弊病不会在几天、几星期或几个月内消失，但它们终将消失。它们之所以终将消失，是因为我们作为现在的美国人，一如既往地有能力去完成需要完成的事情，以保存这个最后而又最伟大的自由堡垒。

在当前这场危机中，政府的管理不能解决我们面临的问题。政府的管理就是问题所在。

我们时常误以为，社会已经越来越复杂，已经不可能凭借自治方式加以管理，而一个由杰出人物组成的政府要比民享、民治、民有的政府高明。可是，假如我们之中谁也管理不了自己，那么，我们之中谁还能去管理他人呢？我们大家——不论政府官员还是平民百姓——必须共同肩负起这个责任，我们谋求的解决办法必须是公平的，不要使任何一个群体付出较高的代价。

We hear much of special interest groups. Our concern must be for a special interest group that has been too long neglected. It knows no sectional boundaries or ethnic and racial divisions, and it crosses political party lines. It is made up of men and women who raise our food, patrol our streets, man our mines and our factories, teach our children, keep our homes, and heal us when we are sick— professionals, industrialists, shopkeepers, clerks, cabbies, and truck drivers. They are, in short, "We the people," this breed called Americans.

Well, this administration's objective will be a healthy, vigorous, growing economy that provides equal opportunity for all Americans, with no barriers born of bigotry or discrimination. Putting America back to work means putting all Americans back to work. Ending inflation means freeing all Americans from the terror of runaway living costs. All must share in the productive work of this "new beginning" and all must share in the bounty of a revived economy. With the idealism and fair play which are the core of our system and our strength, we can have a strong and prosperous America at peace with itself and the world.

So, as we begin, let us take inventory. We are a nation that has a government—not the other way around. And this makes us special among the nations of the Earth. Our Government has no power except that granted it by the people. It is time to check and reverse the growth of government which shows signs of having grown beyond the

我们听到许多关于对特殊利益集团的谈论。我们必须关心一个被忽视了很久的特殊利益集团。这个集团没有区域之分,没有人种之分,没有民族之分,没有政党之分,这个集团由许许多多的男人与女人组成,他们生产粮食,巡逻街头,管理厂矿,教育儿童,照料家务和治疗疾病。他们是专业人员、实业家、店主、职员、出租汽车司机和货车驾驶员。简而言之,他们就是"我们这个民族"——这个称之为美国人的民族。

本届政府的目标是必须建立一种健全的、生气勃勃的并不断发展的经济,为全体美国人民提供一种不因偏执或歧视而造成障碍的平等机会。让美国重新开始工作,意味着让全体美国人重新开始工作。结束通货膨胀,意味着让全体美国人从失控的生活费用所造成的恐惧中解脱出来。人人都应分担"新开端"的富有成效的工作,人人都应分享经济复苏的硕果。我国制度和力量的核心是理想主义和公正态度,有了这些,我们就能建立起强大、繁荣、国内稳定并同全世界和平相处的美国。

因此,在我们开始之际,让我们看看实际情况。我们是一个拥有政府的国家——而不是一个拥有国家的政府。这一点使我们在世界各国中独树一帜,我们的政府除了人

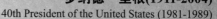

Ronald Reagan
罗纳德·里根(1911-2004)
40th President of the United States (1981-1989)

consent of the governed.

It is my intention to curb the size and influence of the Federal establishment and to demand recognition of the distinction between the powers granted to the Federal Government and those reserved to the States or to the people. All of us need to be reminded that the Federal Government did not create the States; the States created the Federal Government.

Now, so there will be no misunderstanding, it is not my intention to do away with government. It is, rather, to make it work—work with us, not over us; to stand by our side, not ride on our back. Government can and must provide opportunity, not smother it; foster productivity, not stifle it.

If we look to the answer as to why, for so many years, we achieved so much, prospered as no other people on Earth, it was because here, in this land, we unleashed the energy and individual genius of man to a greater extent than has ever been done before. Freedom and the dignity of the individual have been more available and assured here than in any other place on Earth. The price for this freedom at times has been high, but we have never been unwilling to pay that price.

It is no coincidence that our present troubles parallel and are proportionate to the intervention and intrusion in our lives that result from unnecessary and excessive growth of government.

民授予的权力,没有任何别的权力。目前,政府权力的膨胀已显示出超过被统治者同意的迹象,审视并扭转这种状况的时候到了。

我打算压缩联邦机构的规模和影响力,并要求大家承认联邦政府被授予的权力同各州或人民保留的权利这两者之间的区别。我们大家都需要提醒:不是联邦政府创立了各州,而是各州创立了联邦政府。

因此,请不要误会,我的意思不是要取消政府,而是要它发挥作用——同我们一起合作,而不是凌驾于我们之上;同我们并肩而立,而不是骑在我们的背上。政府能够而且必须提供机会,而不是扼杀机会,它能够而且必须促进生产力,而不是抑制生产力。

如果我们要探究这么多年来我们为什么能取得这么大成就,并获得了世界上任何一个民族未曾获得的繁荣昌盛,其原因是在这片土地上,我们使人类的能力和个人的才智得到了前所未有的发挥。在这里,个人所享有并得以确保的自由和尊严超过了世界上任何其他地方。为这种自由所付出的代价有时相当高昂,但我们从来没有不愿意付出这代价。

我们目前的困难,与政府机构因为不必要的过度膨胀而干预、侵扰我们的生活同步增加,这绝不是偶然的巧合。

It is time for us to realize that we are too great a nation to limit ourselves to small dreams. We are not, as some would have us believe, doomed to an inevitable decline. I do not believe in a fate that will fall on us no matter what we do. I do believe in a fate that will fall on us if we do nothing.

So, with all the creative energy at our command, let us begin an era of national renewal. Let us renew our determination, our courage, and our strength. And let us renew our faith and our hope.

We have every right to dream heroic dreams. Those who say that we are in a time when there are no heroes just don't know where to look. You can see heroes every day going in and out of factory gates. Others, a handful in number, produce enough food to feed all of us and then the world beyond. You meet heroes across a counter—and they are on both sides of that counter. There are entrepreneurs with faith in themselves and faith in an idea who create new jobs, new wealth and opportunity. They are individuals and families whose taxes support the Government and whose voluntary gifts support church, charity, culture, art, and education. Their patriotism is quiet but deep. Their values sustain our national life.

I have used the words "they" and "their" in speaking of these heroes. I could say "you" and "your" because I am addressing the heroes of whom I speak—you, the citizens

我们是一个泱泱大国,不能自囿于小小的梦想,现在正是认识到这一点的时候。我们并非注定走向衰落,尽管有些人想让我们相信这一点。我不相信,无论我们做些什么,我们都将命该如此,但我相信,如果我们什么也不做,我们将的确命该如此。

为此,让我们以掌握的一切创造力来开创一个国家复兴的时代吧。让我们重新拿出决心、勇气和力量,让我们重新建立起我们的信念和希望吧。

我们完全有权去做英雄式的梦。有些人说我们正处于没有英雄的时代,那是因为他不知道朝哪里看的缘故。你们每天都可以看到英雄们从工厂进进出出。还有一些英雄,尽管人数很少,却种植了足够满足我国人民,以及世界上其他地方的人们的粮食。你们在柜台前能遇见英雄。他们就站在柜台两边。那些创造新工作、新财富和新机会的企业家们是英雄,他们对自己以及对理想有信心。那些纳税以支持政府,自愿捐献以资助教会、慈善团体、文化、艺术和教育的个人与家庭也都是英雄。他们的爱国主义精神质朴无华却又无限情深。他们的价值观滋养着我们国家的生命。

到现在为止,我一直使用"他们"和"他们的"这两个字眼来谈论这些英雄。我也可

Ronald Reagan

罗纳德·里根(1911-2004)
40th President of the United States (1981-1989)

of this blessed land. Your dreams, your hopes, your goals are going to be the dreams, the hopes, and the goals of this administration, so help me God.

We shall reflect the compassion that is so much a part of your makeup. How can we love our country and not love our countrymen, and loving them, reach out a hand when they fall, heal them when they are sick, and provide opportunities to make them self-sufficient so they will be equal in fact and not just in theory?

Can we solve the problems confronting us? Well, the answer is an unequivocal and emphatic "yes". To paraphrase Winston Churchill, I did not take the oath I have just taken with the intention of presiding over the dissolution of the world's strongest economy.

In the days ahead I will propose removing the roadblocks that have slowed our economy and reduced productivity. Steps will be taken aimed at restoring the balance between the various levels of government. Progress may be slow—measured in inches and feet, not miles—but we will progress. Is it time to reawaken this industrial giant, to get government back within its means, and to lighten our punitive tax burden? And these will be our first priorities, and on these principles, there will be no compromise.

On the eve of our struggle for independence a man who

以说"你们"和"你们的",因为我正在向我所提及的英雄们说话——你们,这块上帝赐福的土地上的公民们。你们的梦想、希望和目标,将成为本届政府的梦想、希望和目标,愿上帝帮助我。

本届政府将体现出在你们的禀性中占很大比重的同情心。我们怎么能爱我们的国家而又不爱我们的同胞呢?我们热爱我们的同胞,在他们跌倒时向他们伸出援助之手,在他们生病受苦时对他们进行治疗,并且要使他们有机会自给自足,使他们能在事实上而不只是在理论上享有平等。

我们能否解决我们面临的问题呢?回答是斩钉截铁、洪亮有力的"能"字。用温斯顿·丘吉尔的话来说,我刚才庄严地宣誓,绝不是为了看到这个世界上最强大的经济在我的主持下土崩瓦解。

在今后的日子里,我要建议搬开那些阻碍经济发展和导致生产力下降的拦路石。我将采取步骤来恢复各级政府之间的平衡。进展可能是缓慢的——不积跬步,无以至千里——但我们一定会前进。难道现在不正是使这个工业大国重新复苏、使政府归本还原、减轻惩罚性的税收负担的时候吗?这些问题将是我们的当务之急,对这些原则问题,没有任何妥协的余地。

在我们为争取独立而战斗

might have been one of the greatest among the Founding Fathers, Dr. Joseph Warren, President of the Massachusetts Congress, said to his fellow Americans, "Our country is in danger, but not to be despaired of.... On you depend the fortunes of America. You are to decide the important questions upon which rests the happiness and the liberty of millions yet unborn. Act worthy of yourselves."

Well, I believe we, the Americans of today, are ready to act worthy of ourselves, ready to do what must be done to ensure happiness and liberty for ourselves, our children and our children's children.

And as we renew ourselves here in our own land, we will be seen as having greater strength throughout the world. We will again be the exemplar of freedom and a beacon of hope for those who do not now have freedom.

To those neighbors and allies who share our freedom, we will strengthen our historic ties and assure them of our support and firm commitment. We will match loyalty with loyalty. We will strive for mutually beneficial relations. We will not use our friendship to impose on their sovereignty, for our own sovereignty is not for sale.

As for the enemies of freedom, those who are potential adversaries, they will be reminded that peace is the highest aspiration of the American people. We will negotiate for it, sacrifice for it; we will not surrender for it—now or ever.

的前夕，马萨诸塞州议会主席约瑟夫·沃伦博士（他差一点就成为我国的开国元勋之一）曾对他的美国同胞们说："我国正处在危急之中，但不要对它失望……美国的命运取决于你们。关系到尚未出世的千百万人的幸福和自由的重大问题将由你们来决定。你们的行动要无愧于你们自己。"

我相信，我们这些当代美国人正准备采取无愧于我们自己的行动，准备完成必须完成的使命，以保证我们自己和我们子孙后代的幸福和自由。

随着我们在自己的这片土地上除旧布新，全世界必将认为我们的实力更为强大。对于那些现在尚未获得自由的人来说，我们必将再度成为自由的楷模和希望的灯塔。

至于那些与我们具有共同自由理想的邻国和盟邦，我们将加强彼此之间具有历史意义的联系，并保证我们对他们的支持与坚定的承诺。我们将坦诚相见。我们将为建立互惠的关系而努力。我们绝不会利用友谊去骗取他国的主权，因为我们自己的主权也是不能出卖的。

至于自由的敌人，那些潜在的对手，我们要提醒他们，和平是美国人民最崇高的愿望。我们将为争取和平而谈判，为争取和平而作出牺牲；但我们永远不会为了和平而投降——现在不会，将来也永远不会。

Ronald Reagan
罗纳德·里根(1911-2004)
40th President of the United States (1981-1989)

Our forbearance should never be misunderstood. Our reluctance for conflict should not be misjudged as a failure of will. When action is required to preserve our national security, we will act. We will maintain sufficient strength to prevail if need be, knowing that if we do so we have the best chance of never having to use that strength.

Above all, we must realize that no arsenal, or no weapon in the arsenals of the world, is so formidable as the will and moral courage of free men and women. It is a weapon our adversaries in today's world do not have. It is a weapon that we as Americans do have. Let that be understood by those who practice terrorism and prey upon their neighbors.

I am told that tens of thousands of prayer meetings are being held on this day, and for that I am deeply grateful. We are a nation under God, and I believe God intended for us to be free. It would be fitting and good, I think, if on each Inauguration Day in future years it should be declared a day of prayer.

This is the first time in history that this ceremony has been held, as you have been told, on this West Front of the Capitol. Standing here, one faces a magnificent vista, opening up on this city's special beauty and history. At the end of this open mall are those shrines to the giants on whose shoulders we stand.

Directly in front of me, the monument to a monumental man: George Washington, Father of our country. A man of humility who came to greatness reluctantly.

对我们的忍耐绝不应误解。我们不愿发生冲突不应被误解为意志不坚。一旦需要我们采取行动以保卫我国的安全,我们一定会采取行动。如有必要,我们将保持足够的实力去争取优势,因为我们知道,如果我们这样做,我们就永远有不必动用这支力量的最大可能。

最重要的是,我们必须认识到,世界上任何武器库或任何武器的威力都比不上自由人的意志及其维护道德的勇气。这是目前世界上我们的对手所没有的武器。我们美国人所掌握的正是这样一种武器。让那些从事恐怖活动并劫掠邻国的人理解这一点。

我听说,今天正在举行数万个祷告会,对此我表示由衷的感谢。我们是上帝保佑下的国家,我相信上帝希望我们永享自由。我认为,如果今后每一次就职典礼日都成为祷告日,那将是件合情合理的好事。

你们已经听说,这次典礼在国会大厦西侧举行,这在我国历史上尚属首次。我们站在此地,面对着一幅壮丽的景色,本市特殊的美景和历史古迹尽收眼底。在这条开阔大道的尽头,坐落着为美国奠定基础的伟人纪念堂。

我的正前方矗立着一位不朽人物的纪念碑。他就是我们的国父乔治·华盛顿,一

He led America out of revolutionary victory into infant nationhood. Off to one side, the stately memorial to Thomas Jefferson. The Declaration of Independence flames with his eloquence.

And then beyond the Reflecting Pool the dignified columns of the Lincoln Memorial. Whoever would understand in his heart the meaning of America will find it in the life of Abraham Lincoln.

Beyond those monuments to heroism is the Potomac River, and on the far shore the sloping hills of Arlington National Cemetery with its row on row of simple white markers bearing crosses or Stars of David. They add up to only a tiny fraction of the price that has been paid for our freedom.

Each one of those markers is a monument to the kinds of hero I spoke of earlier. Their lives ended in places called Belleau Wood, The Argonne, Omaha Beach, Salerno and halfway around the world on Guadalcanal, Tarawa, Pork Chop Hill, the Chosin Reservoir, and in a hundred rice paddies and jungles of a place called Vietnam.

Under one such marker lies a young man—Martin Treptow—who left his job in a small town barber shop in 1917 to go to France with the famed Rainbow Division. There, on the western front, he was killed trying to carry a message between battalions under heavy artillery fire.

We are told that on his body was found a diary. On the flyleaf under the heading, "My Pledge," he had written these words: "America must win this war. Therefore, I will work, I will save, I will sacrifice, I will

位不愿接受殊荣的谦谦君子。他领导美国取得革命胜利,进入建国时期。这座纪念碑旁边是雄伟的托马斯·杰斐逊纪念馆。《独立宣言》闪烁着他那激扬的文思。

穿过倒映池是庄严的圆柱形林肯纪念堂。凡想透彻理解美国真谛的人,都能在亚伯拉罕·林肯的一生中找到答案。

英雄纪念碑和纪念堂的后面是波托马克河,河对岸的坡地就是阿林顿国家公墓,那儿竖立着一排排镶刻着十字架或大卫星的素白色墓碑。这些仅仅是为我们的自由所付出的代价中的一小部分。

公墓中的每一座墓碑都是为着纪念我在前面所提到过的那类英雄。他们在贝洛丛林、阿尔贡、奥马哈海滩、萨莱诺港以及在相隔半个地球之遥的瓜达卡纳尔岛、塔拉瓦岛、猪排山、乔辛水库和越南那个地方的无数水稻田和丛林中献出了生命。

其中,一块墓碑下安息着一位名叫马丁·特雷普托的青年,他于1917年放弃了一个在小镇理发店的工作,随著名的"彩虹师"开赴法国。就在西线,他冒着密集的炮火为部队传递情报,结果不幸阵亡。

据说在他的遗体上发现了一本日记。他在衬页上以"我的誓言"为题写下了这样一些话:"美国必须赢得这场

Ronald Reagan
罗纳德·里根(1911-2004)
40th President of the United States (1981-1989)

endure, I will fight cheerfully and do my utmost, as if the issue of the whole struggle depended on me alone."

The crisis we are facing today does not require of us the kind of sacrifice that Martin Treptow and so many thousands of others were called upon to make. It does require, however, our best effort, and our willingness to believe in ourselves and to believe in our capacity to perform great deeds; to believe that together, with God's help, we can and will resolve the problems which now confront us.

And, after all, why shouldn't we believe that? We are Americans.

God bless you, and thank you.

战争。因此,我一定要像整个战争的胜败全靠我一个人那样去工作、去拯救、去牺牲、去经受考验、去欣然战斗,去竭尽全力。"

我们今天面临的危机并不需要我们像马丁·特雷普托和其他成千上万的人那样去作出牺牲。然而,它的确要求我们尽最大努力,要求我们愿意相信自己,相信我们具有做出丰功伟绩的能力,它要求我们相信,我们只要齐心协力,并在上帝的帮助下,就能够而且必将解决面临的各种问题。

我们为什么不应相信这些呢?我们毕竟都是美国人。

愿上帝保佑你们,谢谢大家。

乔治·H·W·布什：又称老布什，美国第41任总统(1989—1993)。他上任前一直作为里根的副手执掌白宫，有丰富的从政经验和外交经验。他还曾任美国驻北京联络处主任。在他的任期内，苏联解体、冷战时代结束、海湾战争爆发。本篇描绘了他心目中的执政蓝图。

George H. W. Bush
乔治·H·W·布什(1924-　)
41st President of the United States (1989-1993)
Political Party: Republican

Unity, Diversity, and Generosity
团结、多样、包容

Mr. Chief Justice, Mr. President, Vice President Quayle, Senator Mitchell, Speaker Wright, Senator Dole, Congressman Michel, and fellow citizens, neighbors, and friends:

There is a man here who has earned a lasting place in our hearts and in our history. President Reagan, on behalf of our Nation, I thank you for the wonderful things that you have done for America.

I have just repeated word for word the oath taken by George Washington 200 years ago, and the Bible on which I placed my hand is the Bible on which he placed his. It is

大法官先生，总统先生，奎尔副总统，米切尔参议员，发言人赖特先生，多尔参议员，麦克尔众议员，全体同胞们，友邻和朋友们：

这里有一个人在我们心中和我国历史上都赢得了永恒的地位。里根总统，我代表我们的民族，感谢您为美国作出了卓越的贡献。

我刚才逐字逐句地复述了乔治·华盛顿在200年前宣读过的誓言，我用手按过的

George H. W. Bush

乔治·H.W. 布什(1924-)
41st President of the United States (1989-1993)

right that the memory of Washington be with us today, not only because this is our Bicentennial Inauguration, but because Washington remains the Father of our Country. And he would, I think, be gladdened by this day; for today is the concrete expression of a stunning fact: our continuity these 200 years since our government began.

We meet on democracy's front porch, a good place to talk as neighbors and as friends. For this is a day when our nation is made whole, when our differences, for a moment, are suspended.

And my first act as President is a prayer. I ask you to bow your heads:

Heavenly Father, we bow our heads and thank You for Your love. Accept our thanks for the peace that yields this day and the shared faith that makes its continuance likely. Make us strong to do Your work, willing to heed and hear Your will, and write on our hearts these words: "Use power to help people." For we are given power not to advance our own purposes, nor to make a great show in the world, nor a name. There is but one just use of power, and it is to serve people. Help us to remember it, Lord. Amen.

I come before you and assume the Presidency at a moment rich with promise. We live in a peaceful, prosperous time, but we can make it better. For a new breeze is blowing, and a world refreshed by freedom seems

《圣经》,就是他按过的那一本。我们今天怀念华盛顿是恰当的,不仅因为这是我们在建国两百周年举行的总统就职典礼,而且因为华盛顿始终是我们的国父。我想,他会为这个日子感到高兴的。因为这个日子具体说明了一个惊人的事实:我们的政府自创建以来已经延续200年了。

我们相聚在象征着民主政治的正门门廊,这是我们作为邻居、作为朋友交谈的好地方,因为今天是我国成为一个整体的日子,是我们的分歧暂时中止的日子。

我作为总统要做的第一件事是进行祈祷——请大家低下头:

天父,我们垂首感谢您的爱。您赐给我们和平,使我们得有今天,您赐给我们共同的信念,使和平得以持久。请您使我们坚强起来以完成您的工作,使我们甘愿聆听和遵从您的旨意,并在我们心中写下这样的话:"运用权力帮助人民。"因为我们被授予权力不是为了实现个人意图,不是为了炫耀于世,也不是为了追逐名声。权力只有一个正当用途,那就是为人民办事。主啊,帮助我们铭记这一点吧。阿门。

我在一个充满希望的时刻来到你们面前就任总统。我们生活在和平、繁荣的时代,我们能够使它更加美好。

reborn; for in man's heart, if not in fact, the day of the dictator is over. The totalitarian era is passing, its old ideas blown away like leaves from an ancient, lifeless tree. A new breeze is blowing, and a nation refreshed by freedom stands ready to push on. There is new ground to be broken, and new action to be taken. There are times when the future seems thick as a fog; you sit and wait, hoping the mists will lift and reveal the right path. But this is a time when the future seems a door you can walk right through into a room called tomorrow.

Great nations of the world are moving toward democracy through the door to freedom. Men and women of the world move toward free markets through the door to prosperity. The people of the world agitate for free expression and free thought through the door to the moral and intellectual satisfactions that only liberty allows.

We know what works: Freedom works. We know what's right: Freedom is right. We know how to secure a more just and prosperous life for man on Earth: through free markets, free speech, free elections, and the exercise of free will unhampered by the state.

For the first time in this century, for the first time in perhaps all history, man does not have to invent a system by which to live. We don't have to talk late into the night

因为现在吹拂着一阵清新的和风，一个为自由所振奋的世界似乎已经重新降生；因为即使不是在事实上，也是在人们心里，独裁者称雄的日子已经过去。极权主义时代正在消逝，它那陈旧的观念就像一株衰老枯萎的树上的叶子已经被风吹走。一阵清新的和风正在吹拂——一个为自由所振奋的国家准备继续奋进。新的天地有待开辟，新的行动有待采取。有时候浓雾沉沉，前途迷茫；大家坐着等待，希望云开雾散，显露出正确的道路。但在目前这个时刻，未来宛如一扇大门，让你直接跨入明天的殿堂。

世界上的伟大国家正在走向民主——经过这道大门，走向自由。世界上的男男女女正在走向自由市场——经过这道大门，走向繁荣。世界各国人民正在宣扬言论自由和思想自由——经过这道大门，走向只有在自由时才能得到的道德上和理智上的满足。

我们知道什么能起作用：自由能起作用。我们知道什么是正确的：自由是正确的。我们知道如何为地球上的人类保障更合理、更富裕的生活：通过自由市场，自由言论，自由选举，和不受国家阻挠地行使自由意志。

本世纪第一次——也许是有史以来第一次——人类不必发明一种赖以生存的制

George H. W. Bush

乔治·H. W. 布什(1924-)
41st President of the United States (1989-1993)

about which form of government is better. We don't have to wrest justice from the kings. We only have to summon it from within ourselves. We must act on what we know. I take as my guide the hope of a saint: in crucial things, unity; in important things, diversity; in all things, generosity.

America today is a proud, free nation, decent and civil, a place we cannot help but love. We know in our hearts, not loudly and proudly, but as a simple fact, that this country has meaning beyond what we see, and that our strength is a force for good. But have we changed as a nation even in our time? Are we enthralled with material things, less appreciative of the nobility of work and sacrifice?

My friends, we are not the sum of our possessions. They are not the measure of our lives. In our hearts we know what matters. We cannot hope only to leave our children a bigger car, a bigger bank account. We must hope to give them a sense of what it means to be a loyal friend, a loving parent, a citizen who leaves his home, his neighborhood and town better than he found it. What do we want the men and women who work with us to say when we are no longer there? That we were more driven to succeed than anyone around us? Or that we stopped to ask if a sick child had gotten better, and stayed a moment there to trade a word of friendship?

度了。我们不必为哪种政体较好而讨论到深夜了。我们不必从国王手里夺取公正了——我们只需从自身内部唤起公正。我们必须按照自己所懂得的道理去行动。我把一位圣人的期望当作行动的指南：关键事情讲统一，重要事情讲变化，一切事情讲慷慨。

今日美国是一个自豪、自由之国，是一个礼仪之邦，我们由衷地热爱她。我们在心里知道——不需炫耀自傲，而是一个简单的事实——这个国家的含义超出了我们的目光所及，我们的力量是为善的力量。然而在当今时代，我们作为一个民族是否已经变了？我们是否迷恋于物质享受，因而不推崇高尚的工作和牺牲精神了？

朋友们，我们不是财富的总和，财富并不是衡量生活的标准。我们心里知道什么重要。我们不能只指望给孩子们留下更豪华的轿车和更多的存款。我们应该希望给予他们一种理念，让他们懂得，做一个忠诚的朋友和慈爱的父母意味着什么；在离开家庭、邻居和家乡时，使这些都变得更好又意味着什么。当我们离开共事过的男男女女，我们希望他们说些什么呢？是说我们比周围的人都渴望成功？还是说我们会把工作放一放，关心生病的孩子，愿意花时间和别人共叙友谊呢？

No President, no government, can teach us to remember what is best in what we are. But if the man you have chosen to lead this government can help make a difference; if he can celebrate the quieter, deeper successes that are made not of gold and silk, but of better hearts and finer souls; if he can do these things, then he must.

America is never wholly herself unless she is engaged in high moral principle. We as a people have such a purpose today. It is to make kinder the face of the Nation and gentler the face of the world. My friends, we have work to do. There are the homeless, lost and roaming. There are the children who have nothing, no love, no normalcy. There are those who cannot free themselves of enslavement to whatever addiction—drugs, welfare, the demoralization that rules the slums. There is crime to be conquered, the rough crime of the streets. There are young women to be helped who are about to become mothers of children they can't care for and might not love. They need our care, our guidance, and our education, though we bless them for choosing life.

The old solution, the old way, was to think that public money alone could end these problems. But we have learned that is not so. And in any case, our funds are low. We have a deficit to bring down. We have more will than wallet; but will is what we need. We will make the hard choices, looking at what we have and perhaps allocating it differently, making our decisions based on honest need and prudent safety. And then we will do the wisest thing of all:

没有哪一位总统,也没有哪一届政府,能够教导我们并让我们记住什么才是最优秀的品质。但是,如果你们选出的领导本届政府的那个人能够有助于创新;如果他可以颂扬不是用金银绸缎,而是用美好心灵构成的更朴实、更深远的成就;如果他可以做这些,那么他就必须努力,责无旁贷。

美国如果不投身于崇高的道德原则,就永远不是一个完善的美国。今天,我们作为一个民族有这样的目标,那就是使国家的面貌更亲切,使世界的面貌更和善。朋友们,我们有许多工作要做。许多人无家可归,迷茫无援,到处流浪;许多儿童一无所有,没有爱,没有正常的生活;许多人沉溺于毒品和依赖救助而不能自拔,贫民窟里道德败坏;街头犯罪有待消除;即将成为母亲,却又不能照顾或者不喜爱孩子的年轻妇女需要帮助,她们需要我们的关心、指导和教育,尽管我们祝福她们选择自己的生活。

旧方案和旧方法认为,仅靠公款就能解决这些问题。但我们已经懂得,事实并非如此。无论如何,我们的资金也嫌不足。我们需要降低赤字,我们是心有余而力不足,但我们需要有这样的心。我们将作出艰难的抉择,慎重地对待我们的财富,或许会在使用上作出调

George H. W. Bush

乔治·H. W. 布什(1924-)
41st President of the United States (1989-1993)

We will turn to the only resource we have that in times of need always grows—the goodness and the courage of the American people.

I am speaking of a new engagement in the lives of others, a new activism, hands-on and involved, that gets the job done. We must bring in the generations, harnessing the unused talent of the elderly and the unfocused energy of the young. For not only leadership is passed from generation to generation, but so is stewardship. And the generation born after the Second World War has come of age.

I have spoken of a thousand points of light, of all the community organizations that are spread like stars throughout the Nation, doing good. We will work hand in hand, encouraging, sometimes leading, sometimes being led, rewarding. We will work on this in the White House, in the Cabinet agencies. I will go to the people and the programs that are the brighter points of light, and I will ask every member of my government to become involved. The old ideas are new again because they are not old, they are timeless: duty, sacrifice, commitment, and a patriotism that finds its expression in taking part and pitching in.

We need a new engagement, too, between the Executive and the Congress. The challenges before us will be thrashed out with the House and the Senate. We must bring the Federal budget into balance. And we must ensure that America stands before the world united, strong, at peace, and fiscally sound. But, of course, things may be difficult. We need compromise; we have had dissension.

整,我们才能按照实际需要万无一失地作出决策。那时,我们将采取最明智的行动,即转向我们唯一拥有的、在需要时总是不断增加的资源——美国人民的善意和勇气。

我说的是一种关心他人生活的新义务,一种动手参与并把工作做好的新的能动精神。我们必须把几代人都调动起来,发挥老一代人的余热和年轻人尚无目标的活力。因为不仅领导权要一代一代地传下去,管理工作也是如此。二战后出生的那代人已经成年。

我谈到了成千上万个闪光点,谈到了像星星一样遍布全国的做好事的社区组织。我们将携手努力,互相鼓励,时而当领导,时而被领导,并且劳有所酬。白宫和内阁各部门将着手研究此事。我将深入人民,深入最灿烂夺目的社区计划,我将要求每一个政府官员都参与其中。许多传统的观念又焕发出了青春,因为这些观念并不陈旧,而是历久常新:责任感、牺牲精神、承担义务,以及在参与和作出贡献过程中表现出来的爱国主义。

在总统和国会之间,我们同样需要承担一种新的义务。我们面临的各种挑战将由总统会同众议院和参议院研究解决。我们必须使联邦预算达到平衡。我们必须确保美国以团结、强大、和谐和财政状况良好

We need harmony; we have had a chorus of discordant voices.

For Congress, too, has changed in our time. There has grown a certain divisiveness. We have seen the hard looks and heard the statements in which not each other's ideas are challenged, but each other's motives. And our great parties have too often been far apart and untrusting of each other. It has been this way since Vietnam. That war cleaves us still. But, friends, that war began in earnest a quarter of a century ago; and surely the statute of limitations has been reached. This is a fact: The final lesson of Vietnam is that no great nation can long afford to be sundered by a memory. A new breeze is blowing, and the old bipartisanship must be made new again.

To my friends—and yes, I do mean friends—in the loyal opposition—and yes, I mean loyal: I put out my hand. I am putting out my hand to you, Mr. Speaker. I am putting out my hand to you Mr. Majority Leader. For this is the thing: This is the age of the offered hand. We can't turn back clocks, and I don't want to. But when our fathers were young, Mr. Speaker, our differences ended at the water's edge. And we don't wish to turn back time, but when our mothers were young, Mr. Majority Leader, the Congress and the Executive were capable of working together to produce a budget on which this nation could live. Let us negotiate soon and hard. But in the end, let us produce. The American people await action. They didn't send us here to bicker. They ask us to rise above the merely

George H. W. Bush

乔治·H.W. 布什(1924-)
41st President of the United States (1989-1993)

partisan. "In crucial things, unity"—and this, my friends, is crucial.

To the world, too, we offer new engagement and a renewed vow: We will stay strong to protect the peace. The "offered hand" is a reluctant fist; but once made, strong, and can be used with great effect. There are today Americans who are held against their will in foreign lands, and Americans who are unaccounted for. Assistance can be shown here, and will be long remembered. Good will begets good will. Good faith can be a spiral that endlessly moves on.

Great nations like great men must keep their word. When America says something, America means it, whether a treaty or an agreement or a vow made on marble steps. We will always try to speak clearly, for candor is a compliment, but subtlety, too, is good and has its place. While keeping our alliances and friendships around the world strong, ever strong, we will continue the new closeness with the Soviet Union, consistent both with our security and with progress. One might say that our new relationship in part reflects the triumph of hope and strength over experience. But hope is good, and so are strength and vigilance.

为生的预算。让我们早日认真地进行协商,最后,让我们也能制订出这样的预算。美国人民期待着行动。他们选出我们到这里来,不是要我们争吵。他们要我们超脱于纯粹党派观念之上。"对重大问题,要有一致性"——而这个问题,朋友们,的确是重大的。

我们也向全世界奉献我们新的承诺和誓言:我们将保持强大和保卫和平。"伸出的手"不愿握成拳;但一旦握成拳就无比强大,就能发挥巨大作用。今天,有一些美国人被外国扣留,这违背了他们的意愿,也没有解释原因。我们在这里表示对他们的声援,这将被人们长期牢记。好心会有好报,好信誉会像螺旋一样永不停息地转动。

伟大的国家像伟人一样必须信守诺言。美国说过的话是算数的,无论是一个条约、一项协议,或在此大理石台阶上立下的誓言。我们将永远毫不含糊地表明看法,因为坦率就是对别人的尊重,不过,出言微妙也很好,也有用武之地。在保持与盟国和世界各国日益强大的友谊的同时,我们将继续与苏联保持新的密切关系,这与维护我国的安全和进步相一致。有人也许会说,美苏两国之间的新关系,部分地反映了希望和实力胜过经验,但充满希望总是好的,保持实力和警惕也一样。

Here today are tens of thousands of our citizens who feel the understandable satisfaction of those who have taken part in democracy and seen their hopes fulfilled. But my thoughts have been turning the past few days to those who would be watching at home to an older fellow who will throw a salute by himself when the flag goes by, and the women who will tell her sons the words of the battle hymns. I don't mean this to be sentimental. I mean that on days like this, we remember that we are all part of a continuum, inescapably connected by the ties that bind.

Our children are watching in schools throughout our great land. And to them I say, thank you for watching democracy's big day. For democracy belongs to us all, and freedom is like a beautiful kite that can go higher and higher with the breeze. And to all I say: No matter what your circumstances or where you are, you are part of this day, you are part of the life of our great nation.

A President is neither prince nor pope, and I don't seek a window on men's souls. In fact, I yearn for a greater tolerance, an easy-goingness about each other's attitudes and way of life.

There are few clear areas in which we as a society must rise up united and express our intolerance. The most obvious now is drugs. And when that first cocaine was smuggled in on a ship, it may as well have been a deadly bacteria, so much has it hurt the body, the soul of our

今天,这里有成千上万个美国公民,他们为参加了民主事业,并看到自己的希望得到实现,而理所当然地感到满意。然而近几天来,我的思绪却转向那些在家里观看实况转播的人们——我想到了一个在国旗经过身旁时会自动敬礼的老伙伴,和一位会将战歌歌词告诉子孙们的妇女。我这样说不是感情冲动。我是说,在像今天这样的日子里,我们不会忘记我们都是一个连续统一体的组成部分,都是必然地由联结着我们的纽带团结起来的。

在我国辽阔的大地上,我们的孩子正在学校里观看着这里的一切。对他们,我要说,谢谢你们观看着民主事业的这个盛大节日。因为民主属于我们全体,自由就像一个随着和风越飞越高的风筝。对全体人民,我要说,不论你们情况如何,也不论你们身在何处,你们都是这个重要日子的组成部分。你们是这个伟大国家的生命的组成部分。

总统不是君王,不是教皇。我不寻求"人们心灵上的窗户"。事实上,我向往的是更大的宽容,和人们对彼此的态度与生活方式不作苛求。

然而,在有些问题上,我们作为一个社会必须团结起来,明确地表示不能留情。目前最明显的是吸毒问题。自从第一批可卡因在一艘船上

George H. W. Bush

乔治·H. W. 布什(1924-)

41st President of the United States (1989-1993)

country. And there is much to be done and to be said, but take my word for it: This scourge will stop.

And so, there is much to do; and tomorrow the work begins. I do not mistrust the future; I do not fear what is ahead. For our problems are large, but our heart is larger. Our challenges are great, but our will is greater. And if our flaws are endless, God's love is truly boundless.

Some see leadership as high drama, and the sound of trumpets calling, and sometimes it is that. But I see history as a book with many pages, and each day we fill a page with acts of hopefulness and meaning.

The new breeze blows, a page turns, the story unfolds. And so today a chapter begins, a small and stately story of unity, diversity, and generosity—shared, and written, together.

Thank you. God bless you and God bless the United States of America.

偷运入境，就完全可以说它是一种致命的毒菌，因为它如此严重地损害了我们国家的肌体与灵魂，这方面有许多事要做，有许多话要说，但请相信我的话：这个祸害必将被制止。

所以，要做的事很多；工作明天就开始。对未来，我毫无怀疑；对前途，我毫无恐惧。因为，我们的问题虽大，我们的勇气更大，我们的挑战虽大，我们的决心更大。而且，如果说我们的缺点无穷无尽，上帝的爱就真正无边无垠。

有人把领袖的作为看作是高亢激越的戏剧，和催人奋进的号角。有时情况正是如此。但是，我把历史看作一部鸿篇巨制——我们每天都以充满希望和意义的行动去填写一页。

一阵清新的和风正在吹拂，一页历史正在揭开，故事展开了——今天就这样开始了新的一章：以一致性、多样性和宽容性为主题的短小而辉煌的篇章——由我们大家一起参加，一起去写。

谢谢你们，上帝保佑你们，上帝保佑美利坚合众国。

比尔·克林顿：美国第42任总统(1993—2001)，第二次世界大战后出生的第一位总统。曾任阿肯色州州长达12年之久，1992年抓住冷战结束的机遇，打出"变革"的旗号问鼎白宫，4年后连任。他的两篇演说文辞优美，多次引用或模仿杰斐逊、威尔逊、富兰克林·罗斯福和肯尼迪(均为"强有力的"民主党人总统)所说过的话，意在表明自己是个继往开来者。

Bill Clinton
比尔·克林顿(1946-)
42nd President of the United States (1993-2001)
Political Party: Democratic

A New Season of American Renewal
复兴美国的新时代

My fellow citizens:

Today we celebrate the mystery of American renewal.

This ceremony is held in the depth of winter. But, by the words we speak and the faces we show the world, we force the spring. A spring reborn in the world's oldest democracy, that brings forth the vision and courage to reinvent America.

When our founders boldly declared America's independence to the world and our purposes to the Almighty, they knew that America, to endure, would have to change.

同胞们：

今天，我们庆祝美国复兴这一奇迹。

这个仪式虽在隆冬举行，然而，我们通过自己的言语和向世界展示的面容，却促使春回大地——回到了世界上这个最古老的民主国家，并带来了重新创造美国的远见和勇气。

当我国的缔造者勇敢地向世界宣布美国独立，并向上帝表明自己的目的时，他们知道，美国若要永存，就必须变革。

Bill Clinton

比尔·克林顿 (1946-)
42nd President of the United States (1993-2001)

Not change for change's sake, but change to preserve America's ideals—life, liberty, the pursuit of happiness. Though we march to the music of our time, our mission is timeless. Each generation of Americans must define what it means to be an American.

On behalf of our nation, I salute my predecessor, President Bush, for his half-century of service to America…

Today, a generation raised in the shadows of the Cold War assumes new responsibilities in a world warmed by the sunshine of freedom but threatened still by ancient hatreds and new plagues.

Raised in unrivaled prosperity, we inherit an economy that is still the world's strongest, but is weakened by business failures, stagnant wages, increasing inequality, and deep divisions among our people.

When George Washington first took the oath I have just sworn to uphold, news traveled slowly across the land by horseback and across the ocean by boat. Now, the sights and sounds of this ceremony are broadcast instantaneously to billions around the world.

Communications and commerce are global; investment is mobile; technology is almost magical; and ambition for a better life is now universal. We earn our livelihood in peaceful competition with people all across the earth.

Profound and powerful forces are shaking and remaking our world, and the urgent question of our time is

不是为变革而变革,而是为了维护美国的理想——为了生命、自由和追求幸福而变革。尽管我们随着当今时代的节拍前进,但我们的使命是永恒的。每一代美国人,都必须为作为一个美国人意味着什么下定义。

我代表全体人民,向前任总统布什致敬,他已经为美国服务了半个世纪之久……

今天,在冷战阴影下成长起来的一代人,在世界上负起了新的责任。这个世界虽然沐浴着自由的阳光,但仍受到旧仇宿怨和新的祸患的威胁。

我们在无与伦比的繁荣中长大,继承了仍然是世界上最强大的经济。但由于企业倒闭,工资增长停滞、不平等状况加剧,人民的分歧加深,我们的经济已经衰弱。

当乔治·华盛顿第一次宣读我刚才宣读的誓言时,人们骑马把那个信息缓慢地传遍大地,继而又划船把它传过海洋。而现在,这个仪式的情景和声音即时地向全球几十亿人播放。

通信和商务具有全球性;投资具有流动性;技术几乎具有魔力;改善生活的理想现在具有普遍性。今天,我们美国人通过同世界各地人民进行和平竞争来谋求生存。

各种深远而强大的力量正在震撼和改造我们的世界,

whether we can make change our friend and not our enemy.

This new world has already enriched the lives of millions of Americans who are able to compete and win in it. But when most people are working harder for less; when others cannot work at all; when the cost of health care devastates families and threatens to bankrupt many of our enterprises, great and small; when fear of crime robs law-abiding citizens of their freedom; and when millions of poor children cannot even imagine the lives we are calling them to lead, we have not made change our friend.

We know we have to face hard truths and take strong steps. But we have not done so. Instead, we have drifted, and that drifting has eroded our resources, fractured our economy, and shaken our confidence.

Though our challenges are fearsome, so are our strengths. And Americans have ever been a restless, questing, hopeful people. We must bring to our task today the vision and will of those who came before us.

From our revolution, the Civil War, to the Great Depression to the civil rights movement, our people have always mustered the determination to construct from these crises the pillars of our history.

Thomas Jefferson believed that to preserve the very foundations of our nation, we would need dramatic change from time to time. Well, my fellow citizens, this is our

当今时代的当务之急是我们能否使变革成为我们的朋友，而不是敌人。

这个新世界已经使几百万能够参与竞争并且取胜的美国人过上了富裕的生活。但是，当多数人干得越多反而挣得越少的时候，当有些人根本不可能工作的时候，当医疗保健的重负使众多家庭不堪承受、使大大小小的企业濒临破产的时候，当犯罪活动的恐惧使守法公民不能自由行动的时候，当千百万贫穷儿童甚至不能想象我们呼唤他们过的那种生活的时候，我们就没有使变革成为我们的朋友。

我们知道，我们必须面对严酷的事实真相，并采取强有力的步骤。但我们没有这样做，而是听之任之，以致损耗了我们的资源，破坏了我们的经济，动摇了我们的信心。

我们面临惊人的挑战，但我们同样具有惊人的力量。美国人历来是不安现状、不断追求和充满希望的民族，今天，我们必须把前人的远见卓识和坚强意志带到我们的任务中去。

从革命、内战、大萧条，直到民权运动，我国人民总是下定决心，从历次危机中构筑我国历史的支柱。

托马斯·杰斐逊认为，为了维护我国的根基，我们需要时常进行激动人心的变革。同胞们，我们的时代就是变革

Bill Clinton

比尔·克林顿 (1946-)
42nd President of the United States (1993-2001)

time. Let us embrace it.

Our democracy must be not only the envy of the world but the engine of our own renewal. There is nothing wrong with America that cannot be cured by what is right with America.

And so today, we pledge an end to the era of deadlock and drift; a new season of American renewal has begun.

To renew America, we must be bold.

We must do what no generation has had to do before. We must invest more in our own people, in their jobs, in their future, and at the same time cut our massive debt. And we must do so in a world in which we must compete for every opportunity.

It will not be easy; it will require sacrifice. But it can be done, and done fairly, not choosing sacrifice for its own sake, but for our own sake. We must provide for our nation the way a family provides for its children.

Our Founders saw themselves in the light of posterity. We can do no less. Anyone who has ever watched a child's eyes wander into sleep knows what posterity is. Posterity is the world to come; the world for whom we hold our ideals, from whom we have borrowed our planet, and to whom we bear sacred responsibility.

We must do what America does best: offer more opportunity to all and demand responsibility from all.

的时代,让我们拥抱这个时代吧!

我们的民主制度不仅要成为举世称美的目标,而且要成为举国复兴的动力。美国没有任何错误的东西不能被正确的东西所纠正。

因此,我们今天立下誓言,要结束这个僵持停顿、放任自流的时代,一个复兴美国的新时代已经开始。

我们要复兴美国,就必须鼓足勇气。

我们必须做前人没有做过的事情。我们必须更多地投资于人民,投资于他们的工作和未来,与此同时,我们必须减少巨额债务。而且,我们必须在一个需要为每个机会而竞争的世界上做到这一切。

这样做并不容易:这样做要求作出牺牲。但是,这是做得到的,而且能做得公平合理。我们不是为牺牲而牺牲,我们必须像家庭供养子女那样供养自己的国家。

我国的开国元勋们是用子孙后代的眼光来审视自己的。我们也必须这样做。凡是注意过孩子蒙眬入睡的人,都知道后代意味着什么,后代就是将要到来的世界——我们为其坚持自己的理想,我们向其借用这个星球,我们对其负有神圣的责任。

我们必须做美国最拿手的事情:为所有的人提供更多的机会,要所有的人负起责任。

It is time to break the bad habit of expecting something for nothing, from our government or from each other. Let us all take more responsibility, not only for ourselves and our families but for our communities and our country.

To renew America, we must revitalize our democracy.

This beautiful capital, like every capital since the dawn of civilization, is often a place of intrigue and calculation. Powerful people maneuver for position and worry endlessly about who is in and who is out, who is up and who is down, forgetting those people whose toil and sweat sends us here and pays our way.

Americans deserve better, and in this city today, there are people who want to do better. And so I say to all of us here, let us resolve to reform our politics, so that power and privilege no longer shout down the voice of the people.

Let us put aside personal advantage so that we can feel the pain and see the promise of America. Let us resolve to make our government a place for what Franklin Roosevelt called "bold, persistent experimentation," a government for our tomorrows, not our yesterdays. Let us give this capital back to the people to whom it belongs.

To renew America, we must meet challenges abroad as well as at home. There is no longer division between what is foreign and what is domestic—the world economy, the world environment, the world AIDS crisis, the world arms race—they affect us all.

现在是破除期待向政府和别人无偿索取的恶习的时候了。让我们大家不仅为自己和家庭，而且为社区和国家担负起更多的责任吧！

要复兴美国，我们就必须恢复我们民主制度的活力。

这个美丽的首都，如同文明诞生以来的每一个首都一样，常常是尔虞我诈、明争暗斗之地。大腕人物争权夺势，没完没了地为职位的升降而烦神，却忘记了人民用辛勤和汗水把我们送到这里，为我们买单。

美国人理应得到更好的生活。在这个城市里，现在有人想把事情办得更好一些。因此，我要对所有在场的人说：让我们下定决心改革政治，使权力和特权的喧嚣不再压倒人民的呼声。

让我们撇开个人利益，这样我们就能察觉美国的病痛，看到它的希望。让我们下定决心，使政府成为富兰克林·罗斯福所说的进行"大胆而持久试验"的地方，成为一个面向未来而不是留恋过去的政府。让我们把这个首都归还给它所属的人民。

我们要复兴美国，就必须迎接国内外的种种挑战。国外和国内事务之间已不再有明确的界限——世界经济、世界环境、世界艾滋病危机、世界军备竞赛，这一切都在影响着我们大家。

Bill Clinton
比尔·克林顿 (1946-)
42nd President of the United States (1993-2001)

Today, as an old order passes, the new world is more free but less stable. ... Clearly America must continue to lead the world we did so much to make.

While America rebuilds at home, we will not shrink from the challenges, nor fail to seize the opportunities, of this new world. Together with our friends and allies, we will work to shape change, lest it engulf us.

When our vital interests are challenged, or the will and conscience of the international community is defied, we will act; with peaceful diplomacy when ever possible, with force when necessary. The brave Americans serving our nation today in the Persian Gulf, in Somalia, and wherever else they stand are testament to our resolve.

But our greatest strength is the power of our ideas, which are still new in many lands. Across the world, we see them embraced, and we rejoice. Our hopes, our hearts, our hands, are with those on every continent who are building democracy and freedom. Their cause is America's cause.

The American people have summoned the change we celebrate today. You have raised your voices in an unmistakable chorus. You have cast your votes in historic numbers. And you have changed the face of Congress, the presidency and the political process itself. Yes, you, my fellow Americans have forced the spring. Now, we must do the work the season demands.

今天,随着旧秩序的消逝,新世界更加自由了,然而却不那么稳定。……美国显然必须继续领导我们曾作出巨大努力而创造的这个世界。

我们在国内进行重建的同时,面对这个新世界的挑战不会退缩不前,也不会坐失良机。我们将与盟友一起努力进行变革,以免被变革所吞没。

当我们的重要利益受到挑战,或者当国际社会的意志和良知受到蔑视,我们将采取行动——可能时就采用和平外交手段,必要时就使用武力。今天,在波斯湾、索马里和任何其他地方为国效力的勇敢的美国人,都证明了我们的决心。

但是,我们最伟大的力量是我们思想的威力。这些思想在许多国家仍然处于萌芽阶段。看到这些思想在世界各地被接受,我们感到欢欣鼓舞。我们的希望、我们的心、我们的手与每一个大陆正在建立民主和自由的人们是连在一起的。他们的事业也是美国的事业。

美国人民唤来了我们今天所庆祝的变革。你们毫不含糊地齐声疾呼。你们以前所未有的人数参加了投票。你们使国会、总统职务和政治进程本身全都面目一新。是的,是你们,我的美国同胞们,促使春回大地。现在,我们必须做这个季节需要做的工作。

To that work I now turn, with all the authority of my office. I ask the Congress to join with me. But no president, no Congress, no government, can undertake this mission alone. My fellow Americans, you, too, must play your part in our renewal. I challenge a new generation of young Americans to a season of service; to act on your idealism by helping troubled children, keeping company with those in need, reconnecting our torn communities. There is so much to be done; enough indeed for millions of others who are still young in spirit to give of themselves in service, too.

In serving, we recognize a simple but powerful truth, we need each other. And we must care for one another. Today, we do more than celebrate America; we rededicate ourselves to the very idea of America.

An idea born in revolution and renewed through two centuries of challenge. An idea tempered by the knowledge that, but for fate we, the fortunate and the unfortunate, might have been each other. An idea ennobled by the faith that our nation can summon from its myriad diversity the deepest measure of unity. An idea infused with the conviction that America's long heroic journey must go forever upward.

And so, my fellow Americans, at the edge of the 21st century, let us begin with energy and hope, with faith and discipline, and let us work until our work is done. The scripture says, "And let us not be weary in well-doing, for

现在，我就运用我的全部职权致力于这项工作。我请求国会同我一道做这项工作。任何总统、任何国会、任何政府都不能单独完成这一使命。同胞们，在我国复兴的过程中，你们也必须发挥作用。我向新一代美国年轻人挑战，要求你们投入这一奉献的季节——为你们的理想主义行动起来，使不幸的儿童得到帮助，使有需要的人们得到关怀，使四分五裂的社区恢复联系。要做的事情很多——确实够多的，以至几百万在精神上仍然年轻的人也可作出奉献。

在奉献过程中，我们认识到相互需要这一简单而又强大的真理。我们必须相互关心。今天，我们不仅是在赞颂美国，我们再一次把自己奉献给美国的理想。

这个理想在革命中诞生，在两个世纪的挑战中更新；这个理想经受了认识的考验，大家认识到，若不是命运的安排，幸运者或不幸者有可能互换位置；这个理想由于一种信念而变得崇高，即我国能够从纷繁的多样性中实现最深刻的统一性，这个理想洋溢着一种信心：美国漫长而英勇的旅程必将永远继续。

同胞们，在我们即将跨入21世纪之际，让我们以旺盛的精力和满腔的希望，以坚定的信心和严明的纪律开始工

Bill Clinton
比尔·克林顿 (1946-)
42nd President of the United States (1993-2001)

in due season, we shall reap, if we faint not."

From this joyful mountaintop of celebration, we hear a call to service in the valley. We have heard the trumpets. We have changed the guard. And now, each in our way, and with God's help, we must answer the call.

Thank you and God bless you all.

作,直到把工作完成。《圣经》说:"我们行善,不可丧志,若不灰心,到了时候,就要收成。"

在这个欢乐的山巅,我们听见山谷里传来了要我们作出奉献的召唤。我们听到了号角声。我们已经换岗待命。现在,我们必须以各自的方式,在上帝的帮助下响应这一召唤。

谢谢大家。愿上帝保佑你们。

乔治·W.布什：美国第43任总统（2001—2009），21世纪美国第一位总统，又称"小布什"，为第41任总统"老布什"之子。2000年以全面减税和加强防务的竞选政纲勉强赢得选举，上任后发动"反恐战争"和海湾战争。2004年获连任。4年后因经济滑坡、外交政策不得人心、民众怨声载道而下台。本篇以团结为题，字斟句酌，堪称佳作。

George W. Bush
乔治·W. 布什 (1946-   )
43rd President of the United States (2001-2009)
Political Party: Republican

Holding Beliefs beyond Ourselves
超越自我的信念

President Clinton, distinguished guests and my fellow citizens:

The peaceful transfer of authority is rare in history, yet common in our country. With a simple oath, we affirm old traditions and make new beginnings.

As I begin, I thank President Clinton for his service to our nation; and I thank Vice President Gore for a contest conducted with spirit and ended with grace.

I am honored and humbled to stand here, where so many of America's leaders have come before me, and so

克林顿总统，尊贵的来宾，广大美国同胞们：

权利的和平过渡在历史上是罕见的，但在美国是平常的。我们以朴素的宣誓庄严地维护了古老的传统，同时开始了新的历程。

首先，我要感谢克林顿总统为这个国家作出的贡献，也感谢副总统戈尔在竞选过程中的热情与风度。

站在这里，我很荣幸，也有点受宠若惊。在我之前，许

George W. Bush
乔治·W.布什 (1946-)
43rd President of the United States (2001-2009)

many will follow.

We have a place, all of us, in a long story—a story we continue, but whose end we will not see. It is the story of a new world that became a friend and liberator of the old, a story of a slave-holding society that became a servant of freedom, the story of a power that went into the world to protect but not possess, to defend but not to conquer.

It is the American story—a story of flawed and fallible people, united across the generations by grand and enduring ideals.

The grandest of these ideals is an unfolding American promise that everyone belongs, that everyone deserves a chance, that no insignificant person was ever born. Americans are called upon to enact this promise in our lives and in our laws; and though our nation has sometimes halted, and sometimes delayed, we must follow no other course.

Through much of the last century, America's faith in freedom and democracy was a rock in a raging sea. Now it is a seed upon the wind, taking root in many nations. Our democratic faith is more than the creed of our country, it is the inborn hope of our humanity, an ideal we carry but do not own, a trust we bear and pass along; and even after

多美国领导人从这里起步；在我之后，也会有许多领导人从这里继续前进。

在美国悠久的历史中，我们每个人都有自己的位置——我们还在继续推动着历史前进，但是我们不可能看到它的尽头。这是一部新世界的发展史，是一部后浪推前浪的历史。这是一部美国由奴隶制社会发展成为崇尚自由社会的历史。这是一个强国保护而不是占有世界的历史，是捍卫而不是征服世界的历史。

这就是美国的故事。它不是一部十全十美的民族发展史，但它是一部在伟大和永恒理想指导下几代人团结奋斗的历史。

这些理想中最伟大的是正在慢慢实现的美国的承诺，这就是：每个人都有自身的价值，每个人都有成功的机会，每个人天生都会有所作为。美国人民肩负着一种使命，那就是要竭力将这个诺言变成生活中和法律上的现实。虽然我们的国家过去在追求实现这个承诺的途中曾停滞不前甚至倒退，但我们仍将坚定不移地完成这一使命。

在上个世纪的大部分时间里，美国自由民主的信念犹如汹涌大海中的岩石。现在，它更像风中的种子，把自由带给每个民族。在我们的国家，民主不仅仅是一种信念，而是

nearly 225 years, we have a long way yet to travel.

While many of our citizens prosper, others doubt the promise, even the justice, of our own country. The ambitions of some Americans are limited by failing schools and hidden prejudice and the circumstances of their birth; and sometimes our differences run so deep, it seems we share a continent, but not a country.

We do not accept this, and we will not allow it. Our unity, our union, is the serious work of leaders and citizens in every generation; and this is my solemn pledge, "I will work to build a single nation of justice and opportunity."

I know this is in our reach because we are guided by a power larger than ourselves who creates us equal in His image.

And we are confident in principles that unite and lead us onward.

America has never been united by blood or birth or soil. We are bound by ideals that move us beyond our backgrounds, lift us above our interests and teach us what it means to be citizens. Every child must be taught these principles. Every citizen must uphold them; and every immigrant, by embracing these ideals, makes our country more, not less, American.

全人类的希望。民主,我们不会独占,而会竭力让大家分享。民主,我们将铭记于心并且不断传播。225年过去了,我们仍有很长的路要走。

有很多公民取得了成功,但也有人开始怀疑,怀疑我们自己的国家所许下的诺言,甚至怀疑它的公正。失败的教育,潜在的偏见和出身的环境限制了一些美国人的雄心。有时,我们的分歧是如此之深,似乎我们虽身处同一个大陆,但不属于同一个国家。

我们不能接受这种分歧,也无法容许它的存在。我们的团结和统一,是每一代领导人和每一个公民的严肃使命。在此,我郑重宣誓:我将竭力建设一个公正、充满机会的统一国家。

我知道这是我们的目标,因为上帝按自己的身形创造了我们,上帝高于一切的力量将引导我们前进。

对这些将我们团结起来并指引我们向前的原则,我们充满信心。

血缘、出身或地域从未将美国联合起来。只有理想,才能使我们心系一处,超越自己,放弃个人利益,并逐步领会公民的真谛。每个孩子都必须学习这些原则。每个公民都必须坚持这些原则。每个移民,只有接受这些理想,才能使我们的国家更具美国特色。

George W. Bush

乔治·W. 布什 (1946-)
43rd President of the United States (2001-2009)

Today, we affirm a new commitment to live out our nation's promise through civility, courage, compassion and character.

America, at its best, matches a commitment to principle with a concern for civility. A civil society demands from each of us good will and respect, fair dealing and forgiveness.

Some seem to believe that our politics can afford to be petty because, in a time of peace, the stakes of our debates appear small. But the stakes for America are never small. If our country does not lead the cause of freedom, it will not be led. If we do not turn the hearts of children toward knowledge and character, we will lose their gifts and undermine their idealism. If we permit our economy to drift and decline, the vulnerable will suffer most.

We must live up to the calling we share. Civility is not a tactic or a sentiment. It is the determined choice of trust over cynicism, of community over chaos. This commitment, if we keep it, is a way to shared accomplishment.

America, at its best, is also courageous.

Our national courage has been clear in times of depression and war, when defending common dangers defined our common good. Now we must choose if the example of our fathers and mothers will inspire us or condemn us. We must show courage in a time of blessing

今天,我们在这里重申一个新的信念,即通过发扬谦恭、勇气、同情心和个性的精神来践行我们国家的诺言。

美国在它最鼎盛时也没忘记遵循谦逊有礼的原则。一个文明的社会需要我们每个人品质优良,尊重他人,为人公平和宽宏大量。

有人认为我们的政治制度是如此的微不足道,因为在和平年代,我们所争论的话题都是无关紧要的。但是,对我们美国来说,我们所讨论的问题从来都不是什么小事。如果我们不领导和平事业,那么和平将无人来领导;如果我们不引导我们的孩子们真心地热爱知识、发挥个性,他们的天分将得不到发挥,理想将难以实现。如果我们不采取适当措施,任凭经济衰退,最大的受害者将是平民百姓。

我们应该时刻听取时代的呼唤。谦逊有礼不是战术也不是感情用事。这是我们最坚定的选择——在批评声中赢得信任;在混乱中寻求统一。如果遵循这样的承诺,我们将会享有共同的成就。

美国有强大的国力作后盾,将会勇往直前。

在大萧条和战争时期,我们的人民在困难面前表现得无比英勇,克服我们共同的困难体现了我们共同的优秀品质。现在,我们正面临着选

by confronting problems instead of passing them on to future generations.

Together, we will reclaim America's schools, before ignorance and apathy claim more young lives; we will reform Social Security and Medicare, sparing our children from struggles we have the power to prevent; we will reduce taxes, to recover the momentum of our economy and reward the effort and enterprise of working Americans; we will build our defenses beyond challenge, lest weakness invite challenge; and we will confront weapons of mass destruction, so that a new century is spared new horrors.

The enemies of liberty and our country should make no mistake: America remains engaged in the world by history and by choice, shaping a balance of power that favors freedom. We will defend our allies and our interests; we will show purpose without arrogance; we will meet aggression and bad faith with resolve and strength; and to all nations, we will speak for the values that gave our nation birth.

America, at its best, is compassionate.

In the quiet of American conscience, we know that deep, persistent poverty is unworthy of our nation's promise. Whatever our views of its cause, we can agree that children at risk are not at fault. Abandonment and

择,如果我们作出正确的选择,祖辈一定会激励我们;如果我们的选择是错误的,祖辈会谴责我们的。上帝正眷顾着这个国家,我们必须显示出我们的勇气,敢于面对问题,而不是将它们遗留给我们的后代。

我们要共同努力,健全美国的学校教育,不能让无知和冷漠吞噬更多的年轻生命。我们要改革社会保险和医疗制度,在力所能及的范围内拯救我们的孩子。我们要减低税收,恢复经济,酬谢辛勤工作的美国人民。我们要防患于未然,懈怠会带来麻烦。我们还要对抗大规模杀伤性武器,使新的世纪摆脱恐怖的威胁。

反对自由和反对我们国家的人应该明白:美国仍将积极参与国际事务,力求世界力量的均衡,让自由的力量遍及全球。这是历史的选择。我们会保护我们的盟国,捍卫我们的利益。我们将谦逊地向世界人民表示我们的目标。我们将坚决反击各种侵略和不守信用的行径。我们要向全世界宣传孕育了我们伟大民族的价值观。

正处在鼎盛时期的美国也不缺乏同情心。

当我们静心思考,我们就会明了根深蒂固的贫穷绝不是美国的愿望。无论我们如何看待贫穷的原因,我们都必

George W. Bush
乔治·W. 布什 (1946-)
43rd President of the United States (2001-2009)

abuse are not acts of God, they are failures of love. The proliferation of prisons, however necessary, is no substitute for hope and order in our souls.

Where there is suffering, there is duty. Americans in need are not strangers, they are citizens; not problems, but priorities, and all of us are diminished when any are hopeless.

Government has great responsibilities for public safety and public health, for civil rights and common schools. Yet compassion is the work of a nation, not just a government. Some needs and hurts are so deep they will only respond to a mentor's touch or a pastor's prayer. Church and charity, synagogue and mosque lend our communities their humanity, and they will have an honored place in our plans and in our laws.

Many in our country do not know the pain of poverty, but we can listen to those who do. I can pledge our nation to a goal, "When we see that wounded traveler on the road to Jericho, we will not pass to the other side."

America, at its best, is a place where personal responsibility is valued and expected.

Encouraging responsibility is not a search for scapegoats,

须承认,孩子们身处逆境并不是他们的错误。放纵与滥用都为上帝所不容。这些都是缺乏爱的结果。监狱数量的增长虽然看起来是有必要的,但并不能代替我们心中的希望——人人遵纪守法。

哪里有痛苦,我们的义务就在哪里。对我们来说,需要帮助的美国人不是陌生人,而是我们的公民;不是负担,而是急需救助的对象。当有人陷入绝望时,我们大家都会因此变得渺小。

对于公共安全和公众健康,对于民权和学校教育,政府都应负有极大的责任。然而,同情心不只是政府的职责,更是整个国家的义务。有些需要是如此的迫切,有些伤痕是如此的深刻,只有导师的爱抚、牧师的祈祷才能有所感触。不论是教堂还是慈善机构、犹太会堂还是清真寺,这些机构使我们的社会更为人性化,理应在我们的规划和法律上受到尊重。

我们国家的许多人都不知道贫穷的痛苦。但我们可以听到那些感触颇深的人们的倾诉。我敢说我们的国家能实现这样的目标:当我们看见受伤的人倒在远行的路上,我们决不会袖手旁观。

正处于鼎盛期的美国重视并期待每个人担负起自己的责任。

鼓励人们勇于承担责任

it is a call to conscience. Though it requires sacrifice, it brings a deeper fulfillment. We find the fullness of life not only in options, but in commitments. We find that children and community are the commitments that set us free.

Our public interest depends on private character, on civic duty and family bonds and basic fairness, on uncounted, unhonored acts of decency which give direction to our freedom.

Sometimes in life we are called to do great things. But as a saint of our times has said, every day we are called to do small things with great love. The most important tasks of a democracy are done by everyone.

I will live and lead by these principles, "to advance my convictions with civility, to pursue the public interest with courage, to speak for greater justice and compassion, to call for responsibility and try to live it as well." In all these ways, I will bring the values of our history to the care of our times.

What you do is as important as anything government does. I ask you to seek a common good beyond your comfort; to defend needed reforms against easy attacks; to serve your nation, beginning with your neighbor. I ask you to be citizens: citizens, not spectators; citizens, not subjects; responsible citizens, building communities of

不是让人们充当替罪羊,而是对人的良知的呼唤。虽然承担责任意味着牺牲个人利益,但是你能从中体会到一种更加深刻的成就感。我们实现人生的完整不单是通过摆在我们面前的选择,也在于承担责任的承诺。我们知道,通过对整个社会和我们的孩子们尽我们的义务,我们将得到最终自由。

我们的公共利益依赖于我们独立的个性;依赖于我们的公民义务,家庭纽带和基本的公正;依赖于我们无数的、默默无闻的文明行为,正是它们指引我们走向自由。

在生活中,有时我们被召唤着去做一些惊天动地的事情。但是,正如我们时代的一位圣人所言,每一天我们都被召唤带着大爱去做一些小事情。一个民主制度最重要的任务是由大家每一个人来完成的。

我为人处事的原则包括:坚信自己而不强加于人,为公众的利益勇往直前,追求正义而不乏同情心,勇担责任而决不推卸。我要通过这一切,用我们的传统价值观来哺育我们的时代。

你们所做的一切和政府的工作同样重要。我希望你们不要仅仅追求个人享受而忽略公众的利益;要捍卫既定的改革措施,以免轻易遭到破坏;要从身边小事做起,为我

George W. Bush
乔治·W. 布什 (1946-)
43rd President of the United States (2001-2009)

service and a nation of character.

Americans are generous and strong and decent, not because we believe in ourselves, but because we hold beliefs beyond ourselves. When this spirit of citizenship is missing, no government program can replace it. When this spirit is present, no wrong can stand against it.

After the *Declaration of Independence* was signed, Virginia statesman John Page wrote to Thomas Jefferson, "We know the race is not to the swift nor the battle to the strong. Do you not think an angel rides in the whirlwind and directs this storm?"

Much time has passed since Jefferson arrived for his inauguration. The years and changes accumulate, but the themes of this day he would know, "our nation's grand story of courage and its simple dream of dignity."

We are not this story's author, who fills time and eternity with His purpose. Yet His purpose is achieved in our duty, and our duty is fulfilled in service to one another.

Never tiring, never yielding, never finishing, we renew that purpose today, to make our country more just

们的国家效力。我希望你们成为真正的公民,而不是旁观者,更不是臣民。你们应成为有责任心的公民,共同来建设一个互帮互助的社会和有特色的国家。

美国人民慷慨、强大、体面,这并非因为我们信任我们自己,而是因为我们拥有超越我们自己的信念。一旦这种公民精神丧失了,无论何种政府计划都无法弥补它。一旦这种精神出现了,无论任何错误都无法抗衡它。

在《独立宣言》签署之后,弗吉尼亚州的政治家约翰·佩齐曾给托马斯·杰弗逊写信说:"我们知道,身手敏捷不一定就能赢得比赛,力量强大不一定就能赢得战争。难道这一切不都是上帝安排的吗?"

杰斐逊就任总统的那个年代离我们已经很远了。时光飞逝,美国发生了翻天覆地的变化。但是有一点他肯定能够预知,即我们这个时代的主题仍然是:我们国家无畏向前的恢宏故事和它追求尊严的淳朴梦想。

我们不是这个故事的作者,是杰斐逊本人的伟大理想穿越时空,并通过我们每天的努力在变为现实。我们正在通过大家的努力在履行着各自的职责。

带着永不疲惫、永不气馁、永不枯竭的信念,今天我

and generous, to affirm the dignity of our lives and every life.

This work continues. This story goes on. And an angel still rides in the whirlwind and directs this storm.

God bless you all, and God bless America.

们重树这样的目标:使我们的国家变得更加公正、更加慷慨,去验证我们每个人和所有人生命的尊严。

这项工作必须继续下去。这个故事必须延续下去。上帝会驾驭我们航行的。

愿上帝保佑大家!愿上帝保佑美国!

巴拉克·奥巴马:美国第44任总统(2009—2017),美国历史上第一位非洲裔总统,曾任伊利诺伊州参议员和联邦参议员。本篇以"开创负责任的新时代"为主题,批评"幼稚"的上届政府造成了困难局面,号召全体美国人团结并行动起来,继续在"征途"上前进并"领跑"世界。通篇文辞优美,多处模仿杰斐逊、林肯和富兰克林·罗斯福的演说,有较强的感染力。

Barack Obama
巴拉克·奥巴马(1961-)
44th President of the United States (2009-2017)
Political Party: Democratic

Giving Our All to a Difficult Task
为艰巨的使命付出一切

My fellow citizens:

I stand here today humbled by the task before us, grateful for the trust you have bestowed, mindful of the sacrifices borne by our ancestors. I thank President Bush for his service to our nation, as well as the generosity and cooperation he has shown throughout this transition.

Forty-four Americans have now taken the presidential oath. The words have been spoken during rising tides of prosperity and the still waters of peace. Yet, every so often the oath is taken amidst gathering clouds and raging storms. At these moments, America has carried on not simply

同胞们:

我今天站在这里,谦卑地面对重任,感谢大家给予我的信任,并牢记先辈们所作出的牺牲。我感谢布什总统曾为国效劳,还要感谢他在权力交接全过程中的慷慨与合作。

迄今为止,已有44个美国人宣誓就职。他们在宣誓的时候,或正值欣欣向荣、和平安宁,或恰逢乌云密布、风暴肆虐。在后一种情况下,美国仍能继续前行,这不仅仅是

because of the skill or vision of those in high office, but because We the People have remained faithful to the ideals of our forbear, and true to our founding documents.

So it has been. So it must be with this generation of Americans.

That we are in the midst of crisis is now well understood. Our nation is at war, against a far-reaching network of violence and hatred. Our economy is badly weakened, a consequence of greed and irresponsibility on the part of some, but also our collective failure to make hard choices and prepare the nation for a new age. Homes have been lost; jobs shed; businesses shuttered. Our health care is too costly; our schools fail too many; and each day brings further evidence that the ways we use energy strengthen our adversaries and threaten our planet.

These are the indicators of crisis, subject to data and statistics. Less measurable but no less profound is a sapping of confidence across our land—a nagging fear that America's decline is inevitable, and that the next generation must lower its sights.

Today I say to you that the challenges we face are real. They are serious and they are many. They will not be met easily or in a short span of time. But know this, America—they will be met.

On this day, we gather because we have chosen hope over fear, unity of purpose over conflict and discord.

因为领导人的能力和远见，还因为我们人民始终坚信先辈的理想，对立国文献保持忠诚。

前辈们如此，我们这一代美国人也要如此。

我们正处于危机之中，这一点已得到充分的认识。我国正在向一个分布广泛的暴力和仇恨势力体系开战。我国经济严重衰退，原因不仅在于一些人的贪婪和失职，还在于我们作为一个整体，未能明确地进行抉择并为新时代做好准备。于是，家园丢失，就业减少，商业萧条。医疗保健费用过高；学校教育令太多的人失望；而与日俱增的事实表明，我们利用能源的方式助长了对手的威风，并威胁到我们的星球。

这些都是危机的症状，都有资料和数据可查。但还有一些不易衡量却同样严重的症状，那就是全国各地正在丧失信心——一种挥之不去的恐惧感，认为美国将不可避免地走下坡路，下一代人不得不放低眼光。

我今天要对你们说，我们面临的挑战真实存在，它们严重且多重。它们不会轻易地或者在短时间内就能得到解决。但美国人民知道——它们一定会得到解决。

我们今天在这里聚集，是因为我们选择了希望而不是恐惧，选择了目标一致而不是冲突对立。

Barack Obama
巴拉克·奥巴马(1961-)
44th President of the United States (2009-2017)

On this day, we come to proclaim an end to the petty grievances and false promises, the recriminations and worn out dogmas, that for far too long have strangled our politics.

We remain a young nation, but in the words of Scripture, the time has come to set aside childish things. The time has come to reaffirm our enduring spirit; to choose our better history; to carry forward that precious gift, that noble idea, passed on from generation to generation: the God-given promise that all are equal, all are free, and all deserve a chance to pursue their full measure of happiness.

In reaffirming the greatness of our nation, we understand that greatness is never a given. It must be earned. Our journey has never been one of short-cuts or settling for less. It has not been the path for the faint-hearted—for those who prefer leisure over work, or seek only the pleasures of riches and fame. Rather, it has been the risk-takers, the doers, the makers of things—some celebrated but more often men and women obscure in their labor, who have carried us up the long, rugged path towards prosperity and freedom.

For us, they packed up their few worldly possessions and traveled across oceans in search of a new life.

For us, they toiled in sweatshops and settled the West; endured the lash of the whip and plowed the hard earth.

For us, they fought and died, in places like Concord and Gettysburg; Normandy and Khe Sanh.

Time and again these men and women struggled and

我们今天来这里宣告,让无谓的抱怨和虚假的承诺就此结束,让束缚我国政治太久的相互指责和陈词滥调就此告终。

我们是一个年轻的国家,但借用《圣经》的话,现在该是丢弃幼稚的时候了。现在该是重申永恒精神的时候,该是选择更辉煌的历史的时候,该是弘扬那份世代相传的珍贵礼物、那个崇高的理念的时候——那就是上帝承诺的人人平等、人人自由、人人都有机会去追求最大限度的幸福。

在重申我们国家伟大精神的同时,我们懂得,伟大从来不是一种馈赠,而要努力争取。我们的征途从来没有捷径,没有退路。这不是一条懦弱者的路——不是一条好逸恶劳者或贪图名利者的路。相反,是那些甘于承担风险的人、实干家和创造者——其中有一些人闻名遐迩,但更多的是默默无闻的劳动者——带领我们走上了通往繁荣和自由的漫长崎岖之路。

为了我们,他们整理好简陋的行囊,漂洋过海,追求新的生活。

为了我们,他们在血汗工厂劳动,在西部荒原拓植,挨着皮鞭在贫瘠的土地上耕耘。

为了我们,他们奔赴疆场,英勇捐躯,长眠于康科德、葛底斯堡、诺曼底和科萨恩。

为了让我们过上更好的

sacrificed and worked till their hands were raw so that we might live a better life. They saw America as bigger than the sum of our individual ambitions; greater than all the differences of birth or wealth or faction.

This is the journey we continue today. We remain the most prosperous, powerful nation on Earth. Our workers are no less productive than when this crisis began. Our minds are no less inventive, our goods and services no less needed than they were last week or last month or last year. Our capacity remains undiminished. But our time of standing pat, of protecting narrow interests and putting off unpleasant decisions—that time has surely passed. Starting today, we must pick ourselves up, dust ourselves off, and begin again the work of remaking America.

For everywhere we look, there is work to be done. The state of the economy calls for action, bold and swift, and we will act—not only to create new jobs, but to lay a new foundation for growth. We will build the roads and bridges, the electric grids and digital lines that feed our commerce and bind us together. We will restore science to its rightful place, and wield technology's wonders to raise health care's quality and lower its cost. We will harness the sun and the winds and the soil to fuel our cars and run our factories. And we will transform our schools and colleges and universities to meet the demands of a new age. All this we can do. And all this we will do.

Now, there are some who question the scale of our

生活，他们不停地斗争和奉献、不停地工作，直至双手结起层层老茧。在他们看来，美国之伟大，超过了所有个人雄心的总和，也超越了出身、贫富或派系的巨大差异。

这就是我们今天仍在继续的征途。我们仍然是世界上最繁荣、最强大的国家。工人的生产力并没有因为目前的这场危机而减弱。我们的头脑仍然富有创造力，对我们产品和服务的需求并没有比上星期、上个月或去年少。我们的能力丝毫未减。但是，维持现状、保护狭隘利益、推迟困难的抉择的时代无疑已经消逝。我们从今天起就必须振作起来，掸掉身上的尘土，重新开始再造美国。

这是因为，无论我们把目光投向何处，都有工作在等待着我们。经济形势要求我们行动起来，果敢而迅速地行动起来！我们确实将采取行动——不仅要创造新的就业机会，而且要为发展打下新的基础。我们将建造道路和桥梁，架设电网和电子通信线路，满足商务的需要，并把我们大家紧密地联系起来。我们将使科学回归本位，利用技术的奇迹，提高医疗保健的质量并降低成本。我们将利用太阳能、风能和地热，为汽车和工厂提供能源。我们将改造中小学和高等院校，应对新时代的挑战。这一切我们都能做到，也必将做到。

现在，有人怀疑我们的野

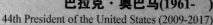

ambitions—who suggest that our system cannot tolerate too many big plans. Their memories are short. For they have forgotten what this country has already done; what free men and women can achieve when imagination is joined to common purpose, and necessity to courage.

What the cynics fail to understand is that the ground has shifted beneath them—that the stale political arguments that have consumed us for so long no longer apply. The question we ask today is not whether our government is too big or too small, but whether it works—whether it helps families find jobs at a decent wage, care they can afford, a retirement that is dignified. Where the answer is yes, we intend to move forward. Where the answer is no, programs will end. And those of us who manage the public's dollars will be held to account—to spend wisely, reform bad habits, and do our business in the light of day—because only then can we restore the vital trust between a people and their government.

Nor is the question before us whether the market is a force for good or ill. Its power to generate wealth and expand freedom is unmatched, but this crisis has reminded us that without a watchful eye, the market can spin out of control—and that a nation cannot prosper long when it favors only the prosperous. The success of our economy has always depended not just on the size of our Gross Domestic Product, but on the reach of our prosperity; on our ability to extend opportunity to every willing heart—not out of charity, but because it is the surest route to our common

心是否太大——说什么我国的体制不能承受太多的宏伟计划。他们很健忘。他们忘记了这个国家所取得的成就,忘记了当共同的目标插上理想的翅膀,现实的要求扬起勇气的风帆,自由的人民就能创造宏图大业。

那些冷嘲热讽的人并不知道,他们的脚下的根基已经动摇——那些长期以来折腾我们的陈腐的政治观点已经不再适用。我们今天提出的问题不是政府太大还是太小,而是它能否起作用——它能否帮助大家找到报酬合理的工作,能否为大家提供负担得起的医疗保健,能否让大家享受体面的退休生活。如果回答是肯定的,我们就向前推进;如果回答是否定的,我们就终止有关计划。公共资金的管理人必须被问责——必须明智地使用资金、改掉不良习惯、在阳光下履行职责——因为只有这样,才能恢复人民和政府之间的至关重要的信任。

我们面临的问题也不是市场是好的动力还是坏的动力。虽然市场具有无与伦比的创造财富和扩展自由的力量,但这场危机提醒我们,缺乏严格的监督,市场就有可能失控——如果一个国家仅仅惠及富人,其富裕便不能持久。我们经济的成功从来不仅仅取决于国内生产总值的规模,而且还取决于繁荣惠及

good.

As for our common defense, we reject as false the choice between our safety and our ideals. Our Founding Fathers, faced with perils we can scarcely imagine, drafted a charter to assure the rule of law and the rights of man, a charter expanded by the blood of generations. Those ideals still light the world, and we will not give them up for expedience's sake. And so to all the other peoples and governments who are watching today, from the grandest capitals to the small village where my father was born: know that America is a friend of each nation and every man, woman, and child who seeks a future of peace and dignity, and that we are ready to lead once more.

...

We are the keepers of this legacy. Guided by these principles once more, we can meet those new threats that demand even greater effort—even greater cooperation and understanding between nations. We will begin to responsibly leave Iraq to its people, and forge a hard-earned peace in Afghanistan. With old friends and former foes, we will work tirelessly to lessen the nuclear threat, and roll back the specter of a warming planet. We will not apologize for our way of life, nor will we waver in its defense, and for those who seek to advance their aims by inducing terror and slaughtering innocents, we say to you now that our spirit is stronger and cannot be broken; you cannot outlast us, and

的范围,取决于我们为每一个愿意获得机会的人提供机会的能力——不是出于施舍,而是因为这才是最可靠的共同富裕之路。

至于共同防御,我们拒绝在安全与理想之间进行非此即彼的荒谬选择。开国元勋们曾面对我们难以想象的危险局面,起草了一部保障法治和人权的宪章,而一代又一代人,又以血的代价使之不断充实。这些理念仍然照耀着世界,我们不会为权宜之计而抛弃这些理念。因此,对于今天正在观看就职典礼的各国人民和政府——从气势宏大的首府到我父亲出生的小村庄——我们希望他们都能知道:凡追求和平与尊严的国家、每一个男人、女人和儿童,美国都是你们的朋友,而且,我们已准备好再次领跑。

……

我们是这一传统的继承者。我们只要重新以这些原则为指导,就能应对新的威胁,而这些新威胁需要我们付出更大的努力——需要国家之间更多的合作与谅解。我们会负责地把伊拉克移交给伊拉克人民,并在阿富汗维持来之不易的和平局面。我们将与老朋友和昔日的对手一道不懈地努力,减少核威胁,扭转全球变暖的趋势。我们不会为我们的生活方式道歉,

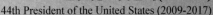

we will defeat you.

For we know that our patchwork heritage is a strength, not a weakness. We are a nation of Christians and Muslims, Jews and Hindus—and non-believers. We are shaped by every language and culture, drawn from every end of this Earth; and because we have tasted the bitter swill of civil war and segregation, and emerged from that dark chapter stronger and more united, we cannot help but believe that the old hatreds shall someday pass; that the lines of tribe shall soon dissolve; that as the world grows smaller, our common humanity shall reveal itself; and that America must play its role in ushering in a new era of peace.

To the Muslim world, we seek a new way forward, based on mutual interest and mutual respect. To those leaders around the globe who seek to sow conflict, or blame their society's ills on the West—know that your people will judge you on what you can build, not what you destroy. To those who cling to power through corruption and deceit and the silencing of dissent, know that you are on the wrong side of history; but that we will extend a hand if you are willing to unclench your fist.

更不会动摇捍卫它的决心。对于那些妄图通过制造恐怖和屠杀无辜来达到目的的人,我们现在就告诉你们,我们的意志更加坚强,不可摧毁;你们无法击垮我们,我们必将战胜你们。

因为我们知道,我国兼收并蓄的传统是一种力量,而不是弱点。我们是一个由基督教徒和穆斯林、犹太教徒和印度教徒以及无宗教信仰者组成的国家。我们受惠于地球上四面八方各种语言和文化的影响。我们饮过南北战争和种族隔离的苦水,在度过了那个黑暗的时代之后,我们变得更加坚强和团结,因此,我们不得不相信:昔日的仇恨终将过去;部族之间的隔阂很快会消失;随着世界变得越来越小,我们共同的人性必将彰显;美国必须为迎来一个和平的新纪元而发挥作用。

对于穆斯林世界,我们将基于共同的利益和相互的尊重,寻求一条新的前进道路。对于世界上那些妄图制造矛盾,将自己社会的弊病归罪于西方的领导人,我们奉劝你们:你们的人民将以你们的建设成就而不是你们的毁灭能力来评判你们。对那些依靠腐败、欺骗、压制不同意见来掌权的人,我们提醒你们:你们站在了历史的反面,但如果你们愿意松开紧握的拳,我们也将伸出相迎的手。

To the people of poor nations, we pledge to work alongside you to make your farms flourish and let clean waters flow; to nourish starved bodies and feed hungry minds. And to those nations like ours that enjoy relative plenty, we say we can no longer afford indifference to suffering outside our borders; nor can we consume the world's resources without regard to effect. For the world has changed, and we must change with it.

As we consider the road that unfolds before us, we remember with humble gratitude those brave Americans who, at this very hour, patrol far-off deserts and distant mountains. They have something to tell us today, just as the fallen heroes who lie in Arlington whisper through the ages. We honor them not only because they are guardians of our liberty, but because they embody the spirit of service; a willingness to find meaning in something greater than themselves. And yet, at this moment—a moment that will define a generation—it is precisely this spirit that must inhabit us all.

For as much as government can do and must do, it is ultimately the faith and determination of the American people upon which this nation relies. It is the kindness to take in a stranger when the levees break, the selflessness of workers who would rather cut their hours than see a friend lose their job which sees us through our darkest hours. It is the firefighter's courage to storm a stairway filled with smoke, but also a parent's willingness to nurture a child, that finally decides our fate.

对于贫困国家的人民，我们保证与你们并肩努力，使农场兴旺，净水长流，饥饿的身体得以饱食，饥渴的心灵受到滋润。对于那些像我们一样比较富裕的国家，我们要说，我们再不能对他人的苦难无动于衷，也再不能肆意消耗世界的资源。世界已经改变，我们必须与时俱进。

在我们思索前方的道路时，我们怀着感激的心情，想起了此刻正在偏远的沙漠和山区巡逻的英勇无畏的美国人。他们有话要对我们说，正如长眠于阿灵顿国家公墓的阵亡英雄，也在透过漫漫岁月向我们轻声诉说。我们崇敬他们，不仅因为他们捍卫我们的自由，而且因为他们代表了为国效劳的精神，体现了超越个人、寻求远大理想的意愿。此时此刻——在这个具有划时代意义的时刻，我们大家必须具备的正是这种精神。

因为无论政府能做多少，必须做多少，归根结底，美国人民的信念和决心才是国家的依靠。正是因为人们在大堤崩裂时接纳陌生人的善良之情，正是因为工人们宁愿减少自己的工时而不愿看到朋友失业的无私精神，才使我们度过了最暗淡的时光。而消防队员们冲进浓烟滚滚的楼道时的大无畏精神，父母亲希望培养子女的殷切心情，将最终决定我们大家的命运。

Barack Obama
巴拉克·奥巴马(1961-)
44th President of the United States (2009-2017)

Our challenges may be new. The instruments with which we meet them may be new. But those values upon which our success depends—hard work and honesty, courage and fair play, tolerance and curiosity, loyalty and patriotism—these things are old. These things are true. They have been the quiet force of progress throughout our history. What is demanded then is a return to these truths. What is required of us now is a new era of responsibility—a recognition, on the part of every American, that we have duties to ourselves, our nation, and the world, duties that we do not grudgingly accept but rather seize gladly, firm in the knowledge that there is nothing so satisfying to the spirit, so defining of our character, than giving our all to a difficult task.

This is the price and the promise of citizenship.

This is the source of our confidence—the knowledge that God calls on us to shape an uncertain destiny.

This is the meaning of our liberty and our creed—why men and women and children of every race and every faith can join in celebration across this magnificent mall, and why a man whose father less than sixty years ago might not have been served at a local restaurant can now stand before you to take a most sacred oath.

So let us mark this day with remembrance, of who we are and how far we have traveled. In the year of America's birth, in the coldest of months, a small band of patriots huddled by dying campfires on the shores of an icy river.

我们可能面临新的挑战,我们可能用新的手段迎接挑战,然而,我们赖以成功的价值观——勤劳和诚实、勇气和公平、宽容和好奇、忠诚和爱国——却是古老的、千真万确的。在美国历史发展的全过程中,这些价值观是无声地推动进步的力量。现在需要的是重归这些真理。我们现在需要做的是开创有责任感的新时代——每一个美国人都要认识到,我们对自己、对国家、对全世界承担着义务。对于这些义务,我们不是勉强接受,而是乐于承担并且坚信:没有什么比全身心地投入一项艰巨的任务更能使我们获得精神上的满足,更能体现我们的特性。

这就是公民的义务和承诺。

这就是我们自信的源泉——我们认识到上帝呼唤我们把握住难以确定的命运。

这就是我们的自由和信条的意义——这就是为什么各个种族、各种信仰的男女老少能在这个华丽的大草坪上欢聚一堂,这就是为什么今天有人能站在这里进行最庄严的宣誓,而不到60年前,他的父亲在当地一家餐馆却有可能得不到接待。

所以,让我们记住这一天,记住我们是什么样的人,记住我们已经走了多远。在美利坚诞生的年代,在最寒

The capital was abandoned. The enemy was advancing. The snow was stained with blood. At a moment when the outcome of our revolution was most in doubt, the father of our nation ordered these words be read to the people:

"Let it be told to the future world…that in the depth of winter, when nothing but hope and virtue could survive…that the city and the country, alarmed at one common danger, came forth to meet it."

America, in the face of our common dangers, in this winter of our hardship, let us remember these timeless words. With hope and virtue, let us brave once more the icy currents, and endure what storms may come. Let it be said by our children's children that when we were tested we refused to let this journey end, that we did not turn back nor did we falter; and with eyes fixed on the horizon and God's grace upon us, we carried forth that great gift of freedom and delivered it safely to future generations.

Thank you. God bless you. And God bless the United States of America.

冷的岁月里，一小队爱国志士聚集在一条冰河的岸边，身旁的篝火即将熄灭。首都已被放弃；敌军正在挺进。鲜血染红了雪地。革命的结局难以确定的时刻，我们的国父发布命令，向人民宣读以下这段话：

"让我们昭告未来世界，在此隆冬时分，万物萧条，唯希望和美德尚存。这个城市和这个国家，受共同危难之召唤，挺身而出，奋起迎战。"

美国同胞们，在我们面临共同危难之际，在这个充满艰难险阻的冬日，让我们牢记这些不朽的话语吧。让我们心怀希望和美德，再一次勇敢地面对寒流，战胜可能到来的风暴吧。让我们的子孙后代这样来评说我们吧——我们在遇到考验的时候，没有半途而废，没有退缩不前，也没有丝毫动摇；我们眺望远方，沐浴着上帝的恩泽，继承了自由的宝贵传统，并让它平稳地世代相传。

谢谢大家。愿上帝保佑你们。愿上帝保佑美利坚合众国。

巴拉克·奥巴马:2012年11月6日,奥巴马在美国总统选举中击败共和党候选人罗姆尼,成功连任。当地时间2013年1月21日中午,奥巴马在国会山公开宣誓后发表连任演讲,演讲强调美国建国精神,阐述了就业、医疗、移民、气候、同性恋、儿童安全等多项议题。该演讲秉承了西方演说修辞的传统,在风格上大量使用隐喻和排比以增强语言的感染力和表现力,语言朴实形象。

Barack Obama
巴拉克·奥巴马(1961-)
44th President of the United States (2009-2017)
Political Party: Democratic

Carrying on what the pioneers began
继续先驱开创的事业

Vice President Biden, Mr. Chief Justice, members of the United States Congress, distinguished guests, and fellow citizens:

　　Each time we gather to inaugurate a President we bear witness to the enduring strength of our Constitution. We affirm the promise of our democracy. We recall that what binds this nation together is not the colors of our skin or the tenets of our faith or the origins of our names. What makes us exceptional—what makes us American—is our allegiance to an idea articulated in a declaration made more than two centuries ago:

拜登副总统、首席大法官先生、国会议员们、尊敬的各位嘉宾、同胞们:

　　每一次我们集会庆祝总统就职都是在见证美国宪法的持久力量。我们都是在肯定美国民主的承诺。我们重申,将这个国家紧密联系在一起的不是我们的肤色,也不是我们信仰的教条,更不是我们名字的来源。让我们与众不同,让我们成为美国人的是我

211

"We hold these truths to be self-evident, that all men are created equal; that they are endowed by their Creator with certain unalienable rights; that among these are life, liberty, and the pursuit of happiness."

Today we continue a never-ending journey to bridge the meaning of those words with the realities of our time. For history tells us that while these truths may be self-evident, they've never been self-executing; that while freedom is a gift from God, it must be secured by His people here on Earth. The patriots of 1776 did not fight to replace the tyranny of a king with the privileges of a few or the rule of a mob. They gave to us a republic, a government of, and by, and for the people, entrusting each generation to keep safe our founding creed.

And for more than two hundred years, we have.

Through blood drawn by lash and blood drawn by sword, we learned that no union founded on the principles of liberty and equality could survive half-slave and half-free. We made ourselves anew, and vowed to move forward together.

Together, we determined that a modern economy requires railroads and highways to speed travel and commerce, schools and colleges to train our workers.

们对于一种理念的恪守。200多年前,这一理念在一篇宣言中被清晰阐述:

"我们认为下述真理是不言而喻的,人人生而平等。造物主赋予他们若干不可剥夺的权利,包括生存、自由和追求幸福的权利。"(注:此句摘自《美国独立宣言》)

今天,我们继续着这一永恒的征程,架起这些理念与我们时代现实之间的桥梁。因为历史告诉我们,即便这些真理是不言而喻的,它们也从来不会自动生效。因为虽然自由是上帝赋予的礼物,但仍需要世间的子民去捍卫。1776年揭竿而起的美国爱国先驱们,推翻英国国王的暴政,并非为着赢得少数人的特权,亦无意于建立暴民之统治。先驱们留给我们一个共和国,一个民有、民治、民享的政府。他们委托每一代美国人捍卫我们的建国信条。

在过去的200多年里,我们做到了。

从奴役的血腥绳索,和刀剑的血光厮杀中我们懂得了:建立在自由与平等原则之上的联邦不能永远维持半奴隶和半自由的状态。我们赢得了新生,誓言共同前进。

我们共同努力,建立起现代的经济体系。架设铁路与高速公路,加速了旅游和商业交流。建立学校与大学,培训我们的工人。

Barack Obama
巴拉克·奥巴马(1961-)
44th President of the United States (2009-2017)

Together, we discovered that a free market only thrives when there are rules to ensure competition and fair play.

Together, we resolved that a great nation must care for the vulnerable, and protect its people from life's worst hazards and misfortune.

Through it all, we have never relinquished our skepticism of central authority, nor have we succumbed to the fiction that all society's ills can be cured through government alone. Our celebration of initiative and enterprise, our insistence on hard work and personal responsibility, these are constants in our character.

But we have always understood that when times change, so must we; that fidelity to our founding principles requires new responses to new challenges; that preserving our individual freedoms ultimately requires collective action. For the American people can no more meet the demands of today's world by acting alone than American soldiers could have met the forces of fascism or communism with muskets and militias. No single person can train all the math and science teachers we'll need to equip our children for the future, or build the roads and networks and research labs that will bring new jobs and businesses to our shores. Now, more than ever, we must do these things together, as one nation and one people.

This generation of Americans has been tested by crises that steeled our resolve and proved our resilience. A decade of war is now ending. An economic recovery has begun.

我们一起发现,自由市场的繁荣只能建立在保障竞争与公平竞争的原则之上。

我们共下决心,让这个伟大的国家关爱弱者,保护她的人民不受生命威胁和不幸侵扰。

一路走来,我们从未放弃对中央集权的质疑。我们同样不屈服于这一谎言:一切的社会弊端都能够只靠政府来解决。我们对积极向上与奋发进取的赞扬,我们对努力工作与个人责任的坚持,这些都是美国精神的基本要义。

我们也理解,时代在变化,我们同样要变革。对建国精神的忠诚,需要我们迎接新的挑战。保护我们的个人自由,最终需要所有人的共同努力。因为美国人不能再独力迎接当今世界的挑战,正如美国士兵们不能再像先辈一样,用步枪和民兵同敌人(法西斯主义与共产主义)作战。一个人无法培训所有的数学与科学老师,我们需要他们为了未来去教育孩子们。一个人无法建设道路、铺设网络、建立实验室来为国内带来新的工作岗位和商业机会。现在,与以往任何时候相比,我们都更需要团结合作。作为一个国家,一个民族团结起来。

这一代美国人经历了危机的考验,经济危机坚定了我们的决心,证明了我们的恢复

America's possibilities are limitless, for we possess all the qualities that this world without boundaries demands: youth and drive; diversity and openness; an endless capacity for risk and a gift for reinvention. My fellow Americans, we are made for this moment, and we will seize it—so long as we seize it together.

For we, the people, understand that our country cannot succeed when a shrinking few do very well and a growing many barely make it. We believe that America's prosperity must rest upon the broad shoulders of a rising middle class. We know that America thrives when every person can find independence and pride in their work; when the wages of honest labor liberate families from the brink of hardship. We are true to our creed when a little girl born into the bleakest poverty knows that she has the same chance to succeed as anybody else, because she is an American; she is free, and she is equal, not just in the eyes of God but also in our own.

We understand that outworn programs are inadequate to the needs of our time. So we must harness new ideas and technology to remake our government, revamp our tax code, reform our schools, and empower our citizens with the skills they need to work harder, learn more, reach higher. But while the means will change, our purpose endures: a nation that rewards the effort and determination of every single American. That is what this moment requires. That is what will give real meaning to our creed.

力。长达十年的战争正在结束，经济的复苏已经开始。美国的可能性是无限的，因为我们拥有当今没有边界的世界所需要的所有品质：年轻与活力、多样性与开放、无穷的冒险精神以及创造的天赋才能。我亲爱的同胞们，我们正是为此刻而生，我们更要在此刻团结一致，抓住当下的机会。

因为我们，美国人民，清楚如果只有不断萎缩的少数人获得成功，而大多数人不能成功，我们的国家就无法成功。我们相信美国的繁荣必须建立在中产阶级壮大的基础上，美国的兴旺意味着每个人能在工作中获得独立和尊严，诚实的劳动者的薪水能使他的家庭脱离经济危机。我们忠诚于我们的事业，保证让一个生于最贫穷环境中的小女孩都能知道，她有同其他所有人一样的成功机会。因为她是一个美国人，她是自由的、平等的。她的自由平等不仅由上帝来见证，更由我们亲手保护。

我们知道，我们已然陈旧的政府项目不足以满足时代的需要。我们必须应用新理念和新技术重塑我们的政府、改进我们的税法、改革我们的学校，让我们的公民拥有他们所需要的技能，更加努力地工作，学更多的知识，向更高的地方发展。这意味着变革，我们的目标是：国家可以奖励每

Barack Obama
巴拉克·奥巴马(1961-)
44th President of the United States (2009-2017)

We, the people, still believe that every citizen deserves a basic measure of security and dignity. We must make the hard choices to reduce the cost of health care and the size of our deficit. But we reject the belief that America must choose between caring for the generation that built this country and investing in the generation that will build its future. For we remember the lessons of our past, when twilight years were spent in poverty and parents of a child with a disability had nowhere to turn.

We do not believe that in this country freedom is reserved for the lucky, or happiness for the few. We recognize that no matter how responsibly we live our lives, any one of us at any time may face a job loss, or a sudden illness, or a home swept away in a terrible storm. The commitments we make to each other through Medicare and Medicaid and Social Security, these things do not sap our initiative, they strengthen us. They do not make us a nation of takers; they free us to take the risks that make this country great.

We, the people, still believe that our obligations as Americans are not just to ourselves, but to all posterity. We will respond to the threat of climate change, knowing that the failure to do so would betray our children and future generations. Some may still deny the overwhelming judgment of science, but none can avoid the devastating impact of raging fires and crippling drought and more

个美国人的努力和果断。这是现在需要的。这将给我们的信条赋予真正的意义。

我们,人民,仍然认为,每个公民都应当获得基本的安全和尊严。我们必须做出艰难抉择,降低医疗成本,缩减赤字规模。但我们拒绝相信,美国必须在照顾老年一代和培育下一代中只能选其一。因为我们记得过去的教训:老年人的夕阳时光在贫困中度过,家有残障儿童的父母无处求助。

我们相信,在这个国家,自由不只是那些幸运儿的专属,或者说幸福只属于少数人。我们知道,不管我们是怎样负责任地生活,我们任何人在任何时候都可能面临失业、突发疾病或住房被可怕的飓风摧毁的风险。我们通过医疗保险、联邦医疗补助计划、社会保障项目向每个人做出承诺,这些不会让我们的创造力衰竭,而是将会让我们强大。这些不会让我们成为充满不劳而获者的国度,这些让我们可以摆脱后顾之忧,为建设伟大的国家勇担风险。

我们,人民,仍然相信,我们作为美国人的义务不只是对我们自己而言,还包括对子孙后代。我们将应对气候变化的威胁,认识到不采取措施应对气候变化就是对我们的孩子和后代的背叛。一些人可能仍在否定科学界压倒性

powerful storms.

The path towards sustainable energy sources will be long and sometimes difficult. But America cannot resist this transition, we must lead it. We cannot cede to other nations the technology that will power new jobs and new industries, we must claim its promise. That's how we will maintain our economic vitality and our national treasure— our forests and waterways, our crop lands and snow— capped peaks. That is how we will preserve our planet, commanded to our care by God. That's what will lend meaning to the creed our fathers once declared.

We, the people, still believe that enduring security and lasting peace do not require perpetual war. Our brave men and women in uniform, tempered by the flames of battle, are unmatched in skill and courage. Our citizens, seared by the memory of those we have lost, know too well the price that is paid for liberty. The knowledge of their sacrifice will keep us forever vigilant against those who would do us harm. But we are also heirs to those who won the peace and not just the war; who turned sworn enemies into the surest of friends—and we must carry those lessons into this time as well.

We will defend our people and uphold our values through strength of arms and rule of law. We will show the courage to try and resolve our differences with other nations peacefully—not because we are naïve about the dangers we face, but because engagement can more durably lift

的判断,但没有人能够避免火灾、严重旱灾、更强力风暴带来的灾难性打击。

通向可再生能源利用的道路是漫长的,有时是困难的。但美国不能抵制这种趋势,我们必须引领这种趋势。我们不能把制造新就业机会和新行业的技术让给其他国家,我们必须声明这一承诺。这将是我们保持经济活力和国家财富(我们的森林和航道,我们的农田与雪峰)的方法。这将是我们保护我们星球的办法,上帝把它托付给我们照顾。这将为我们的建国之父们曾宣布的信条赋予意义。

我们,人民,仍然相信持久的安全与和平,不需要持续的战争。我们勇敢的男女士兵经受了战火的考验,他们的技能和勇气是无可匹敌的。我们的公民依然铭记着那些阵亡者,他们非常清楚我们为自由付出的代价。明白他们的牺牲将让我们永远对那些试图伤害我们的势力保持警惕。但我们也是那些赢得和平而不只是战争的人们的后代,他们将仇敌转变成最可靠的朋友,我们也必须把这些经验带到这个时代。

我们将通过强大的军力和法制保护我们的人民,捍卫我们的价值观。我们将展现试图和平解决与其他国家分歧的勇气,但这不是因为我们

Barack Obama
巴拉克·奥巴马(1961-)
44th President of the United States (2009-2017)

suspicion and fear.

America will remain the anchor of strong alliances in every corner of the globe. And we will renew those institutions that extend our capacity to manage crisis abroad, for no one has a greater stake in a peaceful world than its most powerful nation. We will support democracy from Asia to Africa, from the Americas to the Middle East, because our interests and our conscience compel us to act on behalf of those who long for freedom. And we must be a source of hope to the poor, the sick, the marginalized, the victims of prejudice—not out of mere charity, but because peace in our time requires the constant advance of those principles that our common creed describes: tolerance and opportunity, human dignity and justice.

We, the people, declare today that the most evident of truths—that all of us are created equal—is the star that guides us still; just as it guided our forebears through Seneca Falls, and Selma, and Stonewall; just as it guided all those men and women, sung and unsung, who left footprints along this great Mall, to hear a preacher say that we cannot walk alone; to hear a King proclaim that our individual freedom is inextricably bound to the freedom of every soul on Earth.

对面临的危险持幼稚的态度，而是因为接触能够更持久地化解疑虑和恐惧。

美国将在全球保持强大的联盟，我们将更新这些能扩展我们应对海外危机能力的机构。因为作为世界上最强大的国家，我们在世界和平方面拥有最大的利益。我们将支持从亚洲到非洲、从美洲至中东的民主，因为我们的利益和良心驱使我们代表那些想获得自由的人们采取行动。我们必须成为贫困者、病患者、被边缘化的人士、异见受害者的希望来源，不仅仅是出于慈善，也是因为这个时代的和平需要不断推进我们共同信念中的原则：宽容和机遇，人类尊严与正义。

我们，人民，今天昭示的最明白的事实是——我们所有人都是生而平等的，这是依然引领我们的恒星。它引领我们的先辈穿越纽约塞尼卡瀑布城（女权抗议事件）、塞尔玛（黑人权力事件）和石墙骚乱（同性恋与警察发生的暴力事件），引领着所有的男性和女性，留下姓名和没留姓名的人。在伟大的征程中，一路上留下足迹的人。曾经听一位牧师说，我们不能独自前行。马丁·路德·金说，我们个人的自由与地球上每个灵魂的自由不可分割。

（注：1.（Seneca Falls）塞内卡瀑布：1848年，美国争取妇女投票权的人士在纽约州的塞内卡瀑布地区召开大会。这次大会被认为是现代女权运动的开创

It is now our generation's task to carry on what those pioneers began. For our journey is not complete until our wives, our mothers and daughters can earn a living equal to their efforts. Our journey is not complete until our gay brothers and sisters are treated like anyone else under the law—for if we are truly created equal, then surely the love we commit to one another must be equal as well. Our journey is not complete until no citizen is forced to wait for hours to exercise the right to vote. Our journey is not complete until we find a better way to welcome the striving, hopeful immigrants who still see America as a land of opportunity—until bright young students and engineers are enlisted in our workforce rather than expelled from our country. Our journey is not complete until all our children, from the streets of Detroit to the hills of Appalachia, to the quiet lanes of Newtown, know that they are cared for and cherished and always safe from harm.

That is our generation's task—to make these words,

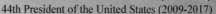

these rights, these values of life and liberty and the pursuit of happiness real for every American. Being true to our founding documents does not require us to agree on every contour of life. It does not mean we all define liberty in exactly the same way or follow the same precise path to happiness. Progress does not compel us to settle centuries-long debates about the role of government for all time, but it does require us to act in our time.

For now decisions are upon us and we cannot afford delay. We cannot mistake absolutism for principle, or substitute spectacle for politics, or treat name-calling as reasoned debate. We must act, we must act knowing that our work will be imperfect. We must act, knowing that today's victories will be only partial and that it will be up to those who stand here in four years and 40 years and 400 years hence to advance the timeless spirit once conferred to us in a spare Philadelphia hall.

My fellow Americans, the oath I have sworn before you today, like the one recited by others who serve in this Capitol, was an oath to God and country, not party or faction. And we must faithfully execute that pledge during the duration of our service. But the words I spoke today are not so different from the oath that is taken each time a soldier signs up for duty or an immigrant realizes her dream. My oath is not so different from the pledge we all make to the flag that waves above and that fills our hearts with pride.

务——让生存、自由和追求幸福的说辞、权力和价值切实体现在每个美国人的身上。我们的立国文本没有要求我们将每个人的生活一致化。这并不意味着，我们会以完全一样的方式去定义自由，沿着同样的道路通向幸福。几个世纪以来关于政府角色的争议，不会随着时代的进步消散，但这更加要求我们立刻采取行动。

目前是由我们决策，我们不能拖延。我们不能将绝对主义当作原则，或者以假象代替政纲，或将中伤视作理性的辩论。我们必须行动，要意识到我们的工作并不完美。我们必须行动，意识到今天的胜利是并不完全的。这些将有赖于未来4年、40年或是400年致力于这项事业的人，去推进当年在费城制宪会议大厅传承给我们的永恒精神。

我的美国同胞，我今天在你们面前宣读的誓词，如同在国会山服务的其他人曾宣读过的誓词一样，是对上帝和国家的誓词，不是对党派或是派别的，我们必须在任期内忠实地履行这些承诺。但我今天宣读的誓词与士兵报名参军或者是移民实现梦想时所宣读的誓词没有多少差别。我的誓词与我们所有的人向我们头顶飘扬的、让我们心怀自豪的国旗所表达的誓言没有多大差别。

They are the words of citizens and they represent our greatest hope. You and I, as citizens, have the power to set this country's course. You and I, as citizens, have the obligation to shape the debates of our time—not only with the votes we cast, but with the voices we lift in defense of our most ancient values and enduring ideals.

Let us, each of us, now embrace with solemn duty and awesome joy what is our lasting birthright. With common effort and common purpose, with passion and dedication, let us answer the call of history and carry into an uncertain future that precious light of freedom.

Thank you. God bless you, and may He forever bless these United States of America.

这些是公民的誓词,代表着我们最伟大的希望。你和我,作为公民,都有为这个国家设定道路的权力。你和我,作为公民,有义务塑造我们时代的辩题,不仅是通过我们的选票,而且要为保卫最悠久的价值观和持久的理想发声。

现在让我们互相拥抱,怀着庄严的职责和无比的快乐,这是我们永久的与生俱来的权利。有共同的努力和共同的目标,用热情与奉献,让我们回答历史的召唤,将宝贵的自由之光带入并不确定的未来。

感谢你们,上帝保佑你们,愿上帝永远保佑美利坚合众国。

唐纳德·特朗普:美国第45任总统(2017—),1946年6月14日生于美国纽约。政治家、商人、作家。这是一次以"唯有美国第一"为主旨,以保护主义为基调的就职演说。在演讲中,特朗普一再强调美国利益至上,他表示这一天美国人民重新掌握国家政权,美国人民要团结起来,改变美国的未来,共同见证美国前所未有的繁荣。

Donald Trump
唐纳德·特朗普(1946-)
45th President of the United States (2017-)
Political Party: Republican

America First
美国利益至上

Chief Justice Roberts, President Carter, President Clinton, President Bush, President Obama, fellow Americans and people of the world: thank you.

We, the citizens of America, are now joined in a great national effort to rebuild our country and restore its promise for all of our people. Together we will determine the course of America and the world for many, many years to come.

We will face challenges. We will confront hardships. But we will get the job done. Every four years, we gather on these steps to carry out the orderly and peaceful transfer

首席大法官罗伯茨先生,卡特总统,克林顿总统,布什总统,奥巴马总统,各位美国同胞,世界人民:感谢你们。

各位美国公民,我们正在参与一项伟大的全国性事业:重建我们的国家,重塑对全体人民的承诺。携起手来,我们将决定美国和世界今后许多许多年的道路。

我们将遭遇挑战。我们会遇到困难。但是我们能将这项事业完成。每过四年,我

of power. And we are grateful to President Obama and First Lady Michelle Obama for their gracious aid throughout this transition. They have been magnificent. Thank you.

Today's ceremony, however, has very special meaning. Because today, we are not merely transferring power from one administration to another or from one party to another. But we are transferring power from Washington D. C. and giving it back to you, the people.

For too long, a small group in our nation's capital has reaped the rewards of government while the people have borne the cost. Washington flourished, but the people did not share in its wealth. Politicians prospered, but the jobs left. And the factories closed.

The establishment protected itself but not the citizens of our country. Their victories have not been your victories. Their triumphs have not been your triumphs. And while they celebrated in our nation's capital, there was little to celebrate for struggling families all across our land.

That all changes starting right here and right now. Because this moment is your moment. It belongs to you. It belongs to everyone gathered here today and everyone watching all across America. This is your day. This is your celebration. And this, the United States of America, is your country.

What truly matters is not which party controls our government but whether our government is controlled by the

们都相聚在这里进行有序、和平的权力交接。我们要感谢奥巴马总统和第一夫人米歇尔·奥巴马,在过渡期间,他们慷慨地给予我帮助。他们真了不起。谢谢。

今天的就职典礼有着特殊的意义。因为,今天,我们不只是将权力由一任总统交接到下一任总统,由一个政党交接给另一政党。今天我们是将权力由华盛顿交接到了人民的手中,即你们的手中。

长久以来,我们国家首都的一小群人攫取了政府的利益果实,代价却要由人民来承受。华盛顿欣欣向荣,人民却没有分享到财富。政客们塞满了腰包,工作机会却越来越少。工厂纷纷倒闭。

当权派保护的是他们自己,而不是我们国家的公民。他们的成功和胜利不属于你们。当他们在我们的首都欢呼庆祝时,这片土地上无数在挣扎奋斗的家庭却没有什么可以庆祝的。

但这些都会改变,在此地改变,在此时改变。因为当下是你们的时刻,这一刻属于你们。这一刻属于今天聚集在这里的所有人,所有观看就职典礼的美国人。这是属于你们的一天。这是你们的庆典。这,美利坚合众国,是你们的国家。

真正重要的并不是政府由哪个党派当政,而是政府是

Donald Trump
唐纳德·特朗普(1946-)
45th President of the United States (2017-)

people. January 20th, 2017 will be remembered as the day the people became the rulers of this nation again.

The forgotten men and women of our country will be forgotten no longer. Everyone is listening to you now. You came by the tens of millions to become part of a historic movement, the likes of which the world has never seen before.

At the center of this movement is a crucial conviction that a nation exists to serve its citizens. Americans want great schools for their children, safe neighborhoods for their families and good jobs for themselves.

These are just and reasonable demands of righteous people and a righteous public. But for too many of our citizens, a different reality exists: Mothers and children trapped in poverty in our inner cities; rusted-out factories scattered like tombstones across the landscape of our nation; an education system flush with cash, but which leaves our young and beautiful students deprived of knowledge; and the crime and gangs and drugs that have stolen too many lives and robbed our country of so much unrealized potential.

This American carnage stops right here and stops right now.

We are one nation and their pain is our pain. Their dreams are our dreams; and their success will be our success. We share one heart, one home, and one glorious destiny. The oath of office I take today is an oath of allegiance to all Americans.

否由人民做主。2017年1月20日,这一天将会被铭记,人民再次成了这个国家的主人。

我们国家被遗忘的男男女女将不再被忘却。现在,所有人都在倾听你们。你们数千万人正加入一场历史运动,这是世间前所未有的一场运动。

这场运动秉承着一个至关重要的信念:国家是为服务人民而存在的。美国人希望孩子们享受优良的学校教育,家人可以享受安全的社区环境,自己可以得到优质的就业岗位。

这些公正、合理的诉求来自正直的民众。但对太多公民而言,现实却是另一番景象:在内陆城市,母亲和孩子们正饱受贫困;生锈的工厂像墓碑一样布满我们国家的土地;教育系统充斥着黑暗的权钱交易,我们年轻美丽的学生们失去汲取知识的机会;犯罪、黑帮和毒品夺走了太多生命,剥夺了我们国家众多尚未释放的潜力。

这种美国式荼毒生灵的惨剧将在此时、此地彻底终结。

我们同属一个国家;他们的痛苦就是我们的痛苦;他们的梦想也是我们的梦想;他们的成就将是我们的成就。我们万众一心,同住一个家园,共享辉煌命运。今天我宣誓就职,就是对全体美国人宣誓效忠。

For many decades, we've enriched foreign industry at the expense of American industry; subsidized the armies of other countries while allowing for the very sad depletion of our military; we've defended other nation's borders while refusing to defend our own; and spent trillions and trillions of dollars overseas while America's infrastructure has fallen into disrepair and decay. We've made other countries rich while the wealth, strength, and confidence of our country has dissipated over the horizon.

One by one, the factories shuttered and left our shores, with not even a thought about the millions and millions of American workers that were left behind. The wealth of our middle class has been ripped from their homes and then redistributed all across the entire world. But that is the past. And now we are looking only to the future.

We assembled here today are issuing a new decree to be heard in every city, in every foreign capital, and in every hall of power. From this day forward, a new vision will govern our land. From this day forward, it's going to be only America First—America First.

Every decision on trade, on taxes, on immigration, on foreign affairs, will be made to benefit American workers and American families. We must protect our borders from the ravages of other countries making our products, stealing our companies, and destroying our jobs. Protection will lead to great prosperity and strength. I will fight for you with every breath in my body—and I will never, ever let you down. America will start winning again, winning like never before.

几十年来，我们牺牲了美国工业，让别国工业得以兴旺；为别国军队施以援助，但对本国军力令人心痛的耗损却视而不见；我们曾经参与保卫其他国家的领地，却疏忽了对自己领土的保护；我们在海外投入成千上万亿美元，自己的基础设施却年久失修、长年荒废。我们帮助其他国家走上了富裕之路，自己的财富、力量和自信却逐渐消失在地平线上。

我们的工厂一个接一个倒闭，却没有考虑被落下的成千上万名工人。我们中产阶级的财富被剥削，再被分配给世界其他国家。但这些都已成过往，现在，我们要面向未来。

我们今天聚集于此，是要发布一道新的法则，让它在每座城市、每个国家的首都、每座权力的殿堂回响。从今天开始，我们的国家将拥有新的愿景。从今天开始，所有一切都只以美国利益为主！美国利益至上！

所有有关贸易、税收、移民或者外交事务的决定，都要有利于美国工人和美国家庭。我们要保护我们的国界不受他国的破坏。这些国家生产了我们的产品，盗取了我们的公司，摧毁了我们的就业。只有自我保护，才能实现真正的富强。我会拼尽全力，为你们奋战到底，永远永远不让你们失望。美国会重新成为胜者，它的胜利将远超昔日的荣光。

Donald Trump
唐纳德·特朗普(1946-)
45th President of the United States (2017-)

We will bring back our jobs. We will bring back our borders. We will bring back our wealth. And we will bring back our dreams. We will build new roads, and highways, and bridges, and airports, and tunnels, and railways all across our wonderful nation. We will get our people off of welfare and back to work—rebuilding our country with American hands and American labor. We will follow two simple rules: Buy American and hire American.

We will seek friendship and goodwill with the nations of the world.

But we do so with the understanding that it is the right of all nations to put their own interests first. We do not seek to impose our way of life on anyone, but rather to let it shine as an example. We will shine for everyone to follow. We will reinforce old alliances and form new ones. And unite the civilized world against radical Islamic terrorism, which we will eradicate completely from the face of the Earth.

At the bedrock of our politics will be a total allegiance to the United States of America, and through our loyalty to our country, we will rediscover our loyalty to each other. When you open your heart to patriotism, there is no room for prejudice. The *Bible* tells us, "How good and pleasant it is when God's people live together in unity." We must speak our minds openly, debate our disagreements honestly, but always pursue solidarity. When America is united, America is totally unstoppable.

我们会拿回属于我们的工作;我们会重新守卫住国界;我们会夺回我们的财富,重新实现我们的梦想。在我们辽阔伟大的国土上,我们要修建新的道路、高速公路、桥梁、机场、隧道和铁路。人民将不再依靠福利,而是回到工作岗位,依靠美国人的双手、美国人的劳动,重建我们的国家。我们将遵循两条最简单的原则——买美国商品,雇美国工人。

我们会与世界各国家和睦相处。

但我们这么做时要明白:把自己的利益放在前面是所有国家的权利。我们不寻求将自己的生活方式强加于人,更期望它能成为典范被所有人追随。我们将以身作则,为别人树立榜样。我们会加固与旧盟友的关系,并建立新的联盟。团结文明世界的国家,以抵御激进的伊斯兰恐怖主义,我们会把他们从地球上抹除。

我们执政的基石是对美利坚合众国的完全效忠。通过忠诚于我们的国家,我们会重新找到彼此之间的忠诚。当你心怀爱国主义,你便不会再心存偏见。《圣经》告诉我们:"上帝子民和睦而居,何等愉悦,何等美好。"我们必须坦率地表达我们的观点,真诚地就不同观点进行辩论,但同时,我们也要追求团结一

There should be no fear—we are protected, and we will always be protected. We will be protected by the great men and women of our military and law enforcement and, most importantly, we are protected by God.

Finally, we must think big and dream even bigger. In America, we understand that a nation is only living as long as it is striving. We will no longer accept politicians who are all talk and no action—constantly complaining but never doing anything about it. The time for empty talk is over. Now arrives the hour of action. Do not allow anyone to tell you it cannot be done. No challenge can match the heart and fight and spirit of America.

We will not fail. Our country will thrive and prosper again. We stand at the birth of a new millennium, ready to unlock the mysteries of space, to free the Earth from the miseries of disease, and to harness the energies, industries and technologies of tomorrow.

A new national pride will stir our souls, lift our sights, and heal our divisions. It is time to remember that old wisdom our soldiers will never forget: that whether we are black or brown or white, we all bleed the same red blood of patriots, we all enjoy the same glorious freedoms, and we all salute the same great American Flag.

And whether a child is born in the urban sprawl of Detroit or the windswept plains of Nebraska, they look up at the same night sky, they fill their heart with the same dreams, and they are infused with the breath of life by the same almighty Creator.

致。当美国人民团结在一起时，美国会变得势不可挡。

我们无需心存恐惧——我们有人保护，我们会永远被保护着。军队、执法部门中的了不起的人们会保护着我们。更重要的是，上帝会庇护我们。

最后，我们必须有雄心壮志和伟大梦想。在美国，我们明白，一个国家只有不断进取，才能生存下去。我们不能再让政客们夸夸其谈，无所作为——只会抱怨，从不行动。讲空话的时代已经结束了。现在是行动的时刻。别让人告诉你这事干不成。美国人的心性、斗志和精神可以克服任何挑战。

我们不会失败。我们的国家会重新发展和繁荣起来。我们即将迎来新的一个世纪，准备解密神秘的太空，将世界从疾病的苦痛中解救，驾驭未来的新能源、新产业和新技术。

一种全新的民族自豪感将激励我们，提升我们的视野，弥合我们的分歧。要记住士兵们永远不会忘记的一句老话——不管是黑皮肤、棕色皮肤，还是白皮肤，我们都流着爱国者的红色血液，我们都同样享有光荣的自由，我们都向同一面美国旗帜敬礼。

我们的孩子，不管是出生在底特律城郊，还是内布拉斯加州风中的平原，他们仰望的都是同一片夜空，他们的内心都承载着同样的梦想，他们的

Donald Trump
唐纳德·特朗普(1946-)
45th President of the United States (2017-)

So to all Americans, in every city near and far, small and large, from mountain to mountain, from ocean to ocean, hear these words: You will never be ignored again. Your voice, your hopes, and your dreams will define our American destiny. And your courage and goodness and love will forever guide us along the way.

Together, We will make America strong again. We will make America wealthy again. We will make America proud again. We will make America safe again. And yes, together, we will make America great again.

Thank you. God bless you. And God bless America.

生命都由同一个万能的造物所赋予。

所有的美国人,无论身在哪个城市,或远或近,或大或小,即使远隔千山万水,你们也要记住:你再也不会被忽视。你们的声音、你们的希望和你们的梦想,将定义美国的命运。

你们的勇气、善良和爱将永远引领我们前行。携起手来,我们要让美国再次强大!我们要让美国再次富有!我们要让美国再次自豪!我们要让美国再次安全!是的,没错,携起手来,我们要让美国再次伟大!

谢谢你们。上帝保佑你们。上帝保佑美国。

乔·拜登:美国第46任总统（2021— ），特拉华州律师和政治家，奥巴马执政时期美国副总统。本篇结合美国国内两党分裂的政治现状，以及新型冠状肺炎带来的种种社会矛盾，提出"团结一心"的主题，号召全体美国人抛开分歧，齐心协力，迎接考验，肩负责任，为后代留下美好新世界，书写美国历史新篇章。

Joe Biden
乔·拜登(1942-)
46th President of the United States (2021-)
Political Party: Democratic

Unity is the path forward
团结是前进的道路

Chief Justice Roberts, Vice President Harris, Speaker Pelosi, Leader Schumer, McConnell, Vice President Pence, my distinguished guests, my fellow Americans.

This is America's day. This is democracy's day. A day of history and hope, of renewal and resolve. Through a crucible for the ages, America has been tested anew and America has risen to the challenge. Today, we celebrate the triumph not of a candidate, but of a cause, the cause of democracy. The will of the people has been heard and the will of the people has been heeded.

首席大法官罗伯茨，哈里斯副总统，佩洛西议长，舒默领袖，麦康奈尔领袖，彭斯副总统，尊敬的嘉宾们，美国同胞们：

今天是美国之日，是民主之日，是充满历史和希望、复兴和决心之日。历经多年考验，美国经受了新的考验，美国已奋起迎接挑战。今天，我们庆祝的不是一位候选人的胜利，而是一项事业，一项民主事业的胜利。人民的意志得到了倾听，人民的意志得到了重视。

Joe Biden
乔·拜登(1942-)
46th President of the United States (2021-)

We've learned again that democracy is precious, Democracy is fragile. At this hour, my friends, democracy has prevailed.

So now, on this hallowed ground where just a few days ago, violence sought to shake this Capitol's very foundation, we come together as one nation, under God, indivisible, to carry out the peaceful transfer of power as we have for more than two centuries.

We look ahead in our uniquely American way—restless, bold, optimistic—and set our sights on the nation we know we can be and we must be.

I thank my predecessors of both parties for their presence here today. I thank them from the bottom of my heart. You know the resilience of our Constitution and the strength, the strength of our nation. As does President Carter, who I spoke with last night, who cannot be with us today, but whom we salute for his lifetime of service.

I've just taken the sacred oath each of those patriots have taken—an oath, first sworn by George Washington. But the American story depends not on any one of us, not on some of us, but on all of us, on "We the People" who seek a more perfect union.

This is a great nation. We are good people. And over the centuries, through storm and strife, in peace and in war, we've come so far. But we still have far to go.

We'll press forward with speed and urgency, for we have much to do in this winter of peril and significant possibility. Much to repair, much to restore, much to heal,

我们再次认识到,民主是宝贵的,民主是脆弱的。朋友们,在这一时刻,民主占了上风。

现在,在这片神圣土地上,这片几天前暴力妄想撼动国会大厦根基的土地上,在上帝的指引下,我们作为一个不可分割的国家团结在一起,遵照我们两个多世纪以来的传统,进行权力的和平交接。

我们以独特的美国方式展望未来:躁动、大胆、乐观,聚焦于我们可以且必须成为的国家。

感谢两党的前任今天能够出席。我由衷地感谢他们。你们知道我们的宪法极具韧性,我们的国家充满力量。正如昨晚与我交谈的卡特总统一样。即使他今天不能到场与我们同在,让我们向他的毕生奉献致敬。

我刚做了神圣的宣誓,诚如乔治·华盛顿以来每个爱国者那样,但美国故事并不取决于我们中任何一个,也不取决于我们中的某些,而是取决于我们所有人,取决于我们这些寻求更完美团结的人民。

这是一个伟大的国家,我们都是善良的人。几个世纪以来,历经风风雨雨,和平与战争,我们已走了这么远,我们还有很长的路要走。

我们将快速而有紧迫感地前进,因为我们在这个危险且充满巨大可能性的冬天有

much to build, and much to gain. Few people in our nation's history have been more challenged or found a time more challenging or difficult than the time we're in now. A once-in-a-century virus that silently stalks the country has taken as many lives in one year as America lost in all of World War Ⅱ.

Millions of jobs have been lost. Hundreds of thousands of businesses closed. A cry for racial justice, some four hundred years in the making, moves us. The dream of justice for all will be deferred no longer. A cry for survivals comes from planet itself. A cry that can't be any more desperate or any more clear now. The rise of political extremism, white supremacy, domestic terrorism that we must confront and we will defeat.

To overcome these challenges to restore the soul and secure the future of America, requires so much more than words. It requires the most elusive of all things in a democracy: unity. Unity.

In another January, on New Year's Day in 1863, Abraham Lincoln signed the Emancipation Proclamation. When he put pen to paper, the president said, and I quote, "If my name ever goes down into history, it'll be for this act. And my whole soul is in it."

My whole soul was in it today, on this January day. My whole soul is in this: Bringing America together, uniting our people, uniting our nation. And I ask every American to join me in this cause. Uniting to fight the foes we face—anger, resentment, hatred, extremism, lawlessness, violence, disease, joblessness and hopelessness.

很多事情要做。我们有太多要完成,太多要治愈,太多要恢复,太多要建设,还有太多要收获。在我们国家的历史上,很少有人遇到过更大的挑战,也很少有人遇到过像如今一样如此充满挑战和困难的时代。百年一遇的病毒潜入我们的国家,在一年中夺走的生命比整个二战还要多。

数百万人失业,数十万的生意停摆。四百年来为种族正义的呐喊令我们动容。人人获得正义的梦想,将不再推延。生存的呐喊来自这个星球本身,这一呐喊从未像现在这样迫切,或者如此清晰。政治极端主义、白人至上、国内恐怖主义兴起,我们必须与之斗争,也必定将之击败。

为了克服这些挑战,重塑灵魂,守卫美国的未来,我们需要的远胜于言语,我们需要民主中最难以捉摸的东西,那就是团结。团结。

在另一个一月,1863年元旦,亚伯拉罕·林肯签署了《解放黑奴宣言》。当他把笔放在纸上的那一刻,林肯总统说道:"如果我能名留青史,一定是因为这一举动,我的整个灵魂都投入在这件事上。"

在今天,一月的这天,我也投入了整个灵魂。我全心全意投入于:让美国团结起来,团结我们的人民,团结我们的国家。我请每个美国人都加入这项事业里来。团结

Joe Biden
乔·拜登(1942-)
46th President of the United States (2021-)

With unity, we can do great things, important things. We can right wrongs. We can put people to work in good jobs. We can teach our children in safe schools. We can overcome the deadly virus. We can reward work, rebuild the middle class and make work secure for all. We can secure racial justice and we can make America once again the leading force for good in the world.

I know speaking of unity can sound to some like a foolish fantasy these days. I know the forces that divide us are deep and they are real, but I also know they are not new.

Our history has been a constant struggle between the American ideal that we're all created equal, and the harsh, ugly reality that racism, nativism, fear, demonization have torn us apart. The battle is perennial and victory is never assured.

Through the Civil War, the Great Depression, World War, 9/11, through struggle, sacrifice and setbacks, our better angels have always prevailed. In each of our moments, enough of us have come together to carry all of us forward, and we can do that now.

History, faith and reason show the way, the way of unity.

We can see each other not as adversaries, but as

起来对抗我们面临的敌人：愤怒、怨恨、仇恨、极端、违法、暴力、疾病、失业和绝望。

有了团结，我们可以做伟大的事情，重要的事情。我们可以更正错误，我们可以让人们有好工作，我们可以在安全的学校里教育我们的孩子，我们可以战胜致命的病毒。我们可以恢复我们的工作，我们可以重振中产阶级，使所有人享有安全的工作。我们可以确保种族正义，我们可以让美国重新成为世界正义的领导力量。

我知道，现在谈论团结可能听起来像是愚蠢的幻想。我知道分裂我们的力量很深厚，而且是真实存在的。但我也知道它们并不新鲜。

我们的历史是一场持续不断的斗争，一方面是我们生来平等的美国理想，另一方面是我们被种族主义、本土主义、恐惧和妖魔化撕裂的残酷而丑陋的现实。这场战斗是长期的，而且胜负难料。

经历了内战、大萧条、世界大战、"9·11"事件，经历了斗争、牺牲和挫折，我们本性中更善良的天使总是占上风。在我们的每一个时刻，都有足够的人团结在一起，带领我们所有人向前。我们现在就能做到。

历史、信仰和理性为我们指明道路，一条团结之路。

我们可以把彼此视为邻

neighbors. We can treat each other with dignity and respect. We can join forces, stop the shouting and lower the temperature. For without unity, there is no peace, only bitterness and fury. No progress, only exhausting outrage. No nation, only a state of chaos. This is our historic moment of crisis and challenge. And unity is the path forward. And we must meet this moment as the United States of America.

If we do that, I guarantee you we will not fail. We have never, ever, ever, ever failed in America when we've acted together. And so today at this time in this place, let's start afresh, all of us. Let's begin to listen to one another again, hear one another, see one another, show respect to one another.

Politics doesn't have to be a raging fire destroying everything in its path. Every disagreement doesn't have to be a cause for total war and we must reject the culture in which facts themselves are manipulated and even manufactured.

My fellow Americans, we have to be different than this. America has to be better than this, and I believe America is so much better than this. Just look around. Here we stand in the shadow of the Capitol dome, as was mentioned earlier, completed in the shadow of the Civil War, when the union itself was literally hanging in the balance. Yet we endured, we prevailed.

Here we stand, looking out in the great Mall where Dr. King spoke of his dream. Here we stand, where 108 years ago at another inaugural, thousands of protesters tried

居，而不是对手。我们可以有尊严地相互尊重。我们可以联合起来，停止喊叫，减少愤怒。因为没有团结，就没有和平，只有痛苦和愤怒。没有进步，只有令人精疲力竭的愤怒。没有国家，只有混乱的状态。这是我们面临危机和挑战的历史性时刻。团结是前进的道路。我们必须以美利坚合众国的名义迎接这一时刻。

如果我们这样做，我保证我们不会失败。当我们齐心协力时，美国就从来没有失败过。所以今天此时此刻，在这里，让我们所有人重新开始。让我们重新开始倾听彼此，看见彼此，尊重彼此。

政治不一定非得是熊熊大火，摧毁道路上的一切。每一个分歧都不一定是全面开战的原因。我们必须拒绝操纵事实甚至捏造事实的文化。

我的美国同胞们，我们必须有所不同。我们必须做得更好，而且我相信美国比这要好得多。看看周围。现在我们站在国会大厦穹顶的阴影下。如前所述，穹顶是在内战阴影中建成的，那时候联邦本身岌岌可危。可是，我们坚持下来了，我们获胜了。

我们站在这里，眺望着马丁·路德·金谈论他梦想的大广场。我们所站立的地方，是108年前那场就职典礼上，

Joe Biden
乔·拜登(1942-)
46th President of the United States (2021-)

to block brave women marching for the right to vote. And today we mark the swearing in of the first woman in American history elected to national office—Vice President Kamala Harris. Don't tell me things can't change.

Here we stand, across the Potomac from Arlington National Cemetery, where heroes who gave the last full measure of devotion rest in eternal peace.

And here we stand just days after a riotous mob thought they could use violence to silence the will of the people, to stop the work of our democracy, to drive us from this sacred ground. It did not happen. It will never happen. Not today, not tomorrow, not ever. Not ever.

To all those who supported our campaign, I'm humbled by the faith you've placed in us. To all those who did not support us, let me say this. Hear me out as we move forward. Take a measure of me and my heart. If you still disagree, so be it. That's democracy. That's America. The right to dissent peaceably, within the guardrails of our Republic, is perhaps this nation's greatest strength.

Yet hear me clearly: disagreement must not lead to disunion. And I pledge this to you: I will be a president for all Americans. All Americans. And I promise you I will fight as hard for those who did not support me as for those who did.

成千上万的抗议者试图阻止勇敢的妇女为争取选举权而游行的地方。而今天,我们见证了美国历史上第一位女性副总统卡玛拉·哈里斯宣誓就职。不要告诉我世事不会改变。

在这里,我们面朝波托马克河边的阿灵顿国家公墓。在那里,献出了最后一份忠诚的英雄们在永恒的和平中安息。

也就在我们所站立的地方,几天前,一群暴徒认为他们可以使用暴力压制人民的意愿,阻止我们的民主事业,把我们从这片神圣的土地上赶走。那没有发生,也永远不会发生,今天不会,明天不会,永远不会,永远都不会。

我要对所有支持我们竞选的人说,你们对我们的信任,让我感到无比谦卑。而对于那些不支持我们的人,请听我说,在前行的路上,请倾听我们的声音,检验我与我的内心。如果你仍然有异议,那就有保留你的意见。这就是民主,这就是美国,在共和国的护栏内,拥有和平表达异议的权利。这也许是我们国家最强大的力量。

请听清楚了,分歧不应该导致分裂。我向你们保证,我会成为所有美国人的总统,所有美国人的总统。我向你们保证,我会像为支持我的人一样那样,也为不支持我的人

Many centuries ago, Saint Augustine—a saint in my church—wrote that a people was a multitude defined by the common objects of their love, defined by the common objects of their love. What are the common objects we as Americans love, that define us as Americans? I think we know. Opportunity, security, liberty, dignity, respect, honor and yes, the truth.

Recent weeks and months have taught us a painful lesson. There is truth and there are lies. Lies told for power and for profit. And each of us has a duty and a responsibility as citizens, as Americans, and especially as leaders—leaders who have pledged to honor our Constitution and protect our nation—to defend the truth and defeat the lies.

Look, I understand that many of my fellow Americans view the future with fear and trepidation. I understand they worry about their jobs. I understand like my dad, they lay in beds staring at nights staring at the ceilings, thinking, "Can I keep my health care? Can I pay my mortgage?" Thinking about their families, about what comes next. I promise you, I get it.

But the answer is not to turn inward, to retreat into the competing factions, distrusting those who don't look like you or worship the way you do, who don't get their news in the same sources you do.

We must end this uncivil war that pits red against blue, rural versus urban, rural versus urban, conservative versus liberal. We can do this if we open our souls instead of hardening our hearts, if we show a little tolerance and

许多世纪以前,教会圣徒圣奥古斯丁写道,一个民族是一个由他们共同热爱的目标所定义的群体。由他们共同的目标来定义。那么我们美国人所热爱的、能将我们定义为美国人的共同目标是什么?我想我们都知道:机会,安全,自由,尊严,尊重,荣誉,是的,还有真理。

最近几周、几个月给了我们惨痛的教训。其中有真相,也有谎言。为了权力和利益而说谎。我们每个人作为公民、作为美国人有义务和责任捍卫真相、战胜谎言。曾承诺遵守《宪法》,保护我们国家的领导人尤其如此。

看,我理解许多美国人对未来充满恐惧和不安。我了解他们担心自己的工作。我知道,他们就像我父亲一样,会在晚上躺在床上盯着天花板想:"我还能继续享受医疗保健吗?"我可以偿还抵押贷款吗?想着他们的家庭,想着接下来会发生什么。我向你们保证,我懂。

但答案不是内斗,不是派系斗争,不信任那些样貌、信仰方式、或新闻来源与自己不同的人。

我们必须结束这场红与蓝、农村对城市、农村对城市、保守对自由的不文明之战。如果我们敞开灵魂,而不是心如坚石,我们就能够做到。如

humility, and if we're willing to stand in the other person's shoes, as my mom would say. Just for a moment, stand in their shoes.

Because here's the thing about life. There's no accounting for what fate will deal you. Some days, when you need a hand. There are other days when we're called to lend a hand. That's how that has to be. That's what we do for one another. And if we are that way, our country will be stronger, more prosperous, more ready for the future. And we can still disagree.

My fellow Americans, in the work ahead of us, we're going to need each other. We need all our strength to persevere through this dark winter. We're entering what may be the toughest and deadliest period of the virus. We must set aside politics and finally face this pandemic as one nation. One nation. And I promise you this, as the Bible says, "Weeping may endure for a night, but joy cometh in the morning."

We will get through this together, together.

Look, folks, all my colleagues I served with in the House, and the Senate up there, we all understand the world is watching. Watching all of us today. So here's my message to those beyond our borders.

America has been tested and we've come out stronger for it. We will repair our alliances, and engage with the world once again—not to meet yesterday's challenges, but today's and tomorrow's challenges. And we'll lead, not merely by the example of our power, but by the power of our example.

We'll be a strong and trusted partner for peace,

果我们展现出一点容忍和谦卑，如果我们愿意替对方着想，就像我母亲常说的那样，站在对方的立场，片刻就好。

因为人生就是这样。没人算得出命运将会如何待你。有时你需要帮助，有时别人向我们求援。必然是这样的，我们互相帮助，这样，我们的国家将变得更强大，更繁荣，更为未来做好准备。而且我们仍然可以保留异议。

同胞们，我们需要彼此来完成我们面前的工作。我们需要所有的力量来度过这个黑暗的冬季。我们进入了疫情最黑暗、最致命的时期。我们必须抛开政治，最终以一个国家的身份面对疫情。一个国家。我保证，正如《圣经》所说的，"悲伤可能持续一夜，但欢乐在清晨来临"。

我们将一起渡过难关，一起。

看，各位，我在众议院和参议院的所有同事们，我们都明白全世界都在看着，看着我们今天所有人。这是我给美国以外的人们传达的信息。

美国经受住了考验，我们因此变得更加强大。我们将修复我们的同盟，并再次与世界互动。不只是应付昨天的挑战，还要迎接今天和明天的挑战。我们将引领世界，不是因为我们所显示的实力，而是因为我们所树立的榜样。

为和平，进步与安全，我

progress and security. Look, you all know, we've been through so much in this nation. In one of my first acts as President, I'd like to ask you to join me in a moment of silent prayer to remember all those who we lost this past year to the pandemic—those four hundred thousand fellow Americans, moms, dads, husbands, wives, sons, daughters, friends, neighbors and co-workers. We will honor them by becoming the people and the nation we know we can and should be.

So I ask you, let's say a silent prayer for those who've lost their lives, those left behind and for our country.

Amen.

Folks, this is a time of testing. We face an attack on our democracy and on truth, a raging virus, growing inequity, the sting of systemic racism, a climate in crisis, America's role in the world. Any one of these will be enough to challenge us in profound ways. But the fact is, we face them all at once, presenting this nation with one of the gravest responsibilities we've had.

Now we're going to be tested. Are we going to step up? All of us?

It's time for boldness, for there is so much to do. And this is certain, I promise you. We will be judged, you and I, by how we resolve these cascading crises of our era.

We will rise to the occasion and the question. Will we master this rare and difficult hour? Will we meet our obligations and pass along a new and better world to our

们将成为强大和值得信赖的合作伙伴。看，你们都知道，我们国家经历了那么多事。作为总统，我的第一个行动是想请您加入我的默祷，以纪念过去一年在疫情中逝去的生命——四十万美国同胞，他们是母亲，父亲、丈夫、妻子、儿子、女儿、朋友、邻居和同事。我们将以他们为荣，成为我们能够且应该成为的人民和国家。

所以，我请求你们，让我们为那些失去生命的人、那些还在的人和我们的国家默祷。

阿门。

各位，这是考验的时刻。我们面临着对我们民主的攻击、对真理的攻击、肆虐的病毒、尖锐的不平等、系统性的种族主义、气候危机，还有美国在世界上扮演的角色。这其中任何一项都足以深刻地挑战我们，但事实是，我们同时面对所有这些问题，让这个国家承担起我们所肩负的最大责任之一。

现在我们要迎接考验了，我们要向前一步吗？所有人？

是时候勇敢了，因为我们还有很多事需要去做。我向你保证，这是肯定的。我们如何解决我们这个时代的多重危机，将成为评判我们的标准。

我们将迎难而上。我们可以掌控这罕见且艰难的时刻吗？我们会履行我们的义

Joe Biden

乔·拜登(1942-)
46th President of the United States (2021-)

children? I believe we must. I'm sure you do as well. I believe we will—and when we do, we'll write the next great chapter in the history of the United States of America. The American story. A story that might sound something like a song that means a lot to me. It's called "American Anthem". There's one verse that stands out, at least for me, and it goes like this:

"The work and prayers of centuries have brought us to this day.

What shall be our legacy? What will our children say?

Let me know in my heart when my days are through.

America, America, I gave my best to you."

Let us add our own work and prayers to the unfolding story of our great nation. If we do this, then when our days are through, our children and our children's children will say of us they gave their best. They did their duty. They healed a broken land.

My fellow Americans, I close the day where I began, with a sacred oath. Before God and all of you, I give you my word. I will always level with you. I will defend the Constitution. I'll defend our democracy. I'll defend America and I will give all—all of you. Keep everything I do in your service, thinking not of power, but of possibilities, not of personal interest, but the public good. And together we shall write an American story of hope, not fear. Of unity, not division, of light, not darkness. A story

务,把一个新的、更美好的世界传给我们的孩子吗?我认为我们必须这样做。我肯定,你们也这样认为。我相信我们将会做到,当我们做到时,我们将书写美利坚历史上下一个伟大篇章。一个美国的故事。一个听起来像是一首歌的故事。这首歌对我而言意义重大。它叫"美国国歌",歌中有一小节至少让我印象深刻,它是这样写的:

"几个世纪的工作和祈祷把我们带到这天,

我们的遗产是什么?我们的后代会会说什么?

我心里明白,当我的岁月将尽时,

美国啊美国,我把我最好的东西给了你。"

让我们把自己的工作和祈祷加入我们伟大国家正在展开的故事之中。如果我们这样做,在我们的岁月将尽时,我们的子子孙孙会这样形容我们:他们尽了全力,他们尽到了责任,他们治愈了破碎的土地。

我的美国同胞们,让我用开始时那句神圣的誓言为这天结尾。在上帝和你们所有人面前,我向你们保证,我将一直与你们真诚相待,我将捍卫宪法,我将捍卫我们的民主。我将捍卫美国,我将付出一切,我所做的一切都是为你们所有人服务。不考虑权力,而是考虑可能性;不为个人利

of decency and dignity, love and healing, greatness and goodness. May this be the story that guides us. The story that inspires us and the story that tells ages yet to come that we answered the call of history. We met the moment. Democracy and hope, truth and justice did not die on our watch, but thrived. That America secured liberty at home and stood once again as a beacon to the world. That is what we owe our forbearers, one another and generations to follow.

So, with purpose and resolve, we turn to those tasks of our time. Sustained by faith, driven by conviction, devoted to one another and the country we love with all our hearts.

May God bless America and may God protect our troops. Thank you, America.

益,而为公共福祉。我们将共同书写一个充满希望而非恐惧、充满团结而非分裂,充满光明而非黑暗的美国故事,一个关于正派和尊严、爱和疗愈、伟大和善良的故事。愿这个故事可以指引我们、激励我们,告诉未来的世世代代,我们回应了历史的召唤,我们相遇在此刻。民主和希望,真理和正义,没有在我们的眼皮底下死去,而是茁壮成长。美国保障了国内的自由,并将再次成为世界的灯塔。这是我们欠我们的祖先、我们彼此和我们后代的。

因此,带着目标和决心,我们开始着手我们时代的这些任务。信仰永存,信念驱使,彼此奉献,全心全意地热爱我们所爱的国家。

愿上帝保佑美国,愿上帝保佑我们的军队。谢谢你,美国。